SO BRAVE...
SO QUIET...
SO LONG!

From The Wildwood Independent Series:

PATRIOTS

Penn Valley, California

SO BRAVE...
SO QUIET...
SO LONG!

An Anthology of Heroes

BY LARRY T. BAILEY

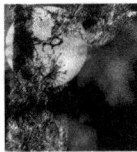

Pine Tree Arts
Penn Valley, CA USA

Pine Tree Arts, P.O. Box 129
Penn Valley, California 95946
www.pinetreearts.com
First Edition: July 4, 2011

*Pine Tree Arts is the creative division of
Pine Tree Press of Penn Valley, California, USA.*

Cover photo: National Archives
via *World War II in Color* website
Other photos are personal property
of the persons depicted and their families.

ISBN 978-061-55088-25

'SO BRAVE...' DEDICATION

Diana, my loving and beautiful spouse
Steven and Kirk, my sons
Wyatt and Kalle, Kirk's progeny and our grandchildren
Bobbi, Steve's wife - our lovely daughter-in-law

July 4, 2011

TABLE OF CONTENTS

FOREWORD

By Mike Dobbins

Owner, Publisher and Editor
The Wildwood Independent
and Owner-Publisher, *Penn Valley Courier*

EVER HAVE THE EXPERIENCE of meeting someone for the first time and knowing in that instant your life will never be the same? Only happens on rare occasions, but when it does, it becomes an instant memory.

It's occurred a couple times in my life (other than the obvious ones, wife, children, etc.), but I'll never forget the day about a decade ago, Larry Bailey walked into my office and said, "I have an idea for the paper you might find interesting."

Interesting? Bailey, master of the understatement!

Thus was born a friendship few are lucky to experience once in a lifetime. That encounter was the "birth-moment" of the *PATRIOTS* series. That "interesting idea" turned into the most successful endeavor ever undertaken by *The Wildwood Independent.*

To this day *PATRIOTS* remains the most talked about, complimented, and popular series in the paper's 30-year history – bar none.

Likewise, the ten years I've been honored in Larry's orbit of influence has been life-altering on several levels.

The uniformed *PATRIOTS* Larry introduced to us experienced the horrors of the 20th Century's most horrific wars.

None ever called themselves "heroes" and yet... ALL are HEROES!

They answered the call and put themselves in harm's way for a belief in their family, home and country – a belief each and every one holds in their hearts today.

But it was Larry's incredible skill in telling their stories up close and personal which brought them to life on our pages.

History tells us who the generals were. How the battles unfolded – all the stuff we think we need to know about the events of the time. Larry tells us the story of the everyday guy (or gal) and how the individual copes suddenly finding oneself in a world gone completely mad.

It began with Peter Leopold, the former general manager of the community served by *The Wildwood Independent*, and the first *PATRIOT* introduced in the series.

Then there was Dick Landis, flying his P-38 or P-51 in some of the fiercest fighting over Europe. Simultaneously on the ground, his then unmet and later lifelong friend, Holger Rasmussen, a very young infantryman, toiled in freezing snow and mud fighting in the nightmare known as the "The Bulge".

Then to my favorite, the young sailor – who would later become my all-time super hero – getting ready for church on an early December Sunday morning when seven Japanese torpedoes suddenly slammed into the side of his ship – USS West Virginia – peacefully moored next to Ford Island in Pearl Harbor.

Of all the lives Larry emblazoned on the pages of *PA-TRIOTS* this one is my favorite. That 21-year-old-just-out-of Kansas farm boy is my Dad. He survived that war and two others and to this day tears up when talking about the experience.

I like to kid Larry on his "gift," at times, to use too many words when fewer will do. When I say this, he mostly smiles. But each word in this series is a sparkling gem in the necklace of a life lived to the fullest by these warriors during unfathomable hardships.

His prose and heart-felt poetry brings these stories out of the darkness in which real history is usually hidden and into the light of today for each of us to cherish.

Thanks, Larry; your friendship, guidance and counsel have enriched my life both professionally and personally on so many levels.

You, my friend, are truly a hero!

— Mike Dobbins

TRIBUTES

"Quietly Living in Our Midst...
Contributing to Our Well-being..."

"So Brave...So Quiet...So Long!" is a superb memoir on human behavior and the emotions felt by that generation of young Americans who answered the call when the wolves came knocking at our nations' door in the early 1940s. Implicit in the telling is a personal portrait of unsurpassed courage, sacrifice, steadfastness and a sense for the mutual affection that these men and women felt for one another when they served in harm's way and in some instances, under intense enemy fire.

A unique feature of this book is the telling of how these same courageous Americans went on in their post-war years to raise their families, lead productive lives and continued to enrich and strengthen American society. Larry Bailey has written a must-read tribute to thirty-four of our neighbors who without any fanfare continue to quietly live in our midst and contribute to the well-being of Nevada County, California, and our country.

By Major General O. K. Steele
U.S. Marine Corps (Ret.)

"Get Busy Living, or Get Busy Dying."

As a newspaper publisher and editor, I've always appreciated a good story and a great story teller. In his book, Larry Bailey shares the fascinating life journeys of 34 hometown heroes and he does so with the skill and sensitivity of a veteran journalist. It's not easy to do justice to lives that have been lived to their fullest and Larry has managed to take his readers around the world and back to a time when young Americans were asked to grow up far too soon.

In his book, Larry Bailey introduces us to Mydell "Myke" Pfanmiller, a Wisconsin girl who would find herself caring for wounded Chinese and American soldiers as a 22-year-old Army nurse in Burma during World War II. She would go on to marry the man who encouraged her to embrace life and to never mix anything but water with good bourbon.

Then there is Al Carver, who logged more than 5,000 hours in the air, starting as a cadet at the controls of a P-38 trainer in 1942 and ending as commander at Beale Air Force Base in Northern California.

One of my all-time favorite movie lines came in the Shawshank Redemption, where the main character reminds his friend to "get busy living, or get busy dying." These thirty-four Americans took those words to heart and Larry Bailey has managed to show us how well they lived.

Their stories should serve as an inspiration to us all.

By Jeff Ackerman, Publisher and Editor
The Union Newspaper and Publishing Co.,
Grass Valley, CA (A Swift Communications Company)

TRIBUTES

"Memories Preserved in Time"

"As I read the fascinating and historic stories these honorable men tell Larry Bailey, I can't help thinking of my own father. How I wish I would have taken the time to document his life experiences to share with future generations in the same colorful, compassionate, and conversational style.

Rotary's motto Service Above Self is never more evident than in this book where men don't think of the sacrifices they made in their youth, but only know the pride of service to their God, their family, and their country.

I have known Larry Bailey for nearly 40 years. We share many memories – I only hope he doesn't write a book about me! I can describe Larry as a successful business manager, a dedicated Rotarian, tender-hearted humanitarian, a loving husband and father, a talented artist, a world traveler, history buff, animal lover, and a dear friend.

Thanks to Larry Bailey's gifted writing, the memories of these patriots are preserved in time."

By Jerry J. Barden
Rotary International Director, 1995-1997

"A Big Impression On Me, Personally"

I wish to first congratulate Larry on his compelling record of the 34 people who served our nation in combat roles primarily during WWII. They were more than just veterans and representatives of our fine country; but in many cases "heroes among us."

This record of the war experiences of such a group of men and women living in the Lake Wildwood area of Penn Valley, California, gives us a better appreciation of their love for our nation and the jobs they did on our behalf.

It goes without saying, in my judgment, service to our nation when necessary is a responsible action on the part of all American citizens.

As I've told Larry before, I've always thought of him as an individual who has been an inspiration to many people who personally know him. I've regarded him as one of the most generous and eloquent in expressing his personal opinion and setting a pattern for life for the many people fortunate to be on familiar terms with him.

Larry is one of the select few I think of who have made a big impression on me personally and affected my individual thinking on many issues.

Once again I thank Larry for the work he has done for the benefit of people in our area who served in the military and those who served all around our wonderful country.

By Richard G. Landis
CEO and Chairman of the Board, Del Monte Corp., and President, Pacific Region, R.J. Reynolds Co. (Ret.)

TRIBUTES

"Extraordinary Behavior and Sacrifice Of Ordinary Men and Women"

As an Air Force officer whose career took me from combat flying in Vietnam to staff Assignments in The White House and The Pentagon and later service as a member of the USAA Board of Directors, I have met and served with many American heroes as well as learned of many more throughout our history.

In capturing the lives and emotions of thirty-four of these heroes, Larry Bailey has done a great service to them in bringing their stories to light and to us in making us aware of the extraordinary behavior and sacrifice of ordinary men and women called to the service of their country. Each personality as engaging as the previous, it is a wonderful read that keeps on giving.

By Leslie G. Denend
Colonel, USAF (Ret.)
USAA Board of Directors (Ret.)

AUTHOR'S INTRODUCTION

By Larry T. Bailey — July 1, 2011

AS AN OCCASIONAL writer for *The Wildwood Independent* newspaper (for Lake Wildwood) in Penn Valley, California, I had an idea for articles primarily about WWII combat veterans (the *PATRIOTS*) living in our community. I approached Mike Dobbins, publisher, owner and editor of the paper (and also owner and publisher of the *Penn Valley Courier*), with modest expectations.

At the time, I played a monthly game of poker with a few pals. One of them was former USMC aviator Peter Leopold, who flew in the rear-facing seat of the SBD 3 Douglas Dauntless Dive Bomber during WWII air battles in the South Pacific. He was the catalyst for my idea.

Peter regularly fleeced me and others at cards. I asked him where he had learned to play. He had honed his skills in the Marine barracks and a troop ship to the combat zones in the South Pacific. He had learned well. One question led to another and to a fifteen hundred word article, which prompted another story about a pair of *PATRIOTS* who had fought the enemy December 7, 1941 and attended the sixtieth anniversary of the Pearl Harbor attack.

Ultimately more than 83,000 words were written about 34 heroes surrounding my home in a tight geographic circle and cocoon of personal assurance and security. Thirty-two of the folks in this book are WWII combat vets. Of the two who are not, one performed acts of extraordinary bravery hovering above a Korean hilltop. The other non-WWII inclusion was an SR-71 warrior who helped push the cause of freedom in the fastest plane the world has ever known.

Two don't live in Lake Wildwood, but were close neighbors of the development and had strong family ties to the community.

Some of the heroes I wrote about became dear friends. All have enriched my life in so many ways.

The series segments were often continued to subsequent editions. As a kid I was a fan of the Saturday morning matinees and their serials – Flash Gordon, Batman, Dick Tracy, Sky King, Buck Rogers, Hoppy and Roy. They always ended with a cliffhanger so you'd return to the theater next week. I, of course, wanted folks to be sure to read the next issue of the paper and focus on the continuing tale of our selected *PATRIOT*. I was just doing my small part to keep the newspaper industry alive and well in America.

If the title *PATRIOTS* was good enough for the newspaper series, why not keep it for the book? There are a couple of reasons for change: The words "patriots/heroes" have been used in book titles, and I'm guessing a million times, maybe more, since the Revolutionary War.

I chose "So Brave... So Quiet... So Long!" for several reasons.

The first two words of the title, "So Brave..." need no explanation. "So Silent..." epitomizes men and women who served in WWII and Korea. For the most part they let their actions speak for them. Think John Wayne, Gary Cooper, Randolph Scott, Humphrey Bogart – strong and silent. Veterans, men and women, worked extraordinarily hard after WWII to build our nation to what it is today. They didn't, and still don't, complain much, sometimes to their detriment. I might add vets from other conflicts, including those in today's headlines, don't do a lot of complaining either. Maybe more squeaky wheel is sometimes called for.

The "So Long..." is what we're saying with alarming frequency, especially to WWII and Korean vets. Too many leave us – too many die – every day. "So long" can be a "good-bye, see you later." Or it can be a sign-off for eternity.

"So Long..." the final two words of the book's title are what I feel compelled to dawdle on.

For many vets, especially in our later conflicts, there are issues like housing, education, intervention treatments and aftercare, job training, other services and items as simple as a hot meal, haircut, basic health checks, dental work and access to benefit services and "needs" counseling. Most vets are fully integrated into society and productive and facing no more or less than any of the rest of us – the non-veterans.

It seems clear to me that for those who served and sacrificed so much we shouldn't be saying "So long..." to their needs, regardless of their war.

This book is definitely not an expose. Rather it tries to accurately reflect the stories of thirty-four brave Americans and my neighbors who laid their lives on the line for our freedom. They did a magnificent job of fighting and serving on our behalf. We can and should do no less for them.

A reminder I want to leave – brave men and women who served in our military in many wars and conflicts surround us regardless of where we live. They are nearly as ubiquitous as the pods in the various movie renditions of "Invasion of the Body Snatchers." They're all around us. They're in line at almost every store. They coach our kids or grandkids in individual and team sports. They sit near us at the theater. Maybe they live next door, across the street, behind us. They are our attorney, EMT, tax person, any job we name, and maybe even standing on a corner with a sign and a hand out. They are very close. They can be any age eighteen and above – Veterans!

I repeat: They did a magnificent job of fighting and serving on behalf of our country and us. We can and should do no less for them.

And now...

SO BRAVE...
SO QUIET...
SO LONG!

For without belittling the courage with which men have died, we
Should not forget those acts of courage with which men have lived.

John F. Kennedy
Profiles in Courage

DAY ONE

Sis and Peter - 62nd Anniversary

Chapter 1. Peter Leopold - USMC

"He did not give much thought to getting killed. It was always the other guy... the unlucky one."

BY MID-MORNING December 7, 1941, Peter Leopold had finished reading the Chicago *Tribune* – a quick scrutiny of the news with special attention to the Sunday comics and the sports section. Around eleven a.m. he was comfortably seated in his future father-in-law's living room anticipating the pending game between his favorite team, the hapless 3-6-1 Chicago Cardinals, and the rival Chicago Bears who had lost but one game mid-season to the Packers.

He was a junior at Northwestern University studying business and getting decent grades. He was in love with Sis, a strikingly beautiful woman. His only sibling, older brother Jim, was doing well at the Army's Officer Training School in Fort Benning, Georgia. Just that summer Peter and his fam-

ily had taken a vacation that took him farther than he had
ever been from Chicago – to Yellowstone Park. It had been
a rare treat for a family that had struggled with dignity
through the depression. At age nineteen and 160 pounds he,
and his life, were in great shape. He was as happy as a young
man could be... until about 11:55 a.m. Chicago time.

He listened incredulously to the early radio bulletins.
The discussion in that cozy living room ultimately climaxed
with anger and outrage at the deliberateness, violence and
enormity of the attack.

While Franklin Roosevelt was formulating his memorable, "Yesterday, Dec. 7, 1941 – a date which will live in in-
famy..." remarks to the Congress of the United States, Peter
Leopold was formulating his own plan.

He did not hear President Roosevelt's live address to
America Dec. 8. He was taking a streetcar to enlist in the
Marine Corp. The ride was smooth, and he read the *Trib's*
front page. The banner screamed in bold print, "HAWAII,
PHILIPPINES, GUAM, SINGAPORE BOMBED."

The editorial cartoon on the front page showed a giant
red, white, and blue American flag flying in the breeze with
a man standing proudly below – saluting. The cartoon's title
read, "Every American". On that day at that moment the
drawing of the man saluting looked very much like young
Mr. Leopold.

He was ordered to report for duty effective January 13,
1942, at age twenty years and one day. That afternoon he
began a trip that would take him far distant from Chicago,
far beyond Yellowstone Park.

First stop, San Diego's Marine Recruit Depot and boot camp.

By May of 1942 he was promoted to PFC, learning the basics of becoming an aviation radioman/gunner. Sis and her mom had traveled to San Diego to see Peter during a brief liberty. He proposed to her. It was agreed that marriage would wait until he was back in civilian clothes. They stood together at the Pacific's edge that proposal day watching the red-orange sunset to the west. Beyond the horizon, beyond the sinking sun, beyond that glorious moment with his bride-to-be, he stared westward across the ocean to...

MAG 14 consisted of several dive bomber squadrons, each flying 6-8 planes out of Henderson Field, Guadalcanal, in the Solomon Islands. Peter had found a home with Headquarter Squadron VMSB 141, as the partner with Naval Aviation Pilot Mickey Jones, the only NCO pilot in the squadron.

The SBD 3 Douglas Dauntless was a two-seat carrier or land-based dive-bomber first delivered to the military in 1940. The pilot faced forward while the radioman/gunner sat facing the tail and scanned where they had been -- 20/20 hindsight – two bookends without the books. The Dauntless had a 9 cylinder Wright R1820, 1200 horsepower cyclone engine and a maximum speed of 252 mph.

It could carry one 500 or 1,000 pound bomb under the fuselage and two 100 or 250 pound bombs under the wings. There were two fixed, forward-firing 0.5-inch Browning machine-guns in the nose. Some said SBD stood for "Slow but Deadly".

Peter's domain included twin manually aimed 30 caliber Browning machine-guns in his rear cockpit. While he had been thoroughly trained on radio operations in San Diego, the machine gun training was strictly OJT. On his first mission he had to ask the enlisted man securing the bombs and ammo how to load the Browning.

"You got to be kidding?"

"No."

"By the way," the armorer concluded, "you got a full 180 degree arc you can swing this thing. Try to remember not to shoot your tail off." Later in the war stops were put in the middle of the arc to preclude shooting one's self down. To his credit, and his pilot partner's gratitude, he managed to remember the armorer's admonition.

Peter had joined the Marines because he wanted to be something special in a special branch of the military. He did not give much thought to getting killed. It was always the other guy... the unlucky one. That's the way it was...that's the way he thought about it. When a man is young, he is almost... almost immortal. In a two-seat airplane you hoped your partner, on those days when you flew together astride 1200 fiery horses, would also share your luck.

Immortality for two, while in the air, seemed a modest favor to ask.

For two months on Guadalcanal, flying missions every day, and sometimes twice a day, they were invincible. From 10,000 feet diving, leveling off at 1000 feet, releasing their bombs and soaring as one, unfriendly enemy fire like sparklers on the fourth of July coming their way – colorful, close and harmless. There was confusion, excitement, and exhilaration those days in the air. Peter remembers a lack of fear and "a strange detachment," in his words, "from the action." He and his partner were doing their job. Aloft there was no time to be afraid. Fear dissipated like wind over the wings.

They were working very hard to even the score with the enemy, a 500-pound bomb flung like a bullet pass from a seasoned quarterback, exploding into the heart of a Japanese warship. Like tossing a football through a tire, shooting a fish in a barrel, falling off a log. That season he and his pilot quarterback, Mickey, did what his Chicago Cardinals could not do... the scoreboard was always in their favor.

By 1943 Pilot Mickey Jones was no longer partnered with Pete. That is the year he died in a non-combat plane crash off the California coast. Go figure.

In the air the fear could not reach Pete.

On the ground... in the dark... some nights in a foxhole on Guadalcanal dug in around the perimeter of camp... flares dropped from enemy planes, punctuated and magnified by catcalls and whistles from unseen enemies who seemed ubiquitous... the fear crept in. It hung like the smell of death and decay. There was no whirling propeller to dispel it, no blue sky to dissipate the anxiety, no rushing wind, no diving plane to leave the trepidation far behind.

With dawn, the red rising sun, came the limitless horizon waiting to be met by the roar of the Dauntless radial engine – the Yin, the Yang. It evened out.

In the air the fear could not reach Peter.

January 1943, new enemies did find and successfully attack him – malaria and jaundice. The hospital in New Zealand was comfortable and safe and the enemy within him was eventually vanquished. He rejoined his squadron, repositioned to Auckland, to train a New Zealand dive-bomber squadron. His unit also knocked around other areas of the Pacific, including Efate in the New Hebrides.

Just before Christmas 1943, after a month at sea on a Liberty ship, he sailed beneath the Golden Gate Bridge. On February 21, 1944, Marine Staff Sergeant Peter Leopold married Sis. The promise to stay single until he was in civilian clothes was not kept. That promise begged to be broken. The promises of marriage vows, however, remain intact – still.

And all the promises he made to himself, the Marine Corps and America that day he enlisted so very long ago Dec.8, 1941, when he was a young man of nineteen, were met with honor and dignity.

The only other combat he saw was as a football player with the Marines. His base, Oak Grove, was playing against the team from the Cherry Point Marine Air Station. He was lined up directly opposite now deceased ex-49er, and Hall-of-Famer, Leo "The Lion" Nomellini.

"Look, kid," growled "The Lion" at Peter , "don't do anything stupid or you might get hurt."

Peter said nothing, but once again he was in the air... soaring, diving, fearless, indestructible, almost immortal.

He is still that way.

Peter passed away a few years ago and is now soaring in a better place.

Holger then... and now

Chapter 2: Holger Rasmussen – Army

"I entered the Battle of the Bulge with thirty six men. When it was over only twelve remained."

HOLGER RASMUSSEN was born in Harrisburg, PA in 1925. He was the third of three boys. About five minutes later his twin, Howard, also became an official Pennsylvania resident. Over the next several years two more boys would join the Rasmussen household.

"My Dad had emigrated from Denmark to America when he was 19 or 20," Holger states, "and he eventually became a professor of agriculture at Penn State, then Secretary of Agriculture for Pennsylvania. At the time of his death, when I was eight years old, he was the Executive Secretary of the International Association of Ice Cream Manufacturers."

His death devastated the family. His mother took what money they had and bought a 160-acre farm near Hummelstown, some twelve miles east of Harrisburg and six miles west of Hershey. Holger's aunt and uncle also moved to the farm and coordinated its day-to-day operations. Additionally, his grandmother joined the family at their new home. Farming, during the height of the Depression, was a difficult way to make a living. There were times when the prices they were paid for their milk, eggs and produce were less than the costs incurred to bring them to market.

"We ate very well." He smiles, "We boys didn't know we were poor." He describes the routine on the farm: "My brothers and I would get up around 5:30 to milk the twenty-five or so cows we had. Sometimes we'd help take the milk to the local dairy, then feed the chickens and pigs, eat breakfast and head to school. After school we'd feed hay to the cows and do other chores, have supper, milk the cows again, spend time as a family, do our school studies and go to bed around ten o'clock." He adds, "We also played sports around the farm and learned how to hunt game."

He describes how his mother worked during the week as secretary to her late husband's successor, some sixty plus miles away, and was home mostly on weekends – much less than he and his brothers would have liked. He credits his grandmother with helping him acquire a passion for learning. "We were also taught the valuable life's lesson that play came *after* work," he adds.

"My grandmother had been a school teacher and would read to us hour after hour – historical novels and English authors – Byron, Wordsworth, Burns, Keats, Shelley, Scott, Tennyson, Shakespeare and other great writers, as well as works about world and United States history." He laughs and continues, "When I was a freshman in high school in nearby Hershey we were all given a state-mandated history test. I was called into the principal's office. He asked me, 'Where did you get the answers to the test?' I didn't know what he was talking about. He told me I had an almost perfect score, the second highest in the state. Finally he realized I was telling the truth and everything was fine."

Holger had paid keen attention while his grandmother read to him and the other boys.

He spent his senior year at Gettysburg High School. The family had purchased another farm so the boys could go to Gettysburg College, a liberal arts school in southern PA with an excellent curriculum and reputation.

He was in his first year of college and joined the Army Reserve, February 28, 1943. His twin brother Howard also enlisted and both were called to active duty that May. They both completed Medical Corpsman training, but in September 1943 were assigned to the Army Specialized Training Program (ASTP) designed to accelerate the college education process for high potential candidates. They were sent to Virginia Polytechnic Institute in Blacksburg.

"My brother and I were assigned to a group of sixty men to help design specialized cams of different types. We spent some months doing that, then the ASTP program for us was terminated." In fact, the motto of the program, run by a highly respected West Point colonel and professor, was, "Soldiers first, students second". As the war continued, the need for men at the front escalated, and the ASTP program was disbanded.

"We were sent to Camp Claibourne, LA and assigned to the 84th Infantry Division as foot soldiers. We trained as infantrymen for a number of months." During that time the brothers were split up due to the public outcry and new military policy developed after the five Sullivan Brothers had been killed in 1942 when their ship was destroyed.

"I went to my captain to see what might be done to keep us together. An army psychiatrist said in the case of twins, due to their closeness, it was a good idea to keep them together. We were reunited in the same unit." The 84th traveled by train to New Jersey, and September 20, 1944 the 334th Infantry Regiment sailed for Europe. They arrived in South Hampton October 1, and left for the Continent a month later, landing on Omaha Beach. They traversed Northern France and by November 12 were in the vicinity of Gulpen, Holland.

"We saw a lot of conflict in the vicinity of the Siegfried Line. My brother and I were in 1st Battalion, Company B, 1st Platoon." During his second day of combat he was promoted to platoon sergeant. Several days later his platoon leader, a lieutenant, was killed in action. He was not replaced until the middle of the Battle of the Bulge when a new platoon leader was finally assigned. After about a week, that leader went on sick call and never returned to the platoon.

"The killed, wounded and captured at times exceeded our ability to replace them," Holger offers. "On the Company organization chart I filled the slot of platoon leader for the majority of my time as a combat soldier. I recall that during this period the average time for an infantryman on the front line for the 84th Infantry Division was thirteen days." His time in command was longer.

The name Holger is ancient Norse in origin and was the name of one of Charlemagne's successful generals, a Danish nobleman. More than 600 years after Charlemagne and his warriors helped unite and pave the way for a modern Europe, another Holger – albeit not a general – was fighting in similar territory for a similar goal.

He recounts one episode that took place the third week of November. "Combat engineers had cleared a pathway through a German minefield. The next morning I took off at 4 a.m. with my men and another platoon toward a big anti-tank ditch about 100 yards past the minefield. Our job was to take three pillboxes not too far away. The Germans heard us and began heavy mortar fire." Thick tule fog had settled over the area. The scene was chaos. Holger and nine men – some from his platoon and some from another – crept forward, along with a British tank, to escape the mortars and advance. As the sun began to climb so, too, did the fog.

"The pillboxes were not in front of us... they were to our right and behind us. We had gone beyond them in the thick fog." He pauses, then continues, "We made our way toward the enemy pillboxes and surprisingly encountered no fire. I ordered one of my men to drop a phosphorous smoke grenade down a ventilator pipe. Germans came running out gasping for air." The scenario of phosphorous grenade and subsequent surrender was successfully repeated for the remaining two pillboxes.

He reflects back on that victory, "The German field of fire was to the front of the pillboxes, not behind. They could not defend themselves from a rear attack." He adds,

"Reinforcements arrived and took our seventy prisoners off our hands."

Near the end of November Holger was rewarded with several three-day passes for a little "R and R" in Paris. One of the men he invited to join him was one of his squad leaders – twin brother Sgt. Howard Rasmussen. When they returned all but three of the men in his platoon had been captured by the Germans. He received new men, most of them rookie replacements sprinkled with some experienced men from other platoons.

"It was painful to lose men who had been friends." His voice is soft as he continues, "The new guys... the replacements... you never make a real attachment to them. It's a defense mechanism, I think."

By mid-December it was bitter cold in Western Europe. Men wisecracked that both the weather and the enemy could kill a man. The morning of December 16 the Germans launched their all-out counterattack against the American-controlled lines in the Ardennes – The Battle of the Bulge.

Ironically, the worst American battle casualties up until the Battle of the Bulge had occurred at Gettysburg, Holger's hometown at the time. Casualties during that Civil War battle exceeded 50,000. Casualties for American forces during the Battle of the Bulge would be fifty percent higher. The third highest number of casualties of any outfit were incurred by the 84th Infantry Division. Holger's regiment, the 334th, was at the heart of major battles all along their portion of the line.

The Battle of the Bulge occurred over an 80-mile front running from the middle of Luxembourg to southern Belgium and encompassing the Ardennes forest. Simply, the German Army hoped to drive through and divide the British and American forces and capture the port of Antwerp. December 20, General Eisenhower assigned command by giving General Bradley responsibility for operations in the southern part of the battle area. British Field Marshal Montgomery was given command in the northern area, including the 84th Infantry Division.

The period, December 16 to the effective conclusion of the battle in Mid-January, was hellish. Holger states, "I entered the Battle of the Bulge with 36 men. When it was over only twelve remained. The other 24 had been killed, wounded or captured."

The bulge was hit on three sides. From the north, four divisions, including the 84th and 83rd Infantry and 2nd and 3rd Armored, led an offensive. From the west there was the British Corps, and from the south the 3rd Army. The 84th and 2nd were teamed, as were the 83rd and 3rd. The 84th/2nd team had a front more than eight miles wide. Their objective, the Belgium town of Houffalize, was nearly twenty miles to the south and east.

Initially, American airpower was not a significant factor as bad weather made flying virtually impossible from just after the start of the German offensive, December 16, until skies partially cleared December 23. In this period the German bulge had expanded to its maximum depth of 50 miles. Over the next five days, more than 16,000 flights lifted off.

"When the fighter planes started flying again," Holger states, "we were very happy to see them." On flying days the planes were in the air from dawn to dusk.

(In Holger and Linda's living room there is a framed print of the P-51 and P-38 flown by Dick Landis – former Chairman of the Board of Del Monte – in Europe during his 2½ tours of duty. He flew a number of missions during the Battle of the Bulge, including five in one day. He was a featured PATRIOT in an issue of The Wildwood Independent and later in this book. The picture has a personal inscription to Holger from Dick. Holger hangs it so the two planes are flying upside down. He smiles impishly as he explains, "It is that way so the pilot, Lt. Landis, can better see the troops on the ground." They are good friends with good humor – each respectful and appreciative of the other's significant contributions and bravery.)

As the month-long battle wore on, the snow deepened, the cold increased, the ice intensified. It took 2-3 hours to dig a foxhole a few feet deep. Frostbite was an issue, and the possibility of a man freezing to death in his sleep was real.

All vehicles, including tanks, had to stay on the roads. At times roads were so icy any vehicle would slide off. Even so, the infantry soldier could always move forward – could always make at least a little progress and hope the armored units would keep up.

By January 15, 1945 Houffalize was captured and the forces from the north had hooked up with Patton's 3rd Army. For all intents and purposes the Battle of the Bulge was over. The 84th was given a five-day breather, then sent back into action. For Holger and his brother the war continued.

"Also in January we were headed across some mountains to take a town. My Captain found me and said a lieutenant from another platoon had gotten lost. He wanted me to take a few men and try to find him. We were moving forward for 30 minutes, meeting no resistance and not finding the missing officer. I saw a man walking along the edge of the forest toward us in a sheepskin jacket. He was carrying an oilskin map bag that looked like the ones used by our tank commanders. I motioned the men to stay out of sight, and as he approached I could see he was a German officer."

Holger yelled at the officer to halt. He did.

"'I'm amazed,' the German said in near-perfect English, 'I didn't think there were any Americans within 20-25 miles.'

"As we walked back to our lines he told me he had been educated in England at Cambridge." Holger continues, "He was relieved he had been captured. He said to me, 'You know you've done me a favor. The war is over for me, and I have lived!'"

By late February Holger, his Brother Howard, and Sgt. Youngblood, a squad leader, were all that remained from the original 36 members of his platoon. On the 26th a runner approached Holger and told him his brother had been wounded.

"I rushed to the aide station. It was a German aide station we had captured. A German doctor who was treating men from *both* sides manned it. My brother had shrapnel in his upper body and face and was temporarily on the sidelines."

The next day, the 27th, Holger was asked by the Captain to lead a scouting mission. At the last minute the officer changed his mind and sent Sgt. Youngblood instead. Sgt. Youngblood was killed by enemy fire while on the patrol.

"The day after Youngblood died I was hit by machine-gun fire in the mid-section at about 4:00 in the afternoon near Homburg, Germany. Part of the bullet shattered the butt of my pistol and drove pieces into my abdomen. I was twenty-plus miles behind enemy lines. Two German prisoners were ordered at gunpoint to carry me to an aide station where I was given morphine." It wasn't until midnight that an ambulance was able to get him to a field hospital in Belgium. The bullet was laid against his spinal column. Two or three units of blood were required for the operation to remove the slug. There are still tiny remnants of the pistol butt embedded in his mid-section.

Slightly less than four months after his platoon had landed on the European continent in early November each of the original 36 warriors of Holger's platoon and many of their replacements had been captured, killed or wounded.

"I spent a few days in a Paris hospital, then was sent to a hospital in Winchester, England. I was there until July. I came down with hepatitis from the blood I had received and also developed jaundice, so there were a number of medical issues to confront. From England I was sent by hospital ship to a medical treatment facility in Wainsborough, Virginia." He continues, "I was released from that hospital in October, and sent to Newport News, Virginia to help process discharges."

His own discharge was Dec. 7, 1945. The next month he returned as a student to Gettysburg College, as did his twin, Howard. Upon graduation from Gettysburg College he took a turn teaching chemistry at the college, then applied to the prestigious Temple University School of Medicine in Philadelphia. He was accepted and began his study in 1948. His twin also went to medical school, but up the road a bit to Harvard.

Five of the Rasmussen brothers served in WWII – two in the Army in Europe, one in the Army in New Guinea, another in the Navy in the South Pacific, and the fifth in the Navy in the U.S. The sixth brother was too young to serve during WWII but did fly B-29's during the Korean War. All came home alive, and all went on to higher education.

Holger explains that his education benefits went beyond the G.I. Bill. All of his medical school tuition was covered under Public Law 16, enacted in 1943 to pay for the rehabilitation of disabled veterans.

"I finished medical school in 1952 during the Korean War and went back in the Army for a year as an officer and physician. I was assigned to Fitzsimmons Hospital in Denver. We were the chest center for the entire armed services. As an intern I did 50-60 Broncoscophies, and with Lowry Air Force Base nearby I delivered some 80 babies."

He was also Battalion Surgeon at two other bases – Fort Carson, CO; and Camp Attebury in Indiana. In 1954 he went into private practice opening an office in Fremont, CA.

"I was in practice in that area for 38 years primarily as a family physician."

He found time to become Chief of Staff at Fremont's Washington Hospital, Head of OBGYN at the same institution, President of the California Academy of Family Physicians, on the Board of Directors of the American Academy

of Family Physicians and a number of other prestigious positions.

For nine years he also was President of the Fremont
Unified School Board and helped start Ohlone College. He
was instrumental in founding the Washington Outpatient
Surgery Center in the Fremont area, and he served on its
board for nine years. During the initial professional liability
crisis in California, he helped develop and was on the Board
of Governors of "The Doctors Company", a physician-
owned-and-operated medical-professional liability insurance
company.

Holger and wife Linda were married in 1975. They
moved to Lake Wildwood in 1991, with Holger commuting
to the Fremont area for a part of each week. He then spent
eight years as a consultant with Milliman and Robertson,
Inc., a health care management company, with emphasis on
promoting the efficiency and quality of healthcare both in
the hospital and the outpatient setting.

He has not yet retired and is currently working in the
area of hormone therapy for aging adults. During life on
the family Pennsylvania farm during the 1930's he learned
the valuable lesson that *work came before play.* Based on Holger Rasmussen's attitude and enthusiasm, he has melded the
concepts of work and play into one harmonious way of life.

Chapter 3: Bill Dobbins – USN

In the whaleboat, "We had to work very fast as men can't last long in near freezing water."

BILL DOBBINS was born Oct. 10, 1920 in the small town of Marion, KS, dead center in the state some 165 miles SE of Kansas City. "I spent my first twelve years in Marion, and learned good Midwestern values." His words: "Hard work, pragmatic, frugal, austere, perseverance," and more are not unlike Carl Sandburg's, who wrote about these same heartland values while Bill was growing up.

During his teens he lived in Omaha and Kansas City, and after high school went to work in a steel mill in the latter city. "I knew I wanted to join the Navy, and I enlisted in

1937." His laugh is nearer a throaty growl. "I went to three different cities to sign up – Kansas City, Omaha and St. Louis. I thought I'd triple my chances of getting in, but they were all in the same naval district so two of the three were a waste of time." He was called up in 1940 and did his basic at Great Lakes Naval Training Center in Illinois.

"After graduation I was assigned to the Battleship *USS West Virginia*, and I headed by train to Bremerton, WA where it was getting refitted." He pauses, and again there is the laugh. "I'd spent a few years in the steel mill and knew..." – he is emphatic – "I *knew* steel didn't float – especially that *much* steel." After refitting, the ship steamed to Long Beach and then on to its' new home port in Pearl Harbor.

"December 7, 1941, I was below decks getting ready to go to church services in Honolulu. At first I thought we had been accidentally rammed by another ship. Then general quarters was sounded. I got topside and saw we were under attack." The *West Virginia* was an easy target for the Japanese attackers. The enemy planes swept down a channel that dead-ended at Ford Island and battleship row. Seven of the nine American battleships were moored alongside Ford Island. Tied directly to the quay was the *Tennessee*, and next to it the *West Virginia*. Behind those two was the *USS Arizona* and beyond it the *USS Nevada*. Directly in front of the *West Virginia* was the *Oklahoma*, with the *Maryland* at its side and tied to the shore. Forward of these two was the *USS California*. More than a half-mile wide string of battleships was directly exposed to enemy torpedo planes and bombers. They were almost impossible targets to miss and the enemy was relentless.

"We were hit again and again. Topside the Japanese planes were so close, guys were shooting .45 pistols and throwing potatoes at them. The ship was on fire and it was going down." By counter-flooding the hull, the ship sank directly to the bottom, some forty feet below, unlike the *Oklahoma* which capsized. "The *Arizona* had exploded and the sea was aflame to our stern. We were ordered to abandon ship over the bow and swim to shore past the heavily damaged *Tennessee* tied up between Ford Island and us." About 100 men did not make it off the *West Virginia* alive, including her captain. He was posthumously awarded the Congressional Medal of Honor.

"Because our ship had sunk I was immediately reassigned to the *USS Honolulu*, a light destroyer. A Japanese bomb came between the ship and dock and the concussion blew a hole in the *Honolulu's* side." He went back to the assembly center on Ford Island for another reassignment. "Early the next morning, around 3 a.m., I volunteered for assignment to the *USS Dewey*." The *Dewey* was a Farragut class destroyer built in 1934. The *Dewey* got underway immediately to patrol the area around Hawaii, then joined a task force sailing to help the Marine garrison on Wake Island and then to another task force in February. She screened the carrier *Lexington* in the attacks on Lae and Salamaua, New Guinea; then on to the Battle of the Coral Sea. May 8, the carrier *Lexington* came under heavy attack. The *Dewey* provided antiaircraft fire, and five of her men were wounded by enemy fire.

When the *Lexington* went down, Bill helped in the rescue effort of 112 of her crew. She screened *Yorktown* into a safe harbor a few days later and returned to Pearl Harbor at the end of May, protecting the carrier *Enterprise*. She sailed three days later and joined the Battle of Midway. During the battle of Guadalcanal in August, the *Dewey* engaged Japanese dive-bombers and brought down several planes. She also rescued 40 men from a sinking ship.

"We were in virtually every major Pacific engagement during 1942, including the Battle of the Eastern Solomons late August and the Japanese campaign to reinforce Tulagi and Guadalcanal. We escorted the damaged *Saratoga* to Pearl, then headed to Mare Island for an overhaul."

His mood shifts and a smile crosses his face. "Vallejo's Mare Island is only 30 miles from San Francisco, and it was a great city to visit during liberty. A buddy and I were in a restaurant in the city. I'd asked for a bushel of fresh salad and a gallon of ice cream, but had to settle for a standard meal. A few tables away I noticed this woman and said to my pal, 'Hey, isn't that beautiful?'

"I asked the waitress, 'How could a guy get to meet a looker like that?' She said, 'Why don't you ask her?' So I did, and a few days later we went on a date to the Golden Gate Theater on Market Street. She was absolutely perfect in every way." Bill and Mary had a whirlwind romance and were married a few weeks after their initial date. "November 15, 1942 we eloped to Reno. For a while we were stuck in a blizzard going over the summit on old Highway 40. I shipped out in December aboard the *Dewey* for Alaskan waters, and 'Honey' settled into her job as bookkeeper for an exclusive local retailer."

The Bering Sea in the winter can be very rough, fueled by arctic gales. "We were supporting the Amchitka Campaign. On January 12, 1943, another Farragut class destroyer, the *USS Worden*, moved toward a harbor to provide cover for an Army security detachment. The weather was bad with waves 20-30 feet high and a fierce wind." His pace quickens. "The *Worden* rode the waves and came down on an uncharted rock formation. Her hull was ripped wide open near the engine room. She had no power, and we tried to tow her off, but she was filling very quickly with water. She began to break up.

"I was in charge of the whaleboat for our ship. We dropped it into the sea from the lee side of the *Dewey*. There were three of us on board – the coxswain, engineer and me. I had a boat hook, and we were able to rescue most of the crew." Fourteen of the *Worden's* crew perished out of a total of 251 men on board. "The water was like black jello – a semi-frozen slick of oil three or four inches thick. We'd get men into the whaleboat, pull up alongside our ship and time it so that a wave would carry us up to deck level. Then the survivors would scramble or be pulled onto the *Dewey*. We had to work very fast as a man can't last long in near-freezing water." Bill's pace slows. "We were exhausted by the time we had finished, and very proud of what we'd accomplished."

Late December 1943 Bill was ordered to a newly launched ship, the jeep carrier *USS Savo Island*. "The navy wanted a few experienced men to help train the new guys on shipboard duties. I was on her for six or eight months, then

transferred to another jeep carrier, the *USS Windham Bay*."
His tour on this ship was also about six months.

"Typically the jeep carriers were hundreds of feet
shorter than regular carriers. One day we were in fairly
rough seas and pilots were having problems landing on the
big carriers. We didn't have any planes up at the time because of the weather. One of our officers radioed the big
carrier and said, "If you'll turn your carrier a bit so the
headwind is blowing toward your side we'll take off and
show you how to land all your planes simultaneously using
the deck width, not length, as the landing area."

Bill laughs, "There was a moment of silence, then this
voice booms in reply, 'This is Admiral Halsey. I'd be very interested in speaking with the wiseass who made that sugges-
tion.' Needless to say, there was radio silence.

"My next ship was a new destroyer commissioned mid-
March, 1945, the *USS Bristol*, the last of the Sumner class. I
was the ship's fire control director. I was on her until the
Japanese surrender. We helped lead the *Missouri* into Tokyo
Bay for the formal surrender ceremony September 2, 1945.
From the *Bristol* I was able to watch this moment of history
through binoculars." For the next few months his ship pa-
trolled Japanese waters, including Hiroshima and Nagasaki.

"When the *Bristol* headed home, I got off in Honolulu
and was assigned to a new ship." The *USS Mugford* was a Ba-
gley class destroyer. "We were headed to the Marshall Islands and the Bikini Atoll. I would be helping to set up the
target ships for atomic bomb testing." The ship he came on,
the *Mugford*, was one of the ships that would ride at anchor
during a bomb burst. "My job was to help set up the target

vessels and examine ship components after the blast for damage."

He recounts the second test in the program, an underwater blast. "One of the target ships was the battleship *Pennsylvania*. She had steamed under her own power to Bikini and was put at anchor. After the detonation, eight of us were to go on board. We each had a specific task that was supposed to take 30 seconds to a minute. After we climbed aboard the *Pennsylvania* the shuttle boat operator left. He later said he thought we were supposed to be there 30 minutes, not 30 seconds.

"Immediately when we got back we were put in a lead-lined room and completely shaved. For three weeks we took a shower every hour, 24 hours a day, and had doctors checking us with Geiger counters. For years I had to undergo testing."

He pauses. "It's been about ten years since my last radiological medical exam, and I never did suffer any ill effects. I really didn't know the other men on the ship with me that day and have no idea if any of them eventually developed radiation related illnesses."

In 1947 a tiny bundle with the energy of several atom bombs entered Bill and Mary's life in San Francisco – their son Michael. "He was so cute," Mary says, "and a very good little boy."

Bill made a career of the Navy, including participating in the 1954 hydrogen bomb test also conducted at the Bikini Atoll. "We were aboard ship about ten miles from ground zero. The fireball was three miles wide, and within minutes the mushroom cloud had reached a height of 135,000 feet and was eight miles wide." The blast was equivalent to 100,000,000 tons of TNT.

Bill served his nation with distinction in WWII, Korea and Vietnam. "I retired with almost 28 years of service to my country. We have a fine son, Mike; two grandchildren, Kim and Seana, and three great-grandchildren. Mary and I moved to this area in 1978." The whirlwind engagement turned into a marathon marriage of more than 60 years – until her 2005 passing.

Chapter 4: Ben West -- AAF

**"It was a steep and terrifying front-row ride
for 17,000 vertical feet."**

THE DAY Ben West was born in 1921, his dad and crew
whooped and hollered in a field near his drilling rig, shout-
ing, "Here it comes," as oil shot to and through the earth's
surface. A few miles away, in Sapulpa, OK, the doctor – no
less enthusiastically – was reassuring Ben's mother with,
"Here he is," as he presented her new son.

Sapulpa, about 14 miles SW of Tulsa, was a small town
of less than 20,000, but important as an oil boomtown and
cattle shipping center for the railroad. It was also the hub
of two major highways – Route 66 and Highway 75.

Says Ben, "Life growing up was good for me and my two older brothers. My dad was an oil well drilling contractor and also owned some farms in Arkansas and Texas." He pauses for a few seconds. "Then the Depression hit and my folks lost the farms for back taxes, and the drilling equipment rusted in the fields because the payments couldn't be made." Again he is silent as he reflects back some seven decades. "But dad was tough and he started a little restaurant in town, then a small dairy and finally back to the oil business, and we did better than most.

"In my early teens I caddied at the local golf course and got pretty good at the game for a kid." At Sapulpa High School, he lettered in basketball as point guard, and in his senior year he was the number-one ranked player on both the golf and tennis varsity teams. "I was too small for football," he offers.

He graduated in 1940, worked in a factory during the day and attended a free government school in the evenings that taught aircraft assembly. In 1941 he headed to L.A. to join one of his brothers who was a foreman at Douglas Aircraft. In 1942 he received a draft notice and was advised by his company they would get him a deferment. "I told them I didn't want one, and I was going to join the service. I went back to Sapulpa because I wanted my home state to get credit for my enlistment, and I joined August, 1942 in the Aviation Cadet Program."

He headed west to the Santa Ana Airbase classification center February 1943. "I had 20/25 vision in one eye and was disqualified for both pilot and bombardier training. I was so disappointed I couldn't be a pilot." He completed preflight basic training near Houston, than attended Navigator School at Hondo Airbase in Hondo, TX. The Monday after he graduated in October 1943, as a new second Lieutenant, he was called to the commander's office and offered the job of being a replacement instructor. "Sir, if I wanted to stay in the states I would have kept my job at Douglas."

Despite not qualifying initially for bombardier because of his right eye, he was sent to that school in Roswell, NM, and graduated in December. "From there I went to Great Bend, Kansas, for B-29 crew training."

The B-29 Superfortress was the most sophisticated bomber of WWII. Maximum speed was 375 MPH at 25,000 feet. Service ceiling was almost 32,000 feet. Normal cruising speed was 200-250 MPH, with a range of 3,200 miles loaded with fuel and bombs. The crew numbered 11 located in three pressurized cabins – six in the forward cabin, four mid-fuselage and the tail gunner. Ben, as bombardier, was located at the very front of the plane. Were the B-29 a ballpoint pen, Ben's nose would scrape the paper as it writes. The pilot and co-pilot sat a few feet above and behind him, one right and one left. In addition to being bombardier, he was also the nose gunner for the aircraft.

"I trained in my plane with my crew for ten months." His B-29 was named *Lady Mary Anna*, a take-off on the name of the islands they'd be flying from, the Marianas, to bomb Japan. The plane's nose-art was a scantily clad and beautiful girl. Oct. 28, 1944 they left Kansas and headed to Saipan via Sacramento, Oahu and Kwajalein in the Marshall Islands. That same day B-29's already on Saipan made the first bombing run on Japanese territory, the island of Truk.

The *Lady Mary Anna* touched down at Isley Field, Saipan Nov. 1, and Superfortress Squadron 874, 498th Bomb Group, 73rd Wing, 20th Air Force was ready to go.

Ben has a 3 X 5" notebook with a leather cover titled "My Life in the Service". It is a diary with small line drawings of servicemen and/or -women in the corners and inspirational sayings at the bottom of each page. November 5, Ben wrote in his journal, "Flew 1st combat mission to Iwo Jima as a prelude to invasion. Our flight bombed by radar and missed. The 2nd flight did considerable damage by bombing visually. Some flak but no fighters." The writing is matter-of-fact, terse and economical like a telegram where you pay by the word.

November 16 his team is briefed for the first raid on Tokyo, some 1,500 miles away, by B-29's. The very first raid on Tokyo had occurred several years before when Doolittle's Tokyo Raiders made their famous assault from the aircraft carrier *Hornet* with 16 B-25's on April 18, 1942. That run was mostly symbolic -- to let the enemy know we were serious. The B-29's would finish the job the Raiders had started.

Every day they were briefed, usually at 2 or 3 a.m., only to have flights cancelled because of bad weather. November 24, he writes in his journal, "This was it!! Finally got off on 1st raid by land-based planes on Tokyo. We've got an artist, photographer and journalist for Air Force Magazine on board. Encountered flak and fighters only after bombs were dropped. Some flak hit very close, but none direct. I got no shots at fighters myself as all attacks came from the sides. Flight back was uneventful. After debriefing we had steak and beer to drink. Happy, yet sad because two B-29's and one crew lost. I hit the sack. I was pretty tired." He'd had a long day – 22 hours from briefing, take-off and return.

Two days later the Japanese retaliated by dropping incendiary and fragmentation bombs on their base, destroying or damaging three B-29's. The next day they returned and five more B-29's were out of action.

December 3 the *Lady Mary Anna* went on its second daylight raid over Tokyo. He writes, "We were in #3 position of lead element and encountered 25-30 fighters after 'bombs away' over target. They got five of our planes and we got 5-7 of theirs. Bomb run was perfect. Our squadron lost two planes and possibly both crews. They were swell guys."

The rest of December and into early January 1945 Ben's team continued making bomb runs from their base on Saipan. January 9, they made another run on Tokyo. "At the coast of Japan," Ben states, "we got on the bomb run. We tried to drop our bombs but we couldn't. One of the bombs had unhooked in the front and was armed, but it stayed attached in the rear. After leaving the target and the Japanese mainland we dropped 15,000 feet, depressurized and the engineer and I went out in the open bomb bay. We tried the emergency bomb drop motor but only burnt it out because the bomb was hung up. I tied a strap around myself and one around the engineer. We managed to shake six bombs out by having the pilot sway the ship while I held down the release switch. If the front, and armed, dangling part of the bomb had hit any part of the plane we would likely have blown up." He chuckles as he wraps up this episode, "We made it back to base and had to land with the bomb bay doors open and four bombs still on board." According to his journal, "The #4 engine did catch fire just before landing, but Captain Greene managed a good 3-point landing."

The next few days, he writes, "We played a couple of ball games with Marines that we won 3 to 2. They gave us beers and treated us pretty nice after the game."

January 27, Ben flew a mission to Tokyo. "We started with ninety planes and lost eight. Our squadron came out okay with no losses. This was the toughest so far."

March 9, they were returning from a run over Tokyo. "We were about 25,000 feet. Our right inboard engine was smoking, then it caught on fire. Of course, I could see it clearly from my position. The engineer tried the remote extinguisher and the fire diminished. A moment later it flared up again and wouldn't go out. The pilot started gradually descending, and the fire continued. We were afraid of an explosion and the wing being blown off. 'I'm going to take us into a dive,' the captain said on the inter-com, 'and hope the increase in speed will blow the fire out.' At about 20,000 feet he put us into a sixty or so degree dive from horizontal. I had a perfect view of the ocean below. Very quickly we gained 100 –110 MPH to about 350-360 MPH... maybe faster." Ben puts a pause on the action, then continues. "I was looking at the engine, then the sea, the engine... like a tennis match." The ride down was swift, yet an eternity. "'It's out,' I told the pilot, 'It's out!' We leveled off at about 3,000 feet above the water. You have to know, I was drastically scared." It was a steep and terrifying front row ride for 17,000 vertical feet.

"April 15 we made an incendiary bomb run on Tokyo. Most of our bomb runs were 25,000 feet or so. This one was at 9,000 feet. Flak was intense, but not too close. Many searchlights, but none caught us. The plane next to us went down. Very sad." The next day, they were informed the bomb run had burned out nine square miles of Tokyo. On some incendiary bomb runs they flew as low as 5,000 feet, with up to 325 B-29's in formation.

"April 12 we had finished another run over Tokyo, and were headed home off the coast of Japan. I saw a lone fighter plane below us. It was a P-51 with the canopy blown off. I contacted the captain, and he radioed the fighter. Not only had he lost his canopy, but his compass was out, and the engine was malfunctioning. We dropped down and escorted him to American controlled Iwo Jima, some 3-400 miles away. It was good payback to the fighter boys who had done so much to protect us. We continued on to our base in Saipan."

He pauses. "By the way, one of my brothers was a Marine who landed with the invasion of Iwo Jima months before. He was wounded and awarded a Purple Heart."

Originally the B-29 crews were supposed to come home after 25 missions.

"When we got to 22 or 23 we were told we'd have to do 30 missions. They just couldn't get the replacement crews trained fast enough. We grumbled a bit, but went on doing our jobs with enthusiasm. When we got close to 30 we had our going home objective raised to 35." Ben completed his final and 35th mission July 4, 1945. This last flight the plane had to make an emergency landing on Iwo Jima, about midway between Tokyo and their Saipan base, because of engine problems.

One of the more famous photos of WWII was taken from *Lady Mary Anna*. It shows a formation of B-29's headed to Tokyo with a snow-clad Mt. Fuji in the background.

Ben was awarded the Distinguished Flying Cross and an Air Medal with six oak leaf clusters. He was credited with one official kill of a Japanese fighter plane headed straight toward their plane. "It was coming from 2 o'clock low. I sighted in and got it just in time. It was on fire, swept just under our fuselage, and went down."

By November 1945 he was home in Oklahoma. He attended Oklahoma A&M (now Oklahoma State), and played varsity golf. He married and has two daughters, seven grandchildren and an equal number of great-grandchildren. He and wife Nadine moved to Lake Wildwood in 1982. She passed away late October of 2000. "I only have one WWII photo," he apologizes, "as our home was destroyed in the catastrophic and huge 49er fire of 1988.

"We loved to dance, and Nadine and I won a few swing and jitter bug contests in past years. I also participated in Lake Wildwood's little theatre." He still plays a mean game of golf. His drives are long and straight, and from 100-150 yards out the greens are like one of his long ago bomb run targets – they don't stand a chance of not getting hit dead center.

Marguerite and George - Wedding Day

Chapter 5: George Leipzig – Army

"George grabbed one soldier and jammed his rifle in the stomach of the other to get them to stop."

GEORGE LEIPZIG was born in Portland, OR, May of 1925. He was the middle child sandwiched by two older brothers and a pair of sisters.

"Dad, known as the 'Mayor of Sellwood,' owned a small restaurant in the southeast section of town. The restaurant was open seven days a week and all us kids worked. Dad was there every day and Mom was a part-timer." He smiles, "Things really took off when Prohibition ended. It was a wonderful place with hardwood floors, a great back bar with large mirrors, booths and stools for the counter trade. It was bright and cheery with high ceilings."

He reflects back seven decades, "I'd wash dishes or sweep the floor – stuff that a 10-11 year old could handle. It was a real family affair." George also had a paper route and caddied from age 11-15. The early grades were a small parochial school with fewer than 100 students. "I was whacked by the nuns half-a-dozen times in eight years... not too bad."

He continues, "High school was Columbia Prep with about 120 students – all boys. All the priests were from Notre Dame." George played four years of basketball – two on JV and the remainder as a varsity forward.

"I had to ride buses to school. Including transfers, it took an hour or so each way." Most summers were spent working to come up with the $120 annual tuition. "It was a great education."

He recalls Dec. 7, 1941, "I was a Junior in high school. I was fishing along the river with three pals and this man approached and told us the Japanese bombed Pearl Harbor. We weren't quite sure where it was. Maybe it was me who thought it was an island in the Aleutians. We sure found out as soon as we got home."

Out of George's 32-member graduating class of May 1943, three were eventually killed in action.

"It was about that mid-May timeframe I met Marguerite Brian. We were introduced by mutual friends one weekend in Seaside, Oregon, the state's largest oceanfront resort." Marguerite was also from Portland. He laughs, "I think it was about fifteen minutes after meeting that she told me she didn't care for my pompadour." He pauses, "What she said made sense, and I thought she was quite a gal, so I went to a barber shop and changed my hair style." They started dating.

George received his draft notice July 15. "Marguerite was upset but realized I had a responsibility to my country." During the first week of August he reported to the Portland Armory for induction, then boarded a train to Fort Lewis, near Tacoma. After a few processing days he began the six-day trip to Fort McClellan, AL, an infantry replacement training center.

It was a 17-week program of close order drill, calisthenics, weapons familiarity, digging holes, bivouacs and camping. During that time he and Marguerite exchanged weekly letters. At the end of the four-month program all the graduates, except six, were given a short furlough then shipped to Anzio, Italy as replacement infantry.

"The six of us held over became a nucleus of instructors for the next two training cycles. I taught for another 35-plus weeks. I guess they kept me because I had a booming voice, was a big kid at more than 190 pounds and 6'2", and had done pretty well in my initial training." He was promoted to corporal, and his first furlough came at the end of his 14th month.

He and another soldier received orders for Fort Ord. "We had to change trains in New Orleans and had a brief layover. I'd been there once before and we headed to Bourbon Street." By the time they returned to the station they were carrying a few bottles of added travel supplies in brown paper bags. They boarded the wrong train.

"We were maybe 20-30 miles out of New Orleans. The conductor checked our tickets. 'You boys s'posed to be going to California. Y'awl headed for Chicago.'

The train came to a stop at the next station. 'Train to California will be along shortly. They know to stop for you.'"

George continues, "We got on the proper train. We thought it was pretty funny. The MP's that came down the aisle weren't amused. They did, however, thank us for relinquishing our paper bags."

George's time at Fort Ord was but a week, then on another train – this with blacked out windows – to San Francisco. "I was one of 1,850 replacement troops who boarded a ship November 4, 1944 for the South Pacific."

The troop ship sailed under the Golden Gate Bridge, westward toward the Far East. It had three decks with six layers of hammocks per deck. By the second day they were in tropical waters as cruise speed was about 17 knots per hour. Their destination, New Caledonia, was about 7,000 miles to the southwest – less than 1,000 miles off the eastern coast of Australia.

"We reached Noumea, the capital, 16 days after sailing," says George, "and went over the side into wooden landing craft – Higgins boats. We knew when we reached New Caledonia that the 1,850 replacement troops on our ship would be heading different directions. I was sent to a camp outside of town awaiting further orders." More than 200,000 men were staged at New Caledonia in 1943.

Days passed with close order drill, calisthenics and other activities to keep the men occupied. There also was free time. "There was a great beach with an Army lifeguard sitting on a tall perch. The thing we couldn't understand was why he had an old Springfield rifle. He told us the rifle was to shoot at the sharks. He added he almost never killed one, but the noise was enough to get most of the swimmers back to shore. He was right – when he shot I got back on dry land." They were in New Caledonia about a week.

Of the 1,850 who had sailed with George from San Francisco, only 200 boarded the liberty ship headed northwest past Guadalcanal and New Georgia to Bougainville. He was officially assigned to the 37th Infantry Division, 148th Regiment.

When he reached Bougainville he discovered his unit had left days earlier. "I waited for another liberty ship. Eventually I continued heading north and west." George still had more than 2,000 miles to go to catch up with the 37th. He and his division were headed to the Lingayen Gulf on the Philippines island of Luzon.

January 9, his division and other units of the Sixth Army moved into the Lingayen Gulf. The Seventh and Third Fleets and the Twentieth Air Force supported them. Shells from big guns aboard battleships, cruisers, destroyers and other ships bombarded the beach area. More than 600 ships were in the gulf to support the landing operation. Bombers and fighter planes hit interior enemy targets. Troops began landing mid-morning.

There was no enemy fire. Instead, a few Filipinos, waving torn flags, greeted the soldiers. They had 160 tough walking miles to reach their main objective – Manila. George's ship arrived February 20th. He was assigned to Company B, 2nd Rifle Platoon.

Three days later George had caught up with his outfit, now in the heart of downtown Manila. The battle turned brutal as the Japanese made their last stand. They had large stocks of ammunition, food and weapons and occupied heavily fortified buildings and pillboxes. Minefields were plentiful throughout the city and many buildings were booby-trapped with high explosives.

By February 24, George's unit began an assault on the Legislative Building. "We were running from bomb crater to bomb crater. Enemy soldiers were on the top of the building and firing out of window openings on all the floors. I was snug up against the side of the building. I heard and felt a drip, drip, drip on my helmet. Then liquid flows over the helmet rim onto my face and clothing. It's blood. I glance up and there is a dead Japanese soldier draped over a windowsill."

His squad entered the building. "I was just inside the main door. I see an enemy soldier down the hall and sight my rifle. I caught him in the throat before he could fire." Americans did not stay in the building for long – it was too heavily fortified and had as many as 750 enemy soldiers.

"We pulled out and returned to a building we had taken earlier – City Hall." The next day 155mm Howitzers shelled the Legislative Building for many hours.

"When we returned we secured the building floor by floor, including the basement area with its two big tunnels and caves built by the Japanese. That night two of us were assigned to stay in a part of the basement area near a tunnel – two hours on and two hours off guard duty to prevent enemy infiltration."

He explains no light was allowed, no matches to glance at a watch. The man on duty would silently count off the seconds and minutes until his time was up. "Not too far away were a half-dozen enemy dead. Throughout the night we could hear the huge Norway rats scampering about and ripping the flesh from the bodies." He adds, "It is a very distinctive and unpleasant sound."

The next day his company was ordered to take the Finance Building manned by some 300 enemy soldiers with 37mm and 75mm guns as well as rifles, machine guns and mortars. "Again we used tanks and heavy weapons to soften them up, then had to take the structure floor-by-floor."

After the civic building operations ended his company was assigned to an adjacent residential area. He was appointed a 2nd platoon squad leader. "My company was walking down a broad residential street, half on one side, half on the other. A jeep comes down the street with a major and General MacArthur. I moved to the center and raised my hand to stop them.

"General, I wouldn't go down there... it hasn't been cleared yet."

MacArthur said, "Hello, Son, we'll be alright." As they drove off I realized I hadn't saluted.

Hours later they were clearing a home. George's platoon leader told him to take some men and check the second floor. "I opened a door to an upstairs bathroom and there's a tub and the water worked. None of us had had a bath for a very long time. We'd fill the tub and 2-3 men would take an individual bath, then drain the tub, fill it again and 2-3 more would bathe. We were concerned the water supply would dry up at anytime which was the reason for men sharing the water. The platoon leader came to the second floor and asked, 'How come you didn't send someone to get me?' I told him I was just getting ready to do that. Eventually the entire platoon took a bath."

The next afternoon they set up a light machine gun on the second floor of a residence with a sweeping view of the street. "The residents were German – Herr and Frau Kruger. They were frightened. One of my grandfathers was from Germany, and I speak some of the language. They were greatly relieved when I told them we meant them no harm and would be gone in the morning."

George continues, "That next day a Catholic chaplain drives up in a jeep and asks if we would like to hear Mass? He sets up a makeshift alter on a school ground. Right in the middle of Mass enemy mortar fire starts getting very close. Everyone ducked for cover except the priest. He didn't miss a beat."

That night his squad dug foxholes in a schoolyard lawn about 25 feet off the street. "It was about 2 a.m. and I hear the barely audible scraping of feet coming down the street. I couldn't see anything, but it sounded like eight or so men who I assumed to be an enemy infantry patrol. I had no grenades in the hole. I didn't want to fire my rifle as that would give away our position. The next day I told an officer in my company what I had and hadn't done. He said I'd made the right decision under the circumstances."

A few days later George's regiment was pulled off the front line and given a three-week rest. "Because I had been an instructor at Infantry Replacement Training School our company commander put me in charge of keeping the men busy. Six days a week from 8:30 to 11:30 a.m., I led the men in exercise, close order drill, rifle inspections and hygiene lectures." He chuckles, "I was a very popular fellow."

He resumes, "About the fifth day a big water tanker pulls up. Our water was stored in big blister bags. The driver tells us to empty the bags. We tell him they're almost full and to just top them off. He explains the San Miguel Brewery was so happy to be liberated that they wanted to give us a little reward. The tanker was full of beer... within hours most of the men were, too."

After their rest period George was made Platoon Guide. With the Americans victorious in Manila and the Central Luzon Plain, the Japanese headed north and east to the rugged mountains. They hoped American firepower and tanks would be less effective. In this large area the Japanese had built cave and tunnel fortifications dug into mountainsides up to 5,000 feet high. Some mountains, terraced with rice fields, rose to 9,000 feet.

The first regiment to head to the mountains was the 129th the end of March. Within a week George's regiment, the 148th, began its mountain trek. Hundreds of Filipinos came to see them off. Some placed garlands around soldier necks while others said prayers for these liberators of Manila. Soldiers boarded 10-MPH narrow gauge rail cars. Whenever the train stopped children would give the "V" for victory sign and cheer the troops onward. The ride, 12 hours long, ended near the Lingayen Gulf area. This was followed by a two-hour truck ride to a staging area.

If Manila was difficult for George, the Baguio operation would be hell.

"As Platoon Guide for Company B, 2nd Platoon, when we would go on patrol in the mountains I would be the last man in line. It was my job to carry supplies, maps, and do the records keeping – a chronicle of who was wounded or killed or injured. I was also in charge of cigarette and beer rationing. In all I carried about an extra twenty pounds."

When George left Fort Ord, he weighed 192 pounds. By the time of the mountain offensive, he was down to 148.

"We were in the mountains and meeting resistance – small arms and machine-gun fire. Some of our men were wounded and Filipino civilians came up with litters to carry them to safety."

He continues, "The next morning I went to company headquarters to pick up three replacements. We came under heavy attack on the way back and two of the three new men were killed."

He pauses. "The following day our platoon sent a patrol down a well-worn path. No talk... all hand signals." Suddenly the men in front began taking and giving fire. Eight feet ahead of George was a big puff of smoke.

"Somebody yelled, 'The Greek got hit!'" George ran to his comrade and lifted him to his feet. The platoon was under attack by a Japanese battalion. The platoon began retreating. George grabbed one soldier and stuck his rifle in the stomach of another to get them to halt. They made a litter out of jackets and rifles and carried the Greek back to a perimeter area. Initially in bad shape, he survived.

Almost an hour later George heard a cry for help. Earlier he had done a head count and recognized the voice, his pal Fergy. He was about forty yards from safety.

During the initial attack Fergy had been shot and had fallen into a mass of leaves. The Japanese, chasing the platoon, had charged all around him. No one stopped to finish him off. Then the enemy fell back. Fergy had waited about 30 minutes, then struggled toward friendly territory. Weakened, he could go no farther and cried out for help. George ran the 120 feet and helped his buddy get back to safety. He, too, survived.

As victory appeared imminent and the war in general began to wind down, President Truman pulled 18-19 year old troops off the front line July 1945. "I had turned twenty just two months earlier. The young men were transferred to a 'Teenage Commando' unit. George was promoted to 1st Sergeant, reporting to the new company commander.

"We got word on the first A-bomb eight days after it fell August 6th on Hiroshima. Everybody went wild." When the war ended George didn't have enough points to go home. Mid-December he received a letter from Marguerite expressing her sympathy about his Dad having a fatal heart attack at age fifty-six. January 25, he was eligible to go home. He landed in San Francisco and several days later caught a train to Fort Lewis. In Eugene, OR, a Pastor pulled him from the train. He drove George to Portland. His Mom was dying with cancer. As they approached the hospital, George was told he might not recognize her.

In her room he leaned to kiss her. She opened her eyes, smiled, and said, "Hello, Sonny." Those were her last words.

George enrolled at Oregon State in Corvallis and earned a B.S. in Agriculture in 1950. He and Marguerite married in June 1947. She worked as a model in an exclusive gown shop in Portland. George worked 34 years as a research chemist and in marketing for American Can Co. They moved to Redwood City north of San Jose early 1951.

They have nine children – six boys and three girls – and six grandchildren.

Marguerite had her own public relations company and handled a number of key accounts including Marine World/ Africa USA and Circle Star Theater as well as professionally coordinating numerous political campaigns. She was a member of the Redwood City Council from 1972-82 and Mayor from 1976-79. Two of their sons are elected city officials – the apple and tree thing.

They moved to Lake Wildwood early 1984. George was on the Western Gateway Park Board 1985-93. Marguerite served ten years on the Lake Wildwood Association Board beginning in 1986 and ending 2001 – three separate terms. She was president three times. George was elected to the Nevada Irrigation District Board 1992, reelected in the 2006 General Election and still serves as a director. He was also a Nevada County Recreation Commissioner and on the county General Plan Update Committee.

Marguerite has been on the Fair board, Park Board and active with the sanitation district.

George was both a founder and president of the Gold Country Senior Softball League. In later years as an umpire he wore his NID ball cap – Never In Doubt.

He earned the Combat Infantry Badge and the Bronze Star along with campaign badges and other awards.

Chapter 6: Jim Baque – USN

"You have five minutes to abandon ship or you will be sunk and you will die."

JIM BAQUE, the first of two children, was born in Sand Coulee, Montana, in 1921.

"Not too long after I was born, we moved to Great Falls, about nine miles away. My parents owned a grocery story, which was run by my mother and an aunt. My Dad was an underground coal miner working the drilling and other equipment used to extract the coal." It was difficult and dangerous work with often disastrous consequences.

His eyes mist over as he talks about his Dad. "He was the greatest fisherman in the state. He loved to hunt and taught me every thing he could about shooting game birds – pheasant, grouse, partridge and prairie chickens."

Great Falls is on the Missouri River near the center of the state, and as it knifes through the city it drops more than 500 feet with five dramatic and thundering waterfalls. Explorers Lewis and Clark wrote they could hear the falls some seven miles away. In the 1920's the town had fewer than 25,000 residents.

"I loved Great Falls. It was a swell place to grow up, with much to do for a young boy." But the Depression had a major impact on the community and Jim's family. "I went to work as a child, delivering the afternoon newspaper and selling the *Saturday Evening Post* and *Ladies Home Journal* door-to-door to bring in a few extra bucks." His sister, three years younger than Jim, helped out at the store. His junior/senior year in high school he worked as a bellhop at a four-story downtown hotel, The Falls. He also played guard for the varsity football Great Falls Bisons. After graduating he worked at a service station and drove a delivery truck for a bakery. For fun he hunted, fished and played industrial league basketball.

"The evening of December 7, 1941," Jim picks up, "six of us were in the local watering hole, the Mint Saloon." (The Mint, now closed, was a haunt of cowboy artist Charles Russell and home to a number of his paintings. The back bar is in the Charles Russell museum in Great Falls.) "Boy, were we mad," says Jim. "But you have to understand, we were Montana boys and thought we were pretty tough." As the evening wore on they got even tougher. "We knew we could help make short work of the Japanese." The next day, Jim and his five pals went to enlist. "A buddy and I joined the Navy, two joined the Air Corps and two the Army." He is pensive a moment. "All six of us had known one another all our lives – three did not make it home from the war."

A month after Pearl Harbor he was sent to the induction center in Salt Lake City, then to San Diego for basic training. "On the train to San Diego," he muses, "I started having second thoughts about the USN – what's a Montana boy doing going to sea since I get sick on a Ferris wheel."

He leaps forward, "Never did get seasick."

He shifts back to 1942. "Because my records said I'd worked for a bakery they wanted to make a cook out of me. I didn't want any part of that and focused on my skills as a game bird hunter... that I'd been doing it since I was a little kid and had a good record of hitting what I aimed at." He was sent to gunnery school at the nearby destroyer base and was made a 3rd class gunners mate when he graduated and was assigned to the USN Armed Guard Gunners.

The Armed Guard Gunners, including USN gunners, pharmacists, radiomen, and a few other key titles, were assigned as primary protectors aboard Merchant Marine ships.

By the end of the war more than 145,000 Navy men had been assigned to more than 6,200 ships.

"My first ship was a small Union Oil tanker, the *Paul M. Gregg.* I had six gunners reporting to me, and we made a run from Los Angeles to Hawaii, then from L.A. to Alaska. I was the senior Navy man on board." That first assignment is where he picked up the nickname, "Guns". It would follow him for the rest of his Navy career.

He chuckles as he recalls an encounter with an Army sergeant in Dutch Harbor. "He came on board asking if anyone could spare some booze. I told him I had an unopened fifth of bourbon, but I couldn't sell it as I was saving it for my birthday the very next day. He pulled out a wad of bills and began making offers. I finally sold it for $100 which was not bad as it had cost me $4.50." He reflects back on his pay. "I think, at the time, I was making a little over $30 a month."

Fall of 1942 his father was reactivated. "My Dad had been in the Navy during WWI." Jim pulls out an old album and proudly shows a photo of his dad in his WWI uniform. "He was called back to service as an interpreter. He was second generation French and spoke the language fluently. I was given a pass to visit home to see him off. It was a very emotional time for the entire family. He served in North Africa, Algeria and Tunisia and returned home unharmed.

"I took the train back to San Francisco and was assigned to the *SS President Polk*, November 1942. It was one of the newest passenger ships in the American President Lines (APL) and was being temporarily manned by the Merchant Marine to transport troops to the Western Pacific." (It was subsequently commissioned as a Naval vessel October of 1943.)

"Our first job was to take 3,000 USMC, including Carlson's Raiders, to the Guadalcanal area. This time I was not in command of all the Navy personnel. There were 48 Armed Guard Gunners on board, which required a few officers." He recounts one amusing encounter with the Marines and USMC officer James Roosevelt, son of FDR.

"The ship's store was run by the Merchant Marine and called the 'Slop Chest'. Everybody had to stand in line, and with 3,000 Marines, plus our Navy team and the Merchant

Mariners, the queue could get long. Our gun crews were four hours on and four hours off and we didn't have time to stand in line when we weren't on duty. The Merchant Marine captain and my officers said ship's company could go to the head of the line, as the Marines didn't have shipboard duties. Unfortunately, no one discussed that policy with the Marine officers. "

He continues, "Coincident with that edict I was just getting off shift. There were 200 or so Marines waiting to enter the Slop Chest. I went to the front and nicely explained how the rules worked for the ship's company, and knew they would understand." He smiles, then continues, "An armed Marine blocked my way and wouldn't let me jump the line." When the Merchant Marine officers and Roosevelt heard about the incident they had different reactions. Roosevelt said tersely, "Nobody steps in front of a Marine!"

"Okay," The Merchant Mariner said, and closed down the facility.

After a few days Roosevelt agreed to let ship's crew go to the head of the line.

"In the New Hebrides the beautiful white-tufted leather-covered piano still on board in the lounge, a carry-over from happier days, disappeared." According to Jim it was off-loaded with Marine battle gear and supplies, along with the 3,000 Marines, and to this day languishes in the jungle, its ivories now silenced for more than six decades.

By December, 1942, the *President Polk* was back in Pearl Harbor. "We picked up about 500 wounded patients that needed to be transported back to the states, plus we were taking military wives and kids. We also were transporting a significant number of prostitutes being sent back to the mainland." Two warships, the *Helena* and *St. Louis*, escorted them. "We had to zigzag across from Hawaii to S.F. and were pummeled by winter storms. Most of the passengers were ill." The hospital personnel took care of the wounded patients. It was left up to Merchant Marine personnel and Jim's Navy team to take care of other passengers in a caring, compassionate way.

From the *Polk* he was assigned to a freighter in the Bayer fleet. "One late afternoon in early 1943 we sailed out of Galveston, Texas into the Gulf of Mexico with a full load of cargo. We had not yet hooked up with a convoy. It was pitch black, the middle of the night." He pauses as he searches the darkness of that long-ago evening, "Our ship was bathed in light from an enemy vessel as a shot crossed the bow. We were ordered to halt."

The ship began to slow, while Jim's crew of eight men manned their guns, ready to fire. As they did so, a voice boomed through a megaphone in German-accented English, "You are ordered to surrender or you will be sunk."

The floodlights from the German vessel bounced off the sides of Jim's ship and outlined a U-boat, with its 4-inch deck gun and machine-guns directed toward them at almost point-blank range. It was official policy for an American merchant ship not to surrender, but if enemy boarding were inevitable, and lives were in great jeopardy, surrender was a last resort. The U-boat had had the element of surprise. Before leaving the ship the crew would do all they could to flood the vessel and destroy sensitive records.

"You have five minutes to abandon ship," – the voice was emphatic – "or you will be sunk and you will die." The Merchant Marine captain notified Jim and his Navy team, with much lighter armaments, to stand down. The ship would surrender.

Jim states, "There was a crew of 25 Merchant Marine and eight Armed Guards. My guys wanted to fight, as did I, but I followed the captain's order." His hands clench and unclench. He still wants to pull the trigger on that battle.

"The Germans boarded as we were preparing our two life boats. They were very businesslike and stood by as we all loaded into the boats." A few of them lent a hand, like humorless pursers responsible for the comfort and safety of their disembarking and disgruntled customers upset because their voyage had been unexpectedly shortened.

The boats were lowered. The merchant sailors had opened valves to flood the ship. The explosives the Germans set would expedite the job. It went down soon after the ship was abandoned. Jim's ship was one of 70 ships sunk or damaged by U-boats in the Gulf of Mexico between May, 1942, and the end of their gulf activity in December, 1943.

U-boat commanders called it, *"Die gluckliche zeit"* – the happy time.

"We were rescued by another ship early the next morning. We had radioed our position before we left the ship."

From there Jim was assigned to a tanker owned by Tidewater, the predecessor to Getty Oil. The ship, the *Tidewater Associated*, was more than 500 feet long and carried crude oil. "We made one trip to Hawaii where we took oil over and came back with molasses, all in the same tanks."

He adds, "The tanks were steam cleaned before the molasses was pumped in." He smiles. "I spent sixteen months on that ship and went around the world. It turned one-million sea miles while I was on board." He mentally recaps the route from San Pedro to Australia, Bombay, the Persian Gulf and the Suez Canal. In the Suez Canal they off-loaded fuel from the temporarily incapacitated Free French Battleship, *Richelieu*, then headed to Italy.

"We anchored in Naples. There was a message waiting for me from the Red Cross. I was told my Dad was in Algiers, and I planned a meeting with him as we were headed that way for a rendezvous with a convoy headed west across the Atlantic."

He continues, "Our ship had engine problems, and we never made it across the Med in time for me to see my Dad. We eventually fixed the engine, got into a convoy and made it to Brooklyn.

"Because I had been gone so long, more than a year, I was able to get a priority trip ticket to Great Falls by airplane. I boarded a plane from Newark to Dayton. I got bumped, but caught a WASP (Women's Air Force Service Pilots) flight to Wichita, then a two-seat fighter to Ogden... from there to Spokane by transport, then to Great Falls. Every stop, I called my Mom to tell her where I was."

When his leave was done, he headed back to the East Coast and boarded another Tidewater Oil ship headed to Liverpool, then Durban, South Africa. "We were headed home to Liverpool out of Durban up the east coast of Africa and through the Suez canal when we were hit by a torpedo in the Eastern Mediterranean." His voice is calm.

"I had my men at the guns in case the sub surfaced. It didn't. It left us there to sink, but the crew was able to isolate the flooding."

A tanker without escort was, at its very best, a slow-moving shooting gallery target for a U-boat. When damaged, it was – as some say – a sitting duck. "Why they didn't finish us off, I'll never know. We limped into Port Said in Egypt. But, then," he reflects, "I'll never know why the U-boat in the Gulf of Mexico gave us a spotlight and megaphone instead of a few torpedoes." Perhaps no one wanted to mess with a Navy gun crew chief from Montana.

One of Jim's last assignments was aboard the *Haiti Victory*, making three round-trips from San Francisco to Saipan and Guam. By then, he was a Petty Officer, and because they carried reconditioned B-29 and other airplane engines critical to the war, they were afforded priority docking.

"Some ships had been there for several months, constantly getting bumped by more important cargoes. One trip we were anchored at Okinawa, and were ordered out to sea because of an approaching typhoon." There were a number of ships with them. It was night and all running lights on all ships were full blast. The typhoon struck, and it was nearly incomprehensible in its fury, according to Jim. The ship wallowed side-to-side like a drunken penguin, tilted front to back like a kinetic see-saw, and rose and fell as though it were manned by a frantically insane elevator operator – all at the same time.

"The ships were spaced far apart, but when we were at the top of a trough, I could see lights from an adjacent ship far below us." When the *Haiti Victory* bottomed out, the adjacent ship was poised high like a circling buzzard ready to swoop down the slope of the wave.

Jim's last ship pulled into Alameda. He was ordered to lead a 150-man crew to Bremerton, WA, in November 1945, for discharge from the Navy. He was included in that count.

Nearly 800 ships of the Merchant Marine were sunk during WWII. Statistics vary on the number of Merchant Mariners who died, as there was no one central point for data collection. But there is no argument that the losses were dramatic – almost 9,500 died as a result of war action with the enemy. In 1988, WWII Merchant Marine personnel were accorded limited veteran status.

Of the 145,000 USN Armed Guard Gunners assigned to protect those ships, some 2,100 died in combat.

Jim returned to Great Falls, then to Woodbury College in Los Angeles.

In August 1946, Gertrude Grundy, his girlfriend from Great Falls, flew into Las Vegas. He drove up from Los Angeles and they were married.

"I was a manufacturer's rep for a large candy company and sold candy-making ingredients to confectioners throughout the Southwest. Our son, Fred, was born in 1950." From there Jim went to work for Whitman Chocolates in Seattle and then became the West Coast manager headquartered in S.F. in 1956.

"I spent 13 great years with Whitman, then went into business for myself as an empty candy-box broker. At that time we lived in Aptos, California. I sold boxes to See's, Brown and Haley and all the great candy producers on the west coast."

Gertrude died in early 1977. Jim met Phyllis, a widow, a year later. The year 1978 was also when his Dad died from Black Lung disease contracted from his time as a coal miner. Jim and Phyllis married in April, 1979. "That, too, was the year we moved to Lake Wildwood in Penn Valley. I used to play golf all the time, but have backed off a bit recently." He still does beautiful bonsai (some plants in their third decade), belongs to the Lake Wildwood hunting and fishing club and enjoys woodworking.

We look at photos of golf and fishing trips to Mexico within the past several years. One photo shows him at the dock scales with a huge Marlin, another with an equally large sailfish.

Between Phyllis and Jim's blended family there are two sons, three grand-daughters and two grand-sons. They point proudly at a recent photo of a grand-son in his navy whites. He looks eager and proud to serve his country – just like Jim's pictures in uniform from so long ago.

Chapter 7: John Griffith, AAF - NACA

(Predecessor to the National Aeronautics and Space Administration - Test Pilot)

"On a potentially big dollar bonus day at 38,000 feet I pointed to at least a 60 degree angle. By 29,000 feet I had slightly over Mach 1. The test went bad."

IN THE EARLY 1930's John Griffith was a boy growing up in Homewood, IL, just south of Chicago. Above his home was a commercial air route that wended its way from Chicago to New York City with stops in between. His memory is vivid: "I remember the old DC-3 passenger planes flying overhead. Sometimes I'd just lie down in the yard and watch a plane until it disappeared, thinking it would be a great thing to be a pilot flying that aircraft to wherever it was headed."

The family home was lost during the Depression, and John went to live with an aunt. He graduated in pre-engineering from Thornton Junior College as class valedictorian. November 1941 he joined the Army Air Corps, and by September of 1942 he was on his way to New Guinea. He was assigned as a P-40 pilot in the 5th Air Force, 49th Fighter Group, 7th Squadron – the "Screamin Demons." The squadron's emblem was the mythical Java jungle demon that signifies fierceness in battle.

John flew 189 missions and was awarded two Distinguished Flying Crosses and four Air Medals. One of the Air Medals was awarded for air combat with a Zero, where John came out the victor. The story is outlined in a yellowed and ragged article dated "May 15 -- FROM SOMEWHERE IN NEW GUINEA" in a 1943 edition of the Chicago *Daily Tribune:*

"A young Chicagoan yesterday spent a busy morning during an enemy raid on Oro bay. He shot down a Zero after a thrilling dogfight during which his own plane was so badly damaged he was forced to make a crash landing...

"'We saw 18 bombers with a Zero escort heading for Oro bay. I peeled off and made a beam attack, but was unable to see the results of my fire because I was going too fast. I found myself in the middle of a bunch of Zeros and saw one below me. I dived on his tail, fired, and saw pieces fly from his cockpit... When I came out of my dive I saw the Zero strike the water...'"

The article continues, "Griffith then regained altitude despite some trouble with his propeller, dove on a second Zero, and exchanged shots with the plane. By this time his engine was running roughly and his landing gear was damaged." After skidding "...to a stop, later he found 16 bullet holes near the cockpit of his plane."

The article is accompanied by the smiling photo of John snapped the day he received his wings.

"There were some eight or ten occasions when I engaged Zeros in combat, but there were no other kills that could be confirmed," he says.

January 1944 he returned to the states as a fighter pilot instructor in Florida for six months. He was reassigned to Panama and was there for VJ Day, Aug. 14, 1945. In October 1946 he left the service for the campus. He graduated with honors from Purdue University in 1948 with a degree in aeronautical engineering.

"In the spring of 1946, *Aviation Week* and a few other magazines were talking about the new X-1 aircraft. I wrote a letter to Bell Aircraft telling them I was a third-year honor student with 1,200 hours in fighter planes. The letter didn't get me a job. However, when I graduated I was interviewed for a job in the NACA's Lewis Flight Propulsion Lab in Cleveland."

(NACA referred to the National Advisory Committee for Aeronautics, which was the forerunner to NASA – the National Aeronautics and Space Administration.)

"They hired me to do in-air ramjet and icing research. I was there for six months until moving to Langley at Hampton, VA. There I got a good introduction to transonic research..." *(air speeds between Mach .75 and 1.2)* "...to try to find out what really took place at those speeds. Wind tunnels couldn't provide good data. In August 1949 I was given the opportunity to fly research airplanes at what is now NASA's Dryden Flight Research Center in Edwards, CA."

October 14, 1947, the first supersonic flight in level or climbing mode was made by Capt. Charles E. Yeager (USAF) in the X-1 at Edwards. John Griffith was the ninth man (and fourth civilian) to break the sound barrier in the X-1 at Mach 1.13. "I flew the X-1 nine times, the X-4 (he was the first civilian to fly it) three times, the D-558-1 sixteen times, and the D-558-2 eight times." All were aircraft used for transonic and supersonic research.

From September 1949 to October 1950 he was the sole pilot flying the NACA X-1 (designated 6063 NACA). During that same time there were four Air Force test pilots flying their X-1 (6062 AF), including Chuck Yeager. John reached his top speed in the X-1 on May 26, 1950 at Mach 1.20 (Mach 1 equals 741 mph at sea level in dry air at 32 degrees Fahrenheit).

"Every X-1 flight had a chase plane. When I flew the X-1, one of the other test pilots would be in the air in an F-80, F-84 or F-86. Sometimes Yeager was my chase plane pilot, and vice-versa. It was difficult to judge height above the ground during landings. Flying alongside, the chase pilot would, as necessary, radio info to the X-1 pilot. It was especially acute if the windshield was fogged.

"When I first went to work with NACA, I was making $3,727 a year as a test pilot. When I started flying the X-1, I was bumped up to $7,600." He begins to describe a typical X-1 flight. "During the morning, the X-1 would be loaded with liquid oxygen, alcohol and nitrogen. Nitrogen at 5,000 psi was regulated to a lower pressure to pressurize the liquid oxygen and alcohol tanks (about 300 gallons each) to move the propellants to the rocket engine. The X-1 was then put in a pit. A specially modified B-29 was towed over the pit and the X-1 was fastened like a bomb in the bomb bay.

"After take-off and the climb to about 10,000 feet, I'd go down a windy ladder and crawl in the cockpit and strap in. I would hook up the 100-percent oxygen mask and then open a little brass valve to run the gyro instruments and pressurize the cockpit with nitrogen.

"At about 29,000 feet the X-1 would be dropped and I would switch on two of the four 1,500-pound-thrust rockets and climb to 50,000 feet at about .8 Mach. I would make a turn to stop the climb, start a shallow descent and turn on two more rocket tubes to make 6,000 pounds of thrust. Between .8 and Mach 1 there would be some buffeting and trim changes, but not as rough as depicted in the movie, *The Right Stuff.*

"As the propellants were about to run out (at about 1.2 Mach), rolls and pull-ups were made. Control effectiveness about all axes was much less than at speeds below .8 Mach. Instrumentation measured pressure distribution over the wing, structural loads, control position and force, airspeed, altitude, 'G' load and other parameters on oscillographs.

"After these maneuvers, the propellants would run out, and I would purge the tanks and glide to Rogers Dry Lake. We had seven miles north-and-south and five miles east-and -west. I usually landed near the 1-mile marker at about 125 MPH."

John is featured in a book published by NASA in 1999, *Toward Mach 2: The Douglas D-558 Program.* His name, along with three other research pilots and the Chief of the Flight Crew Branch at NASA's Dryden Flight Research Center is listed on the book's cover. He is highlighted as one of the original research pilots in that program.

The book's introduction states, "To gather data so the aviation community could understand what was happening when aircraft approached the speed of sound... the AAF preferred a rocket-powered aircraft and funded the X-1. NACA [John's employer] and the Navy preferred a more conservative design and pursued the D-558, with the NACA also supporting the X-1 research."

One of the speakers featured in *Toward Mach 2*, the former curator at the Smithsonian National Air and Space Muscum, stated, "The two programs (the X-1 and D-558) complemented each other extremely well. The X-1 could reach high Mach numbers quickly... but had little duration. The D-558 could loiter in the transonic regime, and collect tremendous amounts of data." John Griffith was a key player in both programs.

In 1950 John left NACA to be a test pilot for Chance Vought Aircraft. "At the time I had three children, and Chance Vought offered me twice the salary, with a bonus program that could earn me four times my current pay. What they didn't tell me was that in the various experimental models of the F7U Cutlass (It was the first tailless plane produced in the U.S. and the Navy's first swept-wing jet fighter), they had crashed five airplanes and killed three pilots. On a potentially big-dollar bonus day at about 38,000 feet, I pointed to at least a 60-degree dive angle, and by 29,000 feet I had slightly over Mach 1. The test went bad. I wound up pulling between six and 6.5 Gs for eight seconds and missed the ground by less than 2,000 feet. The airplane had both fins bent, one rudder fluttered, and there was a jagged piece of the fin still held to its post.

"As I was going down I thought, what's my wife going to do with those three little kids?" He never made another high-speed dive. Some six months later he went to work for United Airlines as a pilot, then as Chief Pilot for Westinghouse's Gas Turbine Division. He was with the FAA from 1960-66 and worked on a project to develop a supersonic transport. In 1966 he returned to United as flight instructor and pilot and logged more than 4,000 hours in 727's.

In addition to the aircraft described, he also has flown the P-38, P-39, P-43, P-47, P-51, P-63, B-24, L-39, F8F, LH-12, B-29, F-80, DC-3, DC-6, F4U-5N, and many other military and civilian planes. His log entries indicate 77 different aircraft.

"If I could, I'd fly again." There is a glint in his 81-year-old eyes... those same eyes that seven decades before watched the planes in the skies above Homewood, IL.

John and his first wife, Cleo, married in 1945. They had four children. She passed away in 1973. John and his spouse Shirley live in Lake Wildwood.

September 16, 2006, John Griffith was inducted into the Aerospace Walk of Honor in Lancaster, CA. Through mid-2011, more than five dozen aerospace pioneers have been honored, including Neil Armstrong, James Doolittle, Bob Hoover, Chuck Yeager and more.

Ray and Robert

Chapter 8: Ray Boedecker – Army

"I saw a German with a burp gun about twenty feet away. I only had my .45 pistol, but I hit him in the shoulder."

RAY BOEDECKER'S mother had quite a time of it one late October day, 1924. Twenty minutes apart she introduced newborn and identical twins Ray and Bob to the city of Milwaukee, WI. For her it was a form of job security as she taught elementary school. For their father, it represented two new customers for his company, Palmolive (later Colgate), where he was a chemist in the soap division.

The family spent their first five years in Wisconsin, then gradually moved eastward starting with half a decade in Chicago. By 1940, they had settled in Short Hills, NJ, with Dad continuing to climb the Colgate corporate ladder. (He ultimately would retire after a 44-year career.)

The brothers entered Millburn High School as sophomores. They were the only twins in their class of 120. Both were athletes, with Ray playing third base on the junior varsity baseball team. "I had a strong throw to first." Each played JV basketball, and Bob threw both the discus and shot-put on the track team. They also worked part-time jobs, were active in high school stage plays and a variety of other scholastic and social activities.

Their senior year they were playing touch football December 7, with friends – their "gang" – when they heard the news about Pearl Harbor. That spring, on an ongoing basis, they helped package soap and other toiletries to send to local area servicemen stationed overseas. When they graduated Millburn High in June, 1942, Ray was number three in his class with Bob one place behind. They were 17 years old.

"We were both accepted to Penn State as engineering students," says Ray. "Because it was a land grant university, ROTC was obligatory. And when we turned 18 we enlisted in the Army, selecting the Engineer Corps." They were permitted to finish their freshman year. Both participated in a number of school activities and were "rushed" by and pledged to Phi Delta Theta Fraternity. Each was also elected to the freshman National Honor Society.

May 1943 they attended basic training at Fort Dix, NJ. While in basic they went to a nearby USO dance. A woman informed them there was a War Department policy allowing twins to be assigned to the same unit if they desired. Ray still has a copy of the early 1943 memo, "To the extent practicable, and when no urgent military reason exists to the contrary, the policy of the War Department is to assign twins to the same organization, unit or station, provided they so desire. By order of the Secretary of War."

From basic in Dix they went on to Fort Belvoir, VA for four months of basic engineering training. They already knew a lot of the material being covered, plus had a year of Penn State ROTC under their belts. Each was promoted to Corporal as a squad leader, then another four months of engineering schools. This included training in assault river crossings, explosives, land mines, booby-traps, TNT, primacord and more. There were a lot of live exercises in disarming booby traps.

The brothers had applied to Officer Candidate School. They were called to Fort Belvoir's headquarters office and told they were eligible to attend West Point. "We turned them down because we wanted to graduate from Penn State. We did, however, accept appointments to OCS at Fort Belvoir." They entered training April 1, 1944 and graduated in July as second lieutenants. Ray was assigned as an instructor in the demolition school and Bob was a heavy equipment instructor."

The brothers took their jobs seriously almost all the time. Bob recounts a weekend where Ray was the Officer-of-the-Day. "Ray had scheduled a date in town and really wanted to go. I took his place and the one Battalion Commander who could tell us apart showed up to inspect. There was a bit of a reprimand and this may have hastened our departure to overseas."

Ray claims they were ordered to Europe November 1944 because Eisenhower wanted them there. He smiles, "He invited us over... he said, 'Send ammo and second lieutenants.' Both were in short supply." They were part of a group of 120 unassigned engineers headed for the front.

They were sent to Camp Shanks, an embarkation point near New York City. Along with 15,000 other men and women they boarded the *Queen Mary* headed for Greenock, Scotland. Eighteen days after departing the states they had moved south from Scotland down the spine of England to a camp just outside of London.

They went by truck to Plymouth, a small boat to France, and over nets to a landing craft. Then via "40&8" boxcars – that could carry 40 men or eight horses – to Nancy, France, south of the "Bulge" conflict. The clock quietly ticked close to 1945, and the brothers continued their trip to the front and the Thunderbirds – the 45th Infantry Division, 120th Engineer Combat Battalion.

It was the calm before a very big storm. A truck dropped them off in the village of Ingweiller in the Low Vosges Mountains in northeast France near the border with Germany – the Alsace area. Ray was assigned as Company B, 3rd Platoon Leader. Bob was given a Company A administrative post. They would not see one another for two months. They had arrived during one of the coldest winters in four decades, and their respective quarters were tents pitched in a foot or more of snow.

For almost six decades the Battle of the Bulge concentrated in the Ardennes has received as much press as any engagement in Europe. But 150 miles to the southeast, Hitler's last offensive – and a critically important engagement – was about to take place: Operation *Norwind.* There would ultimately be some 40,000 allied and German casualties.

Captured German orders listed the beginning of the attack to start Jan.1, 1945. The objective was to cut off the greatest portion of Allied strength in lower Alsace "...and destroy the enemy west of the Vosges." Hitler held a briefing for his commanders prior to *Norwind*. He said his objective was to destroy the 7th Army, forcing a diversion of troops from Ardennes and weakening the Alliance. He compared himself to Alexander the Great, who dismissed suggestions of his generals that they surrender. Instead, Alexander made one last attack and was successful. Operation *Norwind* presented a similar opportunity for the Third Reich, Hitler insisted.

Says Bob Boedecker, "Little did we know that to the north the Battle of the Bulge was winding down. Nor did we have any idea that on New Year's Day the German's would launch an all-out attack in the Vosges Mountains."

Says Ray, "There was a gap between the 3rd Army and the 7th. Beginning the day we arrived at the 120th Battalion they attacked. We were under concentrated mortar and artillery fire. Virtually the entire 45th Division had to pull back a bit and regroup." Some nearby units had been decimated in the *Bitche-Reipertwiller* Area.

According to Bob, "We never knew the big picture. My view of the war was one road, one bridge, one town at a time." Each brother would do his job as best he could and let higher-level officers worry about strategy and tactics.

Ray says, "We were working and fighting around the clock."

The Low Vosges Mountains operation became one of controlling the snow-covered roads and passes. The 45th Division was given the job of closing the hole made by the German attack. "My men dug defensive positions for our infantry using a tank with a blade – a tank dozer." Troops from the 79th Division and another task force were transferred to the 45th to shore up their efforts.

Weeks later the 45th along with other key elements began an advance and continued strengthening the ground they held. Says Ray, "In places the roads were soggy, and we laid corduroy roads. We used compressed-air chain saws to cut logs and laid them side-by-side to make a roadway for the trucks and jeeps. Tanks were too heavy for these roads. The roads actually looked like corduroy.

"We were also responsible for building defensive fences and picking up enemy mines and laying our own defensive mine fields," Ray adds. He was putting his scholastic and military engineering training to work.

But it was more than engineering. "In February I was on recon and rounding a bend in the road," says Ray. "A significant number of retreating Germans opened fire. There were three of us... my driver, Sergeant, and myself. We dove out of the jeep into a ditch and were pinned down for three or four hours. Enemy fire hit the windshield, tires, radiator and engine, but none of us. Like I say, they were retreating. We were badly outnumbered and didn't go on the offensive. We were able to actually drive the jeep back to our HQ."

Later that month, he saw his brother. "He was fine, as was I."

March 15, 1945, started the last big push of the 7th Army against the retreating Germans. As the official Company "B" history states...

"We were charged with building two foot bridges to get parts of the 180th Infantry across the fast-moving Blies

River, just below Sarreguemines and near Frauenberg, France, on the German Border." One man was killed and four wounded after night-and-day attempts were required to successfully complete the bridge.

Says Ray, "The river was about 100 feet wide and very swift. We were trying to build the new bridges adjacent to a blown-up and twisted Bailey Bridge."

(The Bailey Bridge is a pre-fab bridge first used during the 1944 D-Day invasion. It has three parts, including the floor/transom, the stringers, and side panels. It is launched on rollers and pushed nose-high across the river or gap to be bridged.)

"The 1st and 2nd Platoons were building the footbridges. My Platoon, the 3rd, was checking for mines. We would literally get down on our hands and knees trying to find them. My men cleared the mine area and were put in reserve. I stayed to observe the bridge construction."

He continues, "I saw that the rope and cable on the opposite bank being used to construct the new pontoon bridges was starting to sag. I took a little ownership on that one, as my platoon had crossed the river to set the initial cable. Some of the guys working on the bridge tried to paddle across in a flat-bottom engineer boat. It capsized in the swift current. All of us came under mortar and machine-gun fire."

Ray pauses, then continues. "The Bailey Bridge itself was about 120 feet long extending ten feet or so on either side of the river. I was walking on the exposed and mangled steel girders grabbing hold of anything I could to maintain balance." Apparently they were Penn State Nittany Lion moves. The Germans were firing at him with mortars and machine-guns. He says, "I could see the tracers." When he got to the enemy side he jumped to the bank and pulled from the river one of the men who had earlier capsized. "With the help of the soldier I had pulled from the water, we eventually got the rope and cable taut and the bridge was completed by dawn."

The next day his Company Commander told him a Brigadier General had been watching the operation. The general had said it was Ray's actions that helped serve for a more timely kick-off for the 7th Army getting into Germany.

It was that act of bravery under fire that earned him a Silver Star. It would not be the last time nor would he be the only Boedecker to be noted for bravery with the 120th Engineer Combat Battalion of the 45th Division – The Thunderbirds. His organization – Company B – also received a Presidential Citation – one of the few awarded to a Company-sized unit for their successful efforts to build footbridges.

By late March 1945, Company B of the 120th Engineer Combat Battalion, part of the 45th Division Thunderbirds, was working its way to Nuremberg, Germany. Third Platoon leader Ray Boedecker and his men were busy clearing the roads of German land-mines, roadblocks and other obstacles, including retreating tanks destroyed by the Allied advance.

"We would be moving forward, just behind the advancing infantry, and get the yell, *'Engineers!'* That was our signal that immediate help was needed, often under enemy fire." He describes a not-atypical incident. "We'd get the call and find a huge roadblock of logs that needed to be removed. The Germans would be lobbing in mortars. The logs would be tied with explosives. We didn't know if they were on timers or trip wires."

He continues, "My men quietly, quickly and professionally went about their business, day after day." It was dangerous work. His brief stint as a demolition instructor at Fort Belvoir was now invaluable to him and the men under his command. Ray was not watching from afar – he was usually the man to deactivate an enemy explosive device.

"We were inside Germany at the edge of the Siegfried Line. There was a small but heavily fortified town with pillboxes behind it. The Germans had stuck steel rails vertically into the roadway. We called them asparagus. They were also called Dragon's Teeth. There were other obstacles as well, including a large log roadblock." Ray took four of his men to assess what needed to be done. They came under mortar fire and headed back to an infantry command post a very short distance away.

Ray was telling the command post officer what he needed in the way of firepower before his men could get to work. A sentry interrupted and told them enemy soldiers were close. "I saw a German with a burp gun about 20 feet away. I only had my .45 pistol, but I hit him in the shoulder. We wound up getting two prisoners." About 3 or 4 a.m. he also got sufficient firepower so they could get started removing the asparagus.

"I took my Sergeant and two enlisted men. Each of us had 40 pounds of Tetratol and other gear to get the job done." (Tetratol is a solid explosive with performance a little better than C-2 from both a volume and weight perspective.)

"The explosive was packaged in 2.5-pound blocks. Usually we'd pack eight of them into a canvas bag, figure out placement for best effect, and remove the roadblock."

Ray's twin had also become a platoon leader in Company A. April 26, 1945, his 1st Platoon was selecting launch and bridge sites to get advancing forces across the Danube. They took load after load of infantry across the river in engineer boats, often under small arms fire. He and his men also secured cables for the construction of a bridge and destroyed German roadblocks. It was two days of round-the-clock work under fire from the enemy. He, too – like Ray – was subsequently awarded the Silver Star for his leadership in the face of adversity. Coincidentally, each was promoted to First Lieutenant that April.

Ray's platoon also paddled infantry across the Danube, with an engineer on each side of the small boat carrying six infantrymen. From time-to-time, they came under fire. "Water crossings were always tough... I lost good men on the rivers of Germany."

Two weeks before the end of the war, Ray and his driver and Sergeant were on a recon drive when they noticed German troops scurrying across the road. Ray had a machine-gun mounted on the jeep. His Sergeant fired into the woods. More than 50 German troops came out of the woods with their hands up. "They were beat... they were ready to quit fighting." Ray smiles. "We sent them marching up the road, arms raised, toward our infantry so they could be properly processed as POWs."

"We made our way to Munich. We were among the very first troops into Dachau on April 29, 1945."

He shows me some photos he had taken that are now in the archives of the Holocaust Museum – hundreds of bodies in 40&8-sized gondola cars outside a crematorium. "The several days we spent there were unbelievable. I didn't know about the camps."

He is silent as he looks at the horror of the pictures. There were more than 30,000 recorded deaths and thousands more never registered.

On the other hand, thousands of death camp prisoners were liberated – thousands of lives were saved – by Ray's outfit, the 45th Division.

"Our engineering battalion was put in charge of building facilities to house several hundred thousand German prisoners. We had the prisoners build the fences that would keep them secure. We also used our tank dozers to help clear the war rubble in Munich's streets. Our job now was to help a defeated nation begin to rebuild."

He was on a ship headed home when the war in Japan ended Aug. 6, 1945. He stayed in the army until April 1946, and re-enrolled at Penn State for summer school. Both he and his brother returned to their fraternity – Phi Delta Theta. Bob would become chapter president. By 1947 Ray was elected to Tau Beta Pi, the engineering honor society

However, with their return to Penn State their paths began to diverge.

"I met Elizabeth Hutchinson in a technical report writing course," Ray states. His brother described her as a "Cute little redhead." (She is still a cute little redhead.) Liz and

Ray married in January 1948. Their son, Ray Jr., was born that November."

Ray graduated with a degree in Mechanical Engineering June 1949. Liz earned a Master's degree in Bacteriology. He worked a short while for Texaco Research Lab, then migrated to IBM in its manufacturing division in Poughkeepsie, NY on the Hudson River. Their daughter, Anne, was born January 1950.

Brother Bob also graduated with an engineering degree. He took a job with a small manufacturing company in New Jersey. He and his university sweetheart, Harriet, were married December 1949. They still live on the East Coast.

In the early and mid-50's Ray helped select and start up new IBM plant locations around the United States. In 1957 he returned to manufacturing and by 1970 was President of the IBM Manufacturing Division with some 20,000 employees in six U.S. locations.

In 1988 Ray authored a book published by the American Institute of Management entitled, "Eleven Conditions for Excellence: The IBM Total Quality Improvement Process." It was a best-seller, as quality and IBM are synonymous and interchangeable words – the gold standard in the information age. List price was $187 for both the coffee table and office edition copy. It is currently out of print even though the concepts are still applicable to organizations trying to reach or stay on the leading edge.

After Ray retired from IBM in 1987, he did consulting work, including Aerojet, in the Sacramento area. "After visiting Lake Wildwood, Liz and I bought a home here in 1988."

They are supporters of "Music in the Mountains" and other community organizations. They also do foster parent work with AnimalSave. They have some interesting and rewarding tales about that experience.

Ray helped infuse IBM with a corporate culture dedicated to quality and excellence. Ray and Liz also continue to infuse quality and excellence into their daily lives in what they do and those they touch.

Chapter 9: Al Carver – AAF/USAF

" The nurses came running to the cockpit yelling there were bullet holes in the back of the plane."

SOME THIRTEEN YEARS before Colonel Al Carver's distinguished military career drew to a close in 1974, he had logged more than 5,000 pilot-in-command hours.

With Al, you knew you were in the presence of a leader; his back was straight, his eyes alert, his questions and comments direct and relevant. When he talked about friends, comrades, former subordinates, community members and others he had touched, he did so with fondness and respect -- just as they invariably did when talking about him.

You'll find a taste of that in this interview:

"I had a year of Army ROTC at the University of Nebraska," Al says, "and knew I didn't want to be a soldier. I wanted to fly and enlisted as an Army Air Force Aviation Cadet in April of 1942. I thought the twin-engine P-38 looked like a great plane, and I graduated flight training as a qualified twin-engine fighter pilot." He smiles, then continues, "I wound up in North Africa May 1943 piloting Douglas C47's." (Those were cargo planes.)

Al glances at the cat flopping onto a rectangle of sunlight on the living room carpet. "From North Africa, we moved to Sicily about September, then the Italian mainland. I was based in Italy for more than three years... until mid-December of 1946."

Donna, his wife and partner for more than 54 years, adds he flew to many places besides Italy during that period. Al nods agreement, and continues, "We had a 90-day stint where we were temporarily assigned to India to support the campaign in Burma. We flew missions to support Merrill's Marauders and other allied efforts including the British forces." There is a soft laugh, "A couple of times I even flew pack mules from northeast India to Burma... as many as six animals at a time." There is a pause, "One mule would have been enough...

"There were periods in India when we flew more than 100 hours a week. We'd skim the treetops, sometimes behind enemy lines to pick up wounded and deliver supplies." When asked, Al points out the only armament on the plane was the .45 pistol strapped to his side. "We were lucky; we were shot at but missed while flying in Burma."

"That's where Al received his two Distinguished Flying Cross medals," comments Donna. "I'm glad I didn't know him then... I would have been worried sick." The cat, now in shade, stretches then saunters to the slowly migrating patch of sunlight.

The award criteria are straightforward: The DFC is made to recognize those individuals who distinguish themselves through single acts of "heroism or extraordinary achievement while participating in aerial flight." It includes phrases such as "action beyond the call of duty," and "accomplishment so exceptional and outstanding as to clearly set the individual apart from his comrades or other persons in similar circumstances."

Al says, "While based in Italy we'd fly to many different places. We'd fly into Yugoslavia to retrieve downed American airmen. The partisan underground would take them under their wing and get word out to the allies that they were safe. A date and time for pick-up behind enemy lines would be arranged. Sometimes they would be in pretty bad shape; so there was an urgency to do the job quickly."

Al reflects for a moment, then continues, "We'd fly in at night. We didn't want to stir things up. The missions had to be done with as much stealth as possible to ensure the safe return of our people. The navigator would notify me when we were over the target, then I'd start circling down. If those on the ground thought it was safe for me to land they would light a fire in two barrels – one at each end of a dirt road or field. Time on the ground was kept to a minimum. Those missions were wonderful assignments.

"Only one time did my plane get hit by enemy fire. It was in Italy. We were flying to pick up some wounded. I had some nurses in the back. We came under German fire."

He chuckles. "The nurses came running to the cockpit yelling there were bullet holes in the back of the plane. My area was very crowded for a few minutes."

He concludes matter-of-factly with a wry smile, "The rest of the mission went fine."

Al was made Squadron Commander in 1944 with a contingent of 500 men, including 120 officers. He and his team were prepared to go anywhere and do anything asked of them. In the fall of 1944 he pulled gliders from Italy towing the famed and highly decorated second-generation 442nd Nisei forces into the invasion of southern France. "I can't be sure, but 'Doc' Takeda (a long time Lake Wildwood resident) may have been on the same glider that I towed. If he wasn't being pulled by me, at least we shared the same airspace. 'Doc' and his comrades were, and are, great patriots... great Americans."

When the war in Europe concluded May of 1945, Al's role expanded to the whole of the continent. He and his squadron flew support missions throughout Europe until mid-December 1946. He returned home, became an Air Force Reservist and settled in Omaha, where he began flying for a non-scheduled airline. "I met Donna through a married friend of mine. She was training to be a nurse."

"I didn't care for him," Donna volunteers. "I didn't want to be associated with any 'fly-boy', but eventually I went out with him. He was persistent."

"It was okay," says Al. "Although I was in the Reserves, I was also now a civilian." He chortles, "And I guess I was a darn good salesman."

"Yes, you were," she agrees, "but our friends said it would never work out and never last because we were each too independent...too single-minded." She and Al look at one another; the cat is purring, audible from 12 feet away. She continues, "We were married October 2, 1947."

Al's head tilts back as he laughs.

"We had just bought a home when I was called back to active duty August of 1948. I was sent to Lackland AFB as a Squadron Training Officer. We also bought a home in Texas. Our first child, A.W., was born the day I received orders to go to Germany, March 3, 1949, to support the Berlin Airlift."

They have six children and seven grandchildren.

"For six-months I flew two or three missions a day in C-54's. We'd fly solid for a week, then a few days off, and begin again. Most of my flights were out of Celle in the British Zone." American airmen made 189,963 flights, hauling almost 1.8 million tons of cargo.

The UK made almost 88,000 flights and brought in another 542,000 tons of food, coal and other supplies. France was also an airlift participant.

"We'd land, come to a stop, have a cup of coffee raised to the cockpit on a pole, and be told to get going before we could finish our drink. The amazing thing about it was the cargo was unloaded by hand... no machinery. The Germans were amazing in their focus and sense of urgency to off-load needed supplies."

He shakes his head slowly in acknowledgement of their effort. "The Soviets didn't hassle us. I think they thought we would fail, and they weren't interested in starting a new war."

He pauses, "And just think, today we have Rotary Clubs in Russia... since 1995 or so, as I recall." On a wall is a large walnut plaque with a mounted gavel. It is a tribute to Al for his service as President of the Rotary club of Grass Valley, CA, 1980-81. He subsequently joined the Penn Valley club as a charter member in 1993.

"Rotary... there's a force for good in the world," Al says. "I think we have about one and a quarter million members in about 165 countries." His eyes sparkle. "Every time Rotary establishes clubs in a new country the world comes closer to peace and understanding." Nearby is a stack of individual "thank you" cards Al and Donna are reviewing from Penn Valley grade school students. The cards acknowledge his Rotary Club for giving a personal dictionary to every member of their class.

"Al believes in the Rotary concept of 'Service Above Self,'" says Donna. That is obvious when the litany of his past contributions to the community are reviewed. A few of them include his contribution to the Penn Valley Volunteer Fire Department – Firefighter; Assistant Fire Chief; Board Chair of the Firemen's Association; Chair of the District Fire Protection Board; Chairman, Nevada County Republican Central Committee; Co-founder, Penn Valley Rescue Squad; Chairman, Penn Valley Rodeo; President, Lake Wildwood Men's Club; Member of his Senior Softball League; Co-founder of an orphanage in Kunsan, Korea; Fundraiser for the Lake Wildwood outpatient center for Sierra Nevada Memorial Hospital; – the list goes on and touches countless people in Penn Valley, Grass Valley, Nevada City and surrounding communities.

"Last year I participated in the charity 'Jail and Bail' project where you get locked up in a mock cell, and it is individual contributions that set you free. I raised a lot of money for Hospice." He laughs, then continues, "I was in the Hospice program several years ago as a recipient of their wonderful care." The rectangle of sun is about to climb the wall, and the cat is coveting the last bit of warming light.

"The Hospice Executive Director sometimes introduces me as an alumni member of the program."

We return to his Air Force career. "Oh, I had a wonderful time. I spent an intensive period at Command Staff College in 1961-62, then became a Titan II Missile Commander near Wichita, Kansas. I was also a Missile Launch Task Force Commander at Vandenberg AFB in California." In 1966 he was appointed Vice Base Commander at Westover AFB in Massachusetts; Base Commander at Pease AFB in 1968; and Base Commander at Kunsan AFB, Korea, in 1969.

In 1997, Lake Wildwood resident Bev Barnett, Chaplain and Lt. Colonel, USAF (Ret.), authored a two-part article for *The Union* newspaper entitled, "Colonel Al Carver: A Profile in Courage". It outlined Al's dramatic and successful effort to save a Korean orphanage from closure.

Lt. Col. Barnett concluded his article with this short paragraph: "When our paths cross, as they often do, I still salute Col. Carver. But it was for this extraordinary act of courage on behalf of the Kae Chang Orphanage, that I hold him in highest esteem and place him at the top of the heap in my personal 'Hall of Fame'."

Lake Wildwood resident "By" Maynard was his Airborne Missile Maintenance and Avionics Squadron Commander at Beale AFB. "I still call him Colonel Carver. He is a superb officer and friend. There is none better."

Al assumed command of Kadena AFB in Okinawa in 1970. Donna joined him for 2.5 years of his three-year tour. "When we left," says Donna, "one of the Okinawan's that had reported to Al took me aside. He had something he wanted to say to me in private. 'Colonel Carver...' he lightly tapped his chest, then his skull to emphasize his point, 'speaks and acts with heart and mind. He is a very great man'."

One of the most coveted honors our government can bestow is the Legion of Merit, which recognizes "extremely difficult duty performed in an unprecedented and clearly exceptional manner." Al received one while he commanded Kunsan AFB, Korea and the other while he led Kudena in Okinawa. He was also, during his service to our nation, a five-time recipient of the Air Medal.

He came to Beale AFB in 1973 as base commander. "I left the Air Force in 1974; that was the year we bought a home in Penn Valley. We moved to Lake Wildwood in 1981."

"Our home was destroyed by the '49er fire in the mid-eighties. We lost virtually everything."

Al mentions the only keepsake left from his military career is the bolt from Vandenberg that connected the Titan Missile he launched from its pad. "The bolt was fireproof." A relative subsequently sent one photo of him in his WWII AAF uniform.

"Our home in Wichita was damaged by a tornado," laughs Donna, "and our quarters in Okinawa were hit by a typhoon and our home in Lake Wildwood destroyed by fire." In December 2000 they moved to a townhouse in Grass Valley. "There have been no locusts or floods," Donna quips.

The cat has left the room; the rectangle of sunlight has disappeared.

***

Author's Postscript:

I wrote this while Al was under hospice care at their small home at Quail Ridge in 2002. I worked thru the night to finish so I could read it to him the next morning with Donna sitting by my side.

Al was alert and said he liked it. He passed away later that evening.

−LTB

Bob and Doris

Chapter 10: Bob Acorne – USN

**"I felt my blood squishing in my shoe
as I went to help him."**

JULY FOURTH, 1920, there was a small, patriotic parade in Petaluma, CA, some thirty-two miles north of San Francisco. The next day the sound of firecrackers was replaced by a light slap on a tiny butt and the wailing of a new citizen in the community. Bob Acorne had made his entrance.

At the time Petaluma was the self-proclaimed "World's Egg Basket," producing some 50 million dozen eggs a year. It was a toss-up whether the 4th of July celebration or the National Egg Day festivities was the bigger event. Dairy products were close behind patriotism and eggs in importance to the community. Bob's Dad was a PR man with one of the local dairies.

"I loved growing up in Petaluma," Bob states. "It was a wonderful, close-knit community." The 1920 census listed the population at 6,226, and less than 2,000 more 20 years later.

For Bob, athletics was a dominant part of his life, and his relentless desire to excel paid off. He set rushing records and was accorded all-conference honors as a halfback for Petaluma High School's football team. In track he won the 100 and 220-yard races in the North Bay high school league championships.

Spring of 1938 he was president of the high school boys club. That fall, he continued his athletic triumphs by setting records as a halfback on the Santa Rosa J.C. championship football team. He had that all-American look – blond, wavy hair; tanned, muscular and handsome with a wide smile and perfect teeth. Wearing a leather football helmet since 1934 without a facemask had left no visible marks.

After two years at Jr. College, in the summer of 1940, he took a job with Union Oil as a management trainee and was assigned to the Turlock district in the Central Valley.

When the war started he and his brother Jack, two years younger than Bob, decided they would join the military. In April of 1942, Bob headed home to Petaluma. Then he and Jack drove to San Francisco to enlist.

"The enlistment center we chose was in the Ferry Building at the foot of Market Street. Both of us wanted to be fighter pilots." Bob pauses for a few seconds, then continues, "Jack made it... I didn't." He explains an issue with his vision that precluded flight training. "We were both inducted the next month and did our boot camp together at the Livermore Naval Air Station. Jack went off to pilot training in Corsairs and I stayed at Livermore as an enlisted man for the next two years."

Bob and girlfriend Doris were married August 1942. "I was given a 72-hour pass. We headed to Reno in my '41 Chevy club coupe, and honeymooned at Gold Lake near Graeagle." Doris had just graduated from nursing school and was working at Kaiser Hospital in Oakland.

The spring of 1944 Bob was sent to Tacoma, WA and assigned to the newly christened seaplane tender *USS Hamlin* (AV 15). The ship was placed in commission the end of June, 1944, and headed south to San Pedro, then to Hawaii in August.

Prior to 1944, the seaplane flights for the spotting of enemy ships and planes, anti-submarine patrols, and search and rescue flights originated from shore bases usually a long way from the front lines. A considerable portion of flight time was getting to and from a destination, with a minimal amount of time over the designated area. As the Pacific front moved westward, the need to have flights originate closer to the action hastened the development of seaplane tenders like the *Hamlin*.

Simply, the *Hamlin* was a floating air base, refueling station and repair depot, much like an aircraft carrier, without a landing deck. Once a seaplane had landed in the water, it was either tethered to the ship or hoisted aboard by crane, if shipboard repairs were required. Many repairs were done while the planes were in the water.

The *Hamlin* was almost 500 feet long, 70 feet wide, with a crew of 1,100. The ship had a thin hull and carried about 400,000 gallons of high-octane aircraft fuel. Anti-submarine air patrols around the *Hamlin* were a welcome sight in hostile waters.

"My non-combat role aboard ship was fairly mundane – I worked in the ship's stores department, running the fountain – the ship's ice cream parlor." He also made about 40 gallons of ice cream a day. However, when general quarters was sounded his role changed. There were four enlisted men and one gunnery officer assigned to a tub near the highest point of the ship on the Signal Bridge. Bob was one of those men. The tub was ten feet or so across and 5-5 ½ feet deep. "Quite simply, we were the eyes of the ship when we were under attack. We each faced a different point on the compass and shouted out incoming enemy planes to the gunnery officer." He in turn notified the gun batteries so they could begin their defense of the ship.

September 1944 the ship arrived in Saipan, and initially three seaplane squadrons were assigned to her. The *Hamlin* stayed in the Saipan area for months, then headed toward Iwo Jima. "We pulled in the day after the initial invasion, Feb 20, 1945." As soon as they arrived they were ordered to pick up a seaplane that had been damaged by a rough landing. Even as they hoisted the plane aboard in choppy seas, landing craft loaded with anxious Marines headed toward the beach. The *Hamlin* remained at Iwo Jima 17 days, establishing a base just offshore from Mt. Surabachi on Feb. 24. Heavy enemy fire from the beach and bad sea conditions prevented establishing the seadrome sooner. The ship was on Red or Yellow alert its entire time while at Iwo. The fountain was closed when Bob and his peers scanned the skies. No one then had time for ice cream.

More than 20 enemy vessels in the Iwo Jima area were sighted by planes assigned to the *Hamlin*, and subsequently all were sunk by armed aircraft or ships. During the first 50 days in combat areas in Iwo Jima, Saipan, Kerama Retto and Okinawa, the *Hamlin's* crew was at General Quarters for hundreds of hours. Bob and his tub mates were responsible for spotting several kamikazes' that were subsequently destroyed before inflicting damage.

"While we were anchored off Iowa Jima, a five-inch shell came down one of our stacks."

Bob slowly shakes his head as he continues, "Why it didn't go off, I'll never know. There was a lot of excitement until it was removed." It was also while they were at Iwo Jima that a 20-mm shell struck inside their tub on the signal bridge.

"All five of us were hit by shrapnel. My wound was to my foot and my shoe began to fill with blood." He laughs as he continues. The following is not the exact anatomical descriptor used by Bob as he describes the frantic words of a wounded comrade. "He was screaming that his manhood had been shot off... his manhood had been destroyed... I felt my blood squishing in my shoe as I went to help him." He laughs again. The wound was to his pal's inside upper thigh and not too serious. "I know," Bob chuckles, "because he asked me to look." As they say, close but... uh... no cigar.

"The medics removed my shrapnel, and I was back on duty in no time." He is mum as to whether he served himself an extra scoop of ice cream while he recuperated. Certainly, his wounded comrades got an extra share.

Rub-a-dub-dub, five gobs in a tub, each with a purple heart.

Bob explains he had seen his brother several times, either in person or flying over their ship, waggling his wings as he headed to or was coming back from a mission. "He'd send a message to our radio room and ask if I could be on deck when he flew over." He continues, "My brother ditched one Corsair in combat but was rescued. And one time he managed to catch a ride with a seaplane and visit the ship." He laughs as he adds, "I think he came as much for the ice cream as to see me."

The *Hamlin* remained an integral part of the fleet in or near the heart of the action until the end of the war. August 28, 1945 she entered Tokyo Bay. Their anchorage was close to the *USS Missouri*. "Our Captain broadcast a message September 2, 1945, the day of the formal ceremonies on the *Missouri* ending the war: 'Many men would give everything they have to be in your place today.'" Virtually every American warplane within distance of Tokyo flew over in formation during that event, including the seaplane squadrons assigned to the *USS Hamlin*. "The roar of the aircraft was deafening," Bob states. "Wave after wave of planes."

He adds, "I flew over Hiroshima a week or two after we moored in Tokyo Bay. We circled the city for 15 to 20 minutes." His voice is a monotone, "I was awestruck by the devastation, but felt no remorse for those that had died. The atomic bombs had ended the war and saved countless lives for both sides."

Not too long after the formal surrender, the *USS Hamlin* sailed back to Long Beach. The ship earned three battle Stars – one for the assault and occupation of Iwo Jima; another for the assault and occupation of Okinawa; and a third for the Fleet Operations against Japan.

"When I returned I went back to work for Union Oil and bought a service station and tire distributorship." He also played semi-pro football and rugby. "In rugby I was a player and a coach." He hung up his cleats in 1956. He was inducted into the Santa Rosa J.C. Sports Hall of Fame in 1991 as the sportsman of the decade for the 30's.

When he was selected as an all-star player in the 30's he was given a small gold football to wear around his neck. When he and Doris were engaged he gave her the charm.

"I lost it," Doris says softly, eyes downcast, yet sparkling.

He pats her hand. "That's not important, we have each other." His eyes sparkle, too.

Bob and Doris have four children, two grandchildren and one great-grandchild. They have had a home in Penn Valley's Lake Wildwood since 1981. And, if a guest is especially polite, he or she can get a nice scoop of ice cream served by Bob.

Jerry and Gwen

Chapter 11:
Jerry Seawright
-- USMC

**"I strapped in and braced for
a water landing in the choppy sea."**

THE YEAR, 1925, was among the great ones for silent movies – *Ben Hur*, starring Ramon Novarro; Chaplain's *The Gold
Rush*, Lon Chaney's *Phantom of the Opera* and the classic ani-
mated feature, *The Lost World*.

They were all shown at the Fischer Theatre in Danville,
IL, the year Jerry Seawright was born. Unlike the movies,
his entry was not accompanied by a musician banging out
music on an upright piano appropriate to the images on the
screen. Jerry provided his own loud and discordant sound
track. The audience for his entry spanned a broad age range
– his Mom and Dad, a brother 15 years older than Jerry, and
two sisters, the youngest some six years older.

"Danville is near the border with Indiana, about half way down the state. It was a small community near the Vermilion River and had superb mid-western values," Jerry reflects. Danville was a 19th century coal center. From 1841 to 1859 Abe Lincoln was a practicing attorney in the community.

Jerry continues, "My Dad was a respected dentist and Mom a homemaker. When I was fourteen he died in my arms from a heart attack." There is silence as he reflects back more than six decades. He continues, "You have to remember, the Depression was winding down. For many years Dad had taken payment for his work in goods and services and seldom money. We came to find out he had let his life insurance lapse because there was no money to pay the premiums. Shortly after he died our home was repossessed. We had nothing."

His voice is near monotone as he continues – much of the emotion and pain having been spent when he was barely in his teens. "My Mom went to live with her mother and was unable to take me. My sisters were already on their own. I became self sufficient, paying board with one sister then another, and sometimes with friends. There were many times I didn't have money for food and had to rely on others."

Jerry describes the jobs he had from age 14 on – putting toys together at Sears, bakery deliveries, paper routes and more. "I loved basketball and briefly tried out for the team, but I had to quit because the afternoon practices conflicted with my newspaper delivery job."

He says, "My first semester as a senior in high school I went to the USMC recruiter. He patted me on the back and told me to finish school. I followed his advice and took the oath in Chicago, June of '43. I only had one night in Chicago before I headed to basic training."

His fingers tap a rhythm as we talk. "I saw Glenn Miller that night at a theatre at Lake and State streets." He pauses. "It was wonderful... absolutely marvelous!"

The next morning Jerry left via train for San Diego. "When we finally arrived in San Diego, this guy in uniform started yelling at us to get off the train. I wondered why he was so mad at us." This was his introduction to drill instructors.

"I went to boot camp in San Diego. I had the upper bunk and there was a loudspeaker directly above my head." It broadcast Reveille with great authority. "The D.I. coming into the barracks loudly beating Morse code messages inside a can was nothing compared to the wake-up music."

From San Diego he went to Miramar for testing. "I was accepted into the aviation program and was sent to Jacksonville, Florida, to radio school. From there I went to Yellow Water, Florida, for gunnery school. We did lots of skeet and trap shooting to learn to follow an object... plus I learned to take a gun apart – over and over and over.

"Late 1944 I was sent to Cherry Point, then Edenton, North Carolina for air crew training school. I learned more about gunnery flying in PBJ's, the equivalent to the Army Air Force B-25. It's there I got my wings."

He was assigned to VMB Squadron 613. "The bomber was equipped with a 75mm cannon in the nose." He chuckles, "When it was fired the plane would fill with cordite." He was putting the last bolts on a shipping crate destined for overseas when the squadron was disbanded. "I was sent to Bogue Expeditionary Field in North Carolina to learn to be the radiøgunner in the SBD Dauntless dive bomber."

Jerry's pace picks up as he relates how he was sent back to Miramar. "I hated that place," he says, "and they had me marking time there." He describes how he vented his frustration at figuratively marching in place. "I took off one morning for the officer's quarters. I entered and said, 'Any of you guys going overseas to a combat area, and do any of you need a gunner and radio man?'"

He smiles as he recounts a Second Lieutenant from Tacoma, WA, Whitey Sagehorn, piping up that he might have an opening for the right guy. A week later he was on a troop ship headed to Guam. From there he went by DC-3 to Kwajalein, Eniwetok and Mujuro in the Carolines, then on to Ulithi Atoll in the Western Pacific islands of Micronesia.

"We were based out of Falalop Island, a one mile by half mile sliver of coral, and assigned to Marine Bombing Squadron VMD MAG 245." It would be his home until the end of the war, some 35 missions later with pilot Whitey.

They flew the Curtiss Helldiver, SB2C-1, sometimes called the S.O.B., Second Class.

A few said it had a great name but was a lousy airplane. According to some aviation experts it was a front-runner for one of the worst warplanes of WWII. Neither Jerry nor Whitey got a vote or choice about what plane they would prefer to fly.

The SB2C was designed to meet a Navy request for an updated dive-bomber. The plane had a two-man crew – the pilot and the radioman/gunner/observer facing rearward with two 0.3 inch machine guns each capable of firing 1,000 rounds. Jerry had to be careful not to shoot off the oversized tail assembly during combat. It had four wing-mounted .50 caliber guns, a top speed of 295 mph, with a comfortable cruise speed of 158 mph. Max range was almost 1,400 miles, with 550 being a typical limit. It had a flight ceiling of slightly over 24,000 feet. Jerry and Whitey's plane typically carried one 500-pound bomb or two 250-pounders.

"We made a number of flights to the Japanese stronghold of Yap and flew a lot of anti-submarine patrols." He recounts some of their dive-bomb runs on Yap. "We'd start our dive at about 13,000 feet using a Hollywood wing-over or a negative dive, which was more accurate." He explains the difference. "The Hollywood dive is the one you see in movies, where the plane rolls to the side and begins its dive, and the planes behind follow the leader. It looks good on film but is the least accurate way to line up a target."

Jerry continues, "The negative dive actually has the tail slightly over vertical so the pilot is looking straight down at the target area. That dive position gives him the best line on accurately hitting the objective. We'd release at about 5,000 feet, then maybe go in for a strafing run."

"We also made some low-level strafing runs over Yap. Sometimes the enemy would put charges in the trees that would explode as we passed over." He adds, "I'm not sure, but I think they might have been detonated by the pitch sound of our propellers."

He and his pilot, Lt. Sagehorn, were relatively close. "When I shipped out for home after the war that was the last I saw and heard from Whitey. I tried to find him, but all my leads were dead ends." He smiles as he relates, "Officers could drink whiskey, but enlisted men were restricted to Blatz potato beer. One day Whitey gave me an officer shirt and took me to the officers club. You could order whiskey one shot at a time. A P-51 pilot sat at our table and started asking me questions about our plane that I couldn't answer. I looked to Whitey for a little help, but he didn't offer any. I was really sweating, figuratively and literally. If I got caught as an enlisted man in the officers club I'd be in a lot of trouble."

Jerry says, "I started to bluff an answer and finally Whitey jumped in. I never went back to the officers club!"

We explore cigarette runs to Yap. "Cigarettes were dirt cheap — five cents for a pack of Lucky Strikes and other popular brands, and Raleigh's were free. We delivered cigarettes three or four times to the Japanese military occupying Yap. First we'd do our bomb run on the airstrip. Then we'd assess the damage and make a low-level run over the airstrip tossing out handfuls of Raleigh's and packs and loose cigarettes of other brands." They would rain these unlit smokes down on the enemy, then fly off into the distance.

"After our bombing run, and following a low-level pass where we threw out hundreds of loose Raleigh's and packs of Luckies, Camels and other brands, we'd head away from the island like we were leaving." His voice is matter-of -fact. "Then we'd do a 180 and come in low. The airstrip would have dozens of the enemy on the runway gathering up the smokes. We'd open fire with the wing mounted guns and my rear-facing machine-guns then head back to our base on

Falalop Island, part of the Ulithi Atoll, some 120 miles distant. We did the cigarette drop on three or four missions, and always wound up with fresh targets scampering on the runway." (The scribe is too dignified to do any cheap shots about cigarettes killing people. Cigarettes don't kill people... smoking the cigarettes and dive-bombers kill people.)

"We were one of three or four planes headed back from a bomb run on Yap and our engine started missing. I don't know if it had been hit by enemy fire or not, but it doesn't matter. We were losing altitude, and Whitey told me to bail out. We were down to about 3,000 feet and I was half out of the plane. I looked at Whitey, and he motioned he was going to stay with the Helldiver."

Jerry almost got sucked out by the airflow, but climbed back into the plane.

"I wasn't going to leave him. I strapped in and braced for a water landing in the choppy sea. We almost landed nose over, but settled back down. I pulled the release on the life raft, and we climbed on board." They were in the raft for 2-½ to 3 hours, sometimes with air cover.

"There was a Coast Guard unit stationed at Lithe. They picked us up in a boat about the size of a PT boat."

We chat about ack-ack he and Whitey experienced. He disappears, then returns with an angry looking piece of shrapnel about 2x1 inches. "This came through the bottom of the plane, through my bucket seat, and almost through the parachute I was sitting on." Sometimes flying, like football, golf or horseshoes is a game of an inch or two. Unconsciously he squirms in his seat... it was a very close call.

He recounts another character tester. "We had been on a bomb run, and the rear bracket holding the 500-pound fuselage-mounted bomb had broken. It was hanging only by the nose bracket, and we weren't sure whether the arming mechanism wire had pulled loose. If it had, when we landed we would have been destroyed." He pauses a few seconds, "It was a tense landing." He laughs, "When we stopped we were out of that plane very, very quickly."

When the war ended, the flight crews were ordered to turn in all their equipment. "We were in a long line with all our stuff. I had my .38 S&W pistol, holster, helmet, flight suit, goggles, Mae West, rifle and bayonet. I saw that after items were turned in someone walked out the back door of the building and threw all the things in a big pile. I returned my equipment to my barracks, then walked around to the pile of items turned in, grabbed one of everything and stood in line again. I received a receipt that all of my items were now in possession of the USMC." He stayed on Ulithi until he had the required points to be shipped home. "We sailed home on the *USS Botetourt*, a troop carrier, from Oct. 16 to the 30th. We berthed at Treasure Island and were supposed to head south to Miramar by train. Unfortunately, the railroads were on strike and we were given two nights in San Francisco, then back on board ship headed for San Pedro and Miramar.

"From there, in December I took a train straight from the cowboy era – no heat, no hot water, windows that wouldn't close, lots of engine smoke and soot and bitter cold as we hit the Midwest.

"I stayed in my South Pacific sleeping bag the whole time – three days and three nights." He smiles as he continues, "I hadn't shaved, showered or changed clothes. I looked and smelled pretty bad. I took a cab to the Sheraton in Chicago. I'd rolled my sleeping bag up, and stuck my rifle through the center. The barrel and part of the stock showed. The lobby was full of people waiting for rooms. I approached the desk clerk. People gave me a wide berth.

"I explained I wanted a room. 'Yes sir, right away,' and the clerk slammed the bell that summoned the bell hop." The clerk remained at attention until Jerry had entered the elevator.

The next day, clean and fresh, he was in Danville, IL on a 30-day leave. "From there I was sent to Cherry Point, NC for discharge. I was bored stiff. They posted a list of people who had had their 30-day leaves. I wasn't on it, so I went back to Danville for another month. I had to follow orders," he shrugs.

He was discharged April 1946 as a sergeant. "I went into construction as a laborer. Since I had been on my own since I was fourteen, I hadn't taken college prep courses in high school because I knew I'd never be able to afford higher education. But the G.I. Bill was there if I could take advantage of it." He took entrance tests and was accepted by Butler University, a prestigious private institution founded in 1855 in Indianapolis.

He enrolled the fall of 1947 as a pre-med major.

"Winter of 1949/50 I was pledge captain for my fraternity, Sigma Nu. I was trying to get dates for some of our pledges. There was this girl named Gwen McCracken that I thought was a freshman. Actually, she was a junior transfer from the University of Indiana. I saw her slowly walking up some marble stairs at school and asked her out." He adds, "She was and still is beautiful. We started dating January of 1950 and were married that August."

Jerry graduated January 1951. "I didn't go to med school. Instead, with my B.S. in Zoology, I took a job with a pharmaceutical firm in L.A. as a sales rep. My territory was the Miracle Mile on Wilshire Boulevard – tons of Doctor's offices. From there I went to Stockton, Walnut Creek and Concord. I'd started an investment club with some of the physicians I worked with and liked it so much I went into the brokerage business in the early '60's."

He retired as a Senior Vice President with Dean Witter in 1991.

Gwen, his wife for more than half a century, chimes in. "Tell them about the Blue Devils." They both grin. "In 1964 the Concord Blue Devils were a drum and bell corps," Jerry says. "One of my daughters was interested in playing a glockenspiel with the corps. They were an organization with a limited budget but a lot of potential. They just needed a slight change in focus and direction. I assumed the role of volunteer director and manager."

He pauses. "Their budget now is about $1,000,000 a year, and they have been a drum and bugle corps since the mid-Sixties. We didn't do well at first... we came in 24th in a competition in the Northwest in 1973, ninth in '74, third in '75 and national champs in 1976."

In early August 2003, Jerry and Gwen accompanied the 135-member team with their entourage of 170 to the international competition in Orlando. August 8, 2003 the team won its eleventh world title.

There are some famous entertainers who grew up in Danville, IL – Donald O'Connor, pianist and singer Bobby Short, Gene Hackman, and Jerry and Dick Van Dyke. Jerry Seawright was a friend and contemporary of several of them. There is a photo of him, Dick Van Dyke, Gene Hackman's brother, and other pals doing a skit on the 1987 Ralph Edwards TV show, *This is Your Life*, honoring Dick Van Dyke. It was good fun and very high jinks.

"In the old days we were known as the Burford's... a goofy name selected by Dick. We were just a bunch of buddies having good, clean fun."

Jerry and Gwen had a house built in Lake Wildwood in 1991. They have two daughters and three grand-daughters. He and Gwen are valued community members, contributors and gracious hosts. However, if you smoke don't ever, ever, ask him to toss you a cigarette... especially if it's a Raleigh.

Chapter 12: Cliff Walton – USN

"Whether I got cheered or booed by my men depended on the orders I'd issued earlier the week of my fight."

MARCH 3, 1920, a passenger train was pulling into the Newton, KS train depot. A few miles away, Cliff Walton, the fourth of six children was also making his entrance. The arrival noise of each was size proportional.

The train left within minutes. Cliff, however, lingered in Newton for sixteen years before heading down the track. And it was by train in 1936 that Cliff and most of his family headed west. "My Dad had had a stroke," Cliff explains, "and times were tough at home. One of my younger sisters was quite a dancer and acrobat, and Mom thought there might be a future for her in the movies."

Getting off the train in Los Angeles they knew they weren't in Kansas any more. "I had an uncle who worked for one of the movie studios. I decided to stay out of school for a while after my sophomore year and went to work for Monogram Pictures as a carpenter's helper and laborer. We needed the money and it was a fantastic job for a kid. I saw many of the great stars at the studios – Gary Cooper, Carole Lombard, Clark Gable.... I helped build the sets for 'Gone With the Wind'." He pauses for a few seconds, then continues, "Of course, I worked on a number of 'B' movies, too. My sister, the dancer, performed in a few of them."

Cliff went back to school at Hollywood High, and graduated in 1939. "I also worked for the studios after graduation and knocked around in some other jobs. I joined the Naval Reserve Sept. 1941 and went to bootcamp in San Diego. December 5, I got a 72 hour pass, but before I could get off base was told all liberties had been cancelled by the naval intelligence boys in Washington."

December 7, they received word almost immediately about the attack at Pearl Harbor. Two hours later every sailor was issued a WWI .30/30 rifle and a bandoleer of ammunition. That night each man slept in his uniform with the rifle at his side. "There was the rumor that the Japanese were going to attack somewhere between Ensenada and Tijuana. Every vehicle on base had been commandeered, including the cars, and we were ready to head south to repel the invaders." He chuckles, "Of course, it didn't happen. Originally, I was supposed to head to Alameda for more training. Instead, I was ordered to Bremerton, Washington to join the Battleship *Tennessee*, now in dry-dock."

The *USS Tennessee* was launched April 30, 1919 some ten months before Cliff's birth. Dec.7, 1941 the ship's starboard side was tied to a mooring quay on Battleship Row at Pearl Harbor. Alongside was the *USS West Virginia*. Directly ahead of the *Tennessee* was the *USS Maryland*, with the *USS Oklahoma* parallel to that ship. Behind the *Tennessee* was the *USS Arizona*. Next to the *Arizona* was a repair ship, the *USS Vestal*.

The attack started about 7:55 a.m. and the *Oklahoma* and *West Virginia* took aircraft torpedo hits as they were moored facing the open channel. The *Oklahoma* capsized and sank bottom up. The *West Virginia* sank to the bottom upright and on an even keel.

At about 8:20 a bomb penetrated the *Arizona's* protective decks and that, along with other hits, resulted in her sinking. The *Tennessee* was boxed in. By the evening of Dec.7, the worst had passed, and thirteen days later, the *Tennessee, Maryland* and *USS Pennsylvania* departed Pearl Harbor for West Coast shipyards for much needed work. On February 25, the *Tennessee* left Puget Sound, its repairs complete. Cliff was on board, and would be for the rest of the war.

"My first job was on one of the 14"/50 caliber guns turrets. I was on that job until May when I was transferred to the ship's 40-millimeter Eighth Division." Cliff was a quick study and by November 1942 was promoted to Boatswain's Mate First Class and in charge of the ship's ten quadruple 40-mm gun mounts and 140 men. "My men on the forty 40-mm's had responsibility for close-in antiaircraft defense. And, in some battles, we had shore targets to go after. The ship also had more than forty 20-mm guns for air defense that weren't my responsibility."

August 2-15, 1943 the *Tennessee* saw her first offensive action participating in the bombardment of Japanese positions on Kiska in the Aleutian Islands. Shortly thereafter, she headed to Southern California and then back to Hawaii.

"By early November, 1943 we were in the New Hebrides, then steamed to the Tarawa Atoll in the Gilbert Islands. Beginning November 20 and for the next several days we participated in shelling positions on the atoll's Beito Island, where the enemy had concentrated their forces." The 22nd, a Japanese sub was forced to the surface and spotted by one of the Tennessee's 5-inch gun crews. "We fired about twenty rounds of five-inch shells and the destroyer Frazier rammed and sank the sub, then picked up survivors."

The *Tennessee* stayed near Tarawa until December 3. "Tarawa was difficult for all of us. We were a long way offshore, but when the wind shifted our way, the smell of death from the island was overpowering... it was horrible." He asks, "Imagine being on the island?"

Over the next months the *Tennessee* would participate in the bombardment of Roi and Namur on the Kwajalein Atoll, and Eniwetok in the Marshall Islands. After Eniwetok was secured, the *Tennessee* turned her attention to the adjacent Parry Island. "The afternoon of February 20th we were firing so close we were able to use our 40-mm's to go after their shore defenses." By the 22nd the atoll was under American control. Less than a month later the ship participated in the shelling of Kavieng, New Ireland then headed to Pearl Harbor.

"We had close to 2,500 men on board at any given time," states Cliff, "and when we weren't in a combat mode it was important to keep everybody occupied. There were constant work parties and other activities, including sporting events." Cliff smiles, and finds a page in the "official" history of the *Tennessee*. He points to a photo showing men surrounding a makeshift shipboard boxing ring. Hundreds of sailors are hanging from, and draped over, every conceivable part of the decks and super structure. "I was a pretty big kid at 175 pounds. I had 3-4 bouts as a light-heavy weight. Whether I got cheered or booed by my men depended on the orders I'd issued earlier the week of my fight. It was all good fun." He is unaware his power hand makes a fighter's fist, then relaxes.

In that same book it lists Cliff's nickname as "Ace". "I guess it's tied in to my first and middle name initials – Arthur and Clifford." He is evasive when asked if it has anything to do with his skills in the ring. This time the other fist tightens, and further fight questions are TKO'd.

Early June of 1944 they were underway to the Marianas Islands, and the 14th began the bombardment and invasion of Saipan.

"D-Day started the morning of the next day," Cliff states. "We had stopped shelling as the Marines began their assault. A Japanese 4.7" gun firing from a cave on Tinian opened up on us. We were hit three times, and eight were killed and 25 wounded. We buried our dead at sea that night," he reflects sadly, "with shell casings put in the canvas covering with the body so it would sink rapidly to the bottom."

The *Tennessee* also saw combat duty at Anguar in the Palau Islands, the assault of Leyte in the Phillipines, the battle with the Japanese Fleet in the Surigao Straits, and the American capture of both Iwo Jima and Okinawa.

April 12, during the battle for Okinawa, five Kamikaze planes headed toward the *Tennessee*. Three were shot down by 40 and 20-mm gun crews. Another came toward the bow at a 45-degree angle, was hit by a 5-inch gun, and plunged into the water. The fifth plane got through, despite the fact it had been spotted 2,500 yards out. "The dive-bomber crashed into the signal bridge. The plane skidded along the superstructure and crushed antiaircraft guns and their crews. The plane and its 250 pound bomb went through the deck and exploded." Cliff's pace picks up; "I was topside within 20-30 seconds. There was fire everywhere, and I was pitching live 40-mm shells and other ammo overboard hoping they didn't explode."

It was a chaotic scene -- the fire, the dead, the wounded, the devastation, and the possibility of shells exploding. "I also helped put out the fire and move the wounded from further harm. Many of the dead and wounded were my guys." Twenty-two men died and another 107 injured.

The *Tennessee* was awarded a Navy Unit Commendation and 10 battle stars for her WWII service. After the war Cliff was awarded a commendation for his valor during the April 12 conflict – one of only a few given.

By April 14, emergency fixes had been completed, and the ship was back on the firing line. After more work by the repair ship *USS Ajax*, the *Tennessee* stayed until the battle for

Okinawa was over June 21, 1945. Until V-J Day the ship patrolled the waters off Shanghai. After the war the *Tennessee* spent time in Tokyo harbor, then via Singapore, Ceylon and Cape Town came home and moored at the Philadelphia Naval Shipyard December 7, 1945. Because of its size a quicker return by the Panama Canal was out of the question.

"My gun crews were responsible for shooting down fourteen enemy planes, and," Cliff continues, "we fired a lot of ammunition." Cliff points to a chart in the ship's book which indicates almost 100,000 rounds of 40-mm were fired by his team. The ship also fired 9,347 14"/50 rounds from the big guns and 46,731 from the 5" guns. From Dec 7, 1941 to the end of the war the *Tennessee* steamed more than 170,000 miles. With the exception of the Dec.20, 1941 trip from Pearl Harbor to Bremerton, WA, Cliff was on board for every mile.

"My mother was happy to see the war end. Both of my brothers also served – one in the Navy and the other as an Army officer. My sisters were USO performers, and my mom was a coastal airplane spotter." The war was a family affair for the Walton's.

He was discharged Dec.22, 1945. He married Gwen, his sweetheart from back in Kansas, and raised a family with a boy and girl. They moved to LWW in 1983. She passed away in 1996. He and his second wife, Norma, wed in 1998. She brought two sons to the marriage. Between them there are nine grandchildren.

The WWII nickname "Ace" may or may not apply to his boxing skills – that is a secret. It certainly applies, however, to other aspects of his life.

Chapter 13: Mac Roberts – AAF

"I tried to remove my flight jacket and parts of it had fused to my flesh and it just peeled off with the jacket …my pants and flesh were burned up to about the knee."

MAC ROBERTS was born in the small town of Cashup in southeastern Washington near the Idaho border January 13, 1919. "I guess I was about three when my folks moved to San Jose, California, and I lived there until 1937. San Jose was a great place to grow up… rolling hills and trees and clean air and a community mostly supported by agriculture."

He describes his first plane ride when he was a junior in high school, "A friend of my parents was a pilot and had his own plane, an open cockpit Waco. One day he took my Mom and me up for a ride. The front cockpit could seat the two of us side-by-side, and the flight was quite a thrill." He laughs as he recalls what the pilot said after they touched down. "Son, no way you were going to fall out of the plane. Your mother had your collar clutched so tight her knuckles were white."

His freshman year at San Jose State he took a flight training class for credit. "We learned in a Taylor Cub and Aeronca. They were tiny planes, and our college instructor was rather hefty. When he was along, the plane was very slow to gain altitude."

After his freshman year he transferred to Washington State University in Pullman, just eight miles from Moscow, Idaho. "I jumped around in my studies between engineering and business. In 1940 I decided to join the military and was inducted in the Army in Spokane. I'd taken survey courses and was sent to the 29th Engineers based out of Portland, Oregon. After my Army survey school I went to Anchorage early in 1941. I was there about nine months." That fall his team left for Yuma, Arizona to do some work in that area.

"We were stationed at the Yuma airport. There was a civilian flying school, and I made a deal with the owner that I would get some of my pals to take lessons from him in exchange for free airtime and instruction. December 7, I was on a solo flight and when I landed a bunch of guys were clustered around my '36 Chrysler and waving at me. I taxied over and a buddy came running to the plane, 'We've been attacked by the Japanese,' he shouted."

Within days Mac had put in a request to go to Army flight training. "I took my physical in Las Vegas, preflight shots and physical training in Santa Ana, basic training in Merced and flight school in Santa Maria at the Hancock Aeronautical School. It was a commercial pilot training facility that was a sub-contractor for the military, and we flew the Stearman biplane painted the bright Army yellow."

From California he went to Williams field near Mesa, Arizona, flying the twin engine, twin tail AT-11, a bombing/gunnery trainer. He was promoted January 1943 to flight officer. "A bit later I was sent to Tucson and B-24 training. I was there for two or three weeks, then sent to Alamogordo, New Mexico and assigned a crew and plane. We trained about four months. Then we were given the opportunity to switch to the B-17 and sent to Salina, Kansas. My personal checkout lasted one hour. I took off, did a touch-and-go, landed and taxied back to the tarmac. The instructor said, 'Good job, you're ready to go.' I couldn't believe it, but didn't argue."

They were only in Kansas for three or four days, barely enough time to get the nose art painted on their plane – the picture and name of cartoonist Al Capp's Earthquake McGoon, "the world's dirtiest wrassler."

"We flew to Scotland and when we arrived were informed we had done a good job ferrying the B-17 overseas. And we'd be flying the type plane we'd been extensively trained in – the B-24 – and not a B-17. We were assigned to the 8th Air Force, 44th Bomb Group, 506th Bomb Squadron in Shipdham, England.

"We didn't get a plane immediately. Besides, there was a requirement that newly assigned pilots fly their first five missions as co-pilot with other crews. The rest of my crew either stayed on base or flew as backfill in case someone was ill or injured. My first three flights were fairly uneventful and based out of Shipdham. September 16, 1943 the bomb group went to Tunisia. My fourth training mission flight was out of Benghazi to the oil fields of Ploesti, Romania.

"When we got to Europe there were times we were flying so low, we had to gain altitude to go over smoke stacks. Headed down one ravine, the nose gunner had to shoot up at the German gunners on the bridge above us. We dropped our load over Ploesti and headed home safely.

"My fifth and last training mission before I was to get my own plane, October 1, 1943, was to bomb the railroad marshalling yard and other targets in Weiner-Neustadt, Austria. We left Tunisia and went in at about 20,000 feet. Over the target the clouds were low, and looking at the surrounding mountains, one could see the peaks poking through the cloud layer. We dropped our bomb load and were about four or five minutes away from the target, forming up to head home. The ack-ack was very heavy, and we were hit. The inside of the plane was in flames.

"The fire was so bad all the crew had to exit from the bomb bays. I was the last one to get out. The captain never made it as the plane exploded into a huge ball of fire just as I exited. I was on fire, and didn't open my chute. I went into free fall and the flames blew out.

"It's really strange. I spread my arms like you see sky divers do today, and even changed direction." Without thinking he puts his arms apart, and tilts his chin back. "I felt like I was gliding through the air and didn't feel any pain." He pauses again. "Then I saw I was getting close to the cloud tops and remembered I'd seen mountain peaks earlier and realized I'd better pull my rip cord. As I entered the cloud layer my chute opened.

"I was hung up between two pine trees, 40 or 50 feet off the ground and four to five feet from the nearest trunk." Like a kid on a swing, he pumped back and forth, and was able to get close to the trunk. "I hit my quick release, and was able to climb down. It was a painful process.

"As I reached the ground I realized I had burns... a lot of them. I was disoriented, but knew I was fairly close to Yugoslavia and if I could get there I'd be safe and I'd be rescued. All my hair was burnt off, my ears were badly burned, my wrists, under my eyes, my neck and more.

"Basically, I hid the first day as I knew the enemy would be looking for survivors. I think I just slept on the ground. The second day, I felt a little safer, but it hurt to walk as my legs were badly burned. As it turned out I had burns of varying degrees over about fifty percent of my body. That night I snuck into a barn to sleep. The third day I was hiding under a tree waiting for night, so I could cross a valley dotted with farms and fields. I must have dozed off. This old man pokes me with his rifle. He was as frightened as I was. His gun was shaking like mad. He walked me to an official of some kind, who tried to turn me over to the police. The police didn't want a prisoner, and sent me and my two escorts down the valley.

"By this time my burns were really starting to ache. We trudged by one cluster of farmhouses and several women came out and were very concerned about me. One of them had a bowl of lard or butter and began to apply it to my injuries. I tried to remove my flight jacket and parts of it had fused to my flesh and it just peeled off with the jacket. She was very upset − not with me − but with what I was going through. My pants were burned up to about the knees. Parts of each shin were really cooked. The pain down there was damn near unbearable." He pauses again. "The women were very kind.

"Anyway, eventually I was put in the back of a truck and taken to Udet Flying School in Vienna. I was alone in a room and some Luftwaffe pilots came in. They were in a good mood and offered me a cigarette. They were very nice, if a bit arrogant. One could speak decent English. They all assumed I had been shot down by one of their fighters; they thought I was one of their trophies. One of them asked what was it like being shot down by the Luftwaffe? I said something to the effect the fighter planes were nothing; it was the ack-ack that had hit my plane. Their demeanor changed immediately, and they stormed out. That day I was transferred by boxcar to Frankfurt with about two dozen other flyers, including two gunners from my plane.

"We were herded from the train station toward a trolley stop several blocks away. Frankfurt had been bombed either that morning or the day before. Civilians wanted to hang us, and some threw rocks. The German officer in charge said in English, 'They really want to hurt you, and I may not be able to stop them.' The officer yelled at the crowd and kept them back and we made it to the trolley without further incident.

"They put me in Dulag Luft." There were dozens of dulags in Axis territory. They were collection points and transit centers for all POWS. Prisoners would be interrogated, processed and ultimately assigned to more permanent quarters. "I was in a very small room with only a cot and tin walls. First they'd heat the walls until the room was almost unbearable, then they'd turn the heat off, and it became incredibly cold. I received absolutely no medical attention. One English pilot was burned so badly, that bone was exposed on his face. He, too, received no medical attention."

Each POW was in a similar room. The rooms opened up to either a large central room or a hallway. "I would be brought to the interrogators. They spoke excellent English, and talking with them was like sitting across the table and chatting over coffee. My second day, one asked, 'What do you think of Captain so-and-so who lives across the hall from you in Shipdham?' Another knew I'd had a seven-day pass to London shortly before being sent to Tunisia. Another time I was asked when we were going to fix the clock in operations that always ran five minutes slow.

I wondered how they knew some of the information they had. It was suggested I might get needed medical attention if I would just cooperate. The only response I gave my interrogators was name, rank and serial number... except to the comment about medical treatment. I told him he wasn't following the Geneva Convention."

October 9th, 1943 – nine days after the explosion of his B-24 – Mac Roberts left the Nazi interrogation and distribution center for newly captured POW's. He was in considerable pain from his burns and had received no medical attention from his captors.

A number of recently captured officers like Mac were loaded on boxcars and began the journey from Frankfurt to Stalag Luft III located in Sagan (now Zagan, Poland) some 100 miles southeast of Berlin.

"Little did I know my new home would become the model for the movie *The Great Escape*.

"It was an uncomfortable, painful journey because of my injuries, but shortly after I climbed down from the box-car I was sent to the camp hospital. I was told I shouldn't be there; instead I should have received treatment at a hospital in Frankfurt better suited to handle my burns. Stalag Luft III was considered an able-bodied camp for allied officers.

"I could hardly walk, especially after I'd been stationary. And then it was like... like grab onto the wall, and it seemed each time the pain was more intense. I didn't see a doctor for a few days, but German orderlies were helping me. By the time the doctor did see me I was crawling to get around... to get to the bathroom."

As the doctor examined Mac, he explained the proposed treatment and prognosis. Mac recalls a few of his comments: "I don't have pain medication that will really help you relative to your legs... Hopefully the infection hasn't gone so far that we can't stop it... Your face is pretty bad... Your ears, I don't know, because sometimes ears don't scar like other tissues... Eventually, you will likely need plastic surgery..."

"The doctor was very caring, but I was worried when he told me they didn't have sulfa and wanted to try a substitute they'd developed. He proposed and implemented a few other treatments that were relatively untried, but the only other choice, like the sulfa alternative, was no treatment at all. They kept putting this stuff on my ears and it just kept building up over the days with each successive application." Mac laughs, "Finally my ears looked like big rubber ears you'd buy for Halloween. And it itched, and I picked at it, and a chunk of covering came off, and another patient said, 'You ought to see the skin under there, it's pink as a baby's bottom.' The doctor came in and was excited and said, 'I don't know why, but your ears and face seem to be coming out of this like you've got brand new skin.' My legs were a different story and took a long time to heal.

"I was in the hospital 3-½ months. The doctor. told me there was more healing to be done, but not in the hospital."

Stalag Luft III had close to 11,000 airmen and was eventually divided into five separate sections. Americans were in the West and Center Compounds, British in the East and North and Russians in the South Camp. Mac was assigned to the Center Compound.

"We had about ten main dormitories," he says, "with at least 200 men per dorm. When I came in we still had some British in Center Camp.

"When I left the hospital I was met at the gate of Center Camp by one of the POW's, Wendell 'Windy' Morris. He welcomed me and asked if I'd like the grand tour. 'Let's swing by the kitchen first,' he said, 'and maybe find a bite to eat.' In the kitchen he pointed to a piece of meat about two inches square. It had maggots crawling on it. He sniffed the meat, then offered it to me. I declined, and he popped it in his mouth. 'If the meat isn't spoiled, eat it. And,' my guide offered, 'the maggots are a good source of protein.' It took me six months before I could do as he suggested."

As POW camps go, Stalag Luft III was considered in compliance with the 1929 Geneva Convention regarding prisoner treatment, with the exception of food rations.

And, with Hitler in charge, there was the possibility that treatment could change for the worse on a whim. Being a POW was a grim experience; however, there was the common objective shared by all the prisoners to make the best of a bad situation and escape if at all possible. Every prisoner was a survivor before he entered camp, and each wanted to leave as a survivor and eventual victor over the enemy – if not physically at least mentally.

"One night shortly after I got out of the hospital a bunch of British musicians came into our building and started playing their music. All of a sudden guys are rushing around, and four of them with poles leveraged the brick and tile stove off its base. There was still a fire in it. That's when I found out we were building a tunnel. About a dozen men entered the hole. An hour or so later they emerged, the stove was moved back and the musicians left our building."

Mac became a penguin – a dirt dispenser. "I had thin burlap bags up my pants legs. I would head to the volley ball court and disperse my load. We had to be very careful. If the sand in my bags was wet, and I dumped it on dry ground, the Germans might see it, and vice-versa with dry sand on wet ground. I'd dump and the volley ball players would move around the court and mix it with their feet. It worked," he adds.

"Stalag Luft III is where I got my nickname, Mac. When we named the B-17 we ferried across the Atlantic, I'd had it painted on my flight jacket – Earthquake McGoon. Guys didn't want to call me by my first name, Edgar, or middle name, Wendell. I became Earthquake McGoon, Earthquake, McGoon and Mac." He laughs, "Years after the war a former POW ran up and threw his arms around me, 'Earthquake... Earthquake... it's great to see you.'"

The German officers in charge of the complex were non-flying Luftwaffe. Most of the guards were older men or had been wounded in Eastern Front battles. For prisoners, it was the luck of the draw relative to the officers and enlisted men in charge of their camp or building. "We were lucky," Mac explains. "If you have ever seen Hogan's Heroes, you remember Sgt. Schultz. The guard who had primary responsibility for our building was also named Sgt. Schultz. We called all our German guards and officers 'Goons'. Schultz would enter our building and yell 'Goon in the building'. Any untoward activity would stop immediately as he strolled through with his rifle.

Late March of 1944 almost 80 prisoners escaped through a tunnel in the British North Compound. Less than a handful made it to freedom. Hitler ordered fifty of the recaptured prisoners to be executed. The rest were returned to prison camps, including some back to Stalag Luft III. Privately, many of the Luftwaffe prison officers and guards were horrified by Hitler's action.

Mac says, "Schultz was a good man. At a reunion of Stalag Luft III we had in Denver in the mid-1980's, we provided a round trip ticket for him and his daughter." Mac is quick to add some of the officers and guards for other buildings and camps were truly hated. Again, luck of the draw.

"January 27, 1945 we were told the Goons had given us less than an hour to get to the front gate and to pack light."

Hitler himself had issued the order to evacuate as the Russians were getting close, and he was afraid the almost

11,000 prisoners would be liberated. At the time of his order they were within 13 miles of the Stalag.

"We left in the middle of the night," Mac offers. "We marched for three or four days. It was rough going and oh so cold." At times they were in blizzard conditions. "My pal, Windy Morris, and I marched together. There was a guard walking along side. I'm guessing he was 65 to 70 years old. He was having a very tough time. By this time I spoke pretty good German. The heaviest thing he had was his rifle. 'Can we carry your gun?' I asked. He looked at me and gave me his rifle. Windy and I traded off carrying it for about three hours. No one else volunteered. I guess another guard reported us. A German officer came back and really chewed out the old man. The officer looked at Windy and me and said, 'That wasn't very smart.' A bit later a truck came alongside and the old guard – with his rifle – climbed in the back."

Thirty-two men tried to escape, and all were quickly recaptured. All the prisoners were crammed into boxcars, with up to 60 men in a car that should hold no more than 40. It was a three-day ride in the dead of winter with no stops. The stench was overpowering. The train ground to a halt at Moosburg – Stalag VIIA -- a few miles north of Munich. It was a facility designed to hold no more than 14,000 prisoners. At the time of Mac's liberation it held 130,000 prisoners of all allied nationalities. It was, literally, a scene out of Dante's Inferno. Mac's weight had dropped from 155 to 115 pounds.

April 29, 1945 Mac and his fellow prisoners were liberated by Patton's Third Army. Patton came to camp two days later. The fourth day the American POW's headed to La-Havre in C-47's. "After we landed we were told it would be days before we left for home. Windy and I hitchhiked to another town. That night we walked back to LaHavre. We took a shortcut through some trees taped off by yellow ribbon. When we got to the other side, this American soldier yelled at us, 'What the hell did you walk through that minefield for? Are you guys nuts?'

"When we got back to New York City we were put on a train for the West Coast. It stopped near Beale AFB and the base commander gave us a dinner and all our back pay. I got to San Francisco by bus where I was met by my family.

"I stayed in the military for twenty-one years and retired as a Major. I worked as a civilian in the Army until 1982 at the San Francisco Presidio. My pal Windy introduced me to Bug (think of 'cute as a bug') back in Oklahoma City not too long after the war." He married Bug (Gertrude Elizabeth) on April 29, 1946. She adds, "April 29, 1945 he got out of one camp; that same day in 1946 he entered another one." They both laugh.

They moved to Lake Wildwood in 1982. "We have two wonderful girls and a boy, and three grandchildren – two boys and a girl," Mac says.

"I learned valuable lessons during WWII. I learned much about myself, my comrades, my enemy, and saw extremes of good and bad in people. I do not dislike the German people," he states. "I dislike their government during WWII."

Ferne and Bill

Chapter 14: Bill Tadlock – AAF

"We also did many supply drops to roving patrols of General Merrill's men. We always flew with the doors off, with aircrew in the cargo area tied off so they couldn't fall out the door while dropping supplies."

BILL TADLOCK was born 1921 in Rosalie, Nebraska, a town of about 250 located 60 miles north of Omaha and 30 south of Sioux City. His dad was with the Chicago, Burlington and Quincy Rail Road and worked as a foreman repairing and building bridges. He spent significant time on the rail routes with his crew in a combination sleeping, dining and tool car. For several years Bill's mom ran the crew's dining area, then devoted herself full-time to raising Bill and his three younger brothers.

At Rosalie High School he lettered in four sports—football quarterback, basketball guard, baseball catcher and track quarter-miler. He was also class president his last two years and president of the student senate.

Bill chuckles, "My senior class had 13 students; so fully participating in school activities was easy." His modesty does not explain why he filled such key athletic and student body leadership roles.

After graduation in 1938 the family moved to Ashland just south of Omaha where his father assumed an administrative job with more responsibility. "I had a few odd jobs, and during 1939 went to visit an uncle in Colusa. I liked northern California so much I stayed and went to work for a local grocery store."

He continues, "Shortly after Pearl Harbor I drove to Sacramento to join the Army Air Corps." He was accepted and told to return to Colusa until he was called to duty.

September 1942 he reported to San Francisco, then boarded a train for pre-flight training at Randolph Field, San Antonio.

"After basic I went to primary and advanced flight training in a Fairchild low-wing trainer, the Vultee BT-13, and the AT-6." He graduated from advanced training May 1943 and was promoted to Second Lieutenant.

"I headed back to Colusa and asked my girl friend, Ferne Shippen, to marry me. May 30, we took a train to Reno. We asked a cab driver if he could take us to get a license and find a church. After the courthouse visit the cabbie walked into a church and interrupted the services. I think he had called ahead while we were filling out the license forms. The minister and wife took us into a separate room and married us with the driver as our witness. Ferne and I stayed at the Riverside Hotel, the best in Reno at the time. I remember the band playing." He pauses, reflecting quietly on a night almost 63 years ago. "The cabbie wouldn't take a penny... not a penny. He was a wonderful guy."

Bill pauses again. "From Reno we took the train to Nebraska to visit my folks." He smiles. "Ferne and I were at the train station in Denver and this army sergeant and his men are coming our way. The sarge stops and barks 'Attention' and they all halt and salute. I was a little flustered, but hopefully didn't show it as I returned their salute. It was the first one I'd received as an officer."

Later that month of June, accompanied by Ferne, Bill reported to his new assignment, basic multi-engine training in Austin, TX. July and August were spent in Mississippi for operational training as a first pilot, then Indiana to pick up a crew and a spanking new C-47.

"Early December 1943 we received orders for overseas. Ferne went back to Colusa to stay with her family. We headed our plane via Florida, Puerto Rico, British Guiana, and Brazil across to Ascension Island." (The island is just south of the equator, 1,450 miles east of Brazil and about 1,000 from Africa. They weren't part of a convoy, just one of a continuous flow of aircraft – all types of planes – making their way to war. They landed in Ghana then to Khartoum, Sudan.) "We skirted north around Ethiopia, as that was under Axis control, to Aden and then to an island off Yemen's east coast and headed to Karachi. We arrived at our Ledo, India base just before Christmas 1943."

Ledo is in the far NE corner of India close to the borders with Burma and China. Mid-1942 the British, Chinese and Indian forces under Lt. General Joseph "Vinegar Joe" Stilwell were defeated by the Japanese military in Burma. The Japanese destroyed the Burma Road, the overland supply route winding from coastal Rangoon, Burma, into China.

The strategy to beat the Japanese depended on ultimately getting that route reopened by building a new feeder route from Ledo, India – some 465 miles long – to hook up with the Burma Road at Bhamo near the Chinese border.

Stilwell requested that American ground forces be sent to perform "a dangerous and hazardous mission." By early 1944 some 3,000 American volunteers from existing Pacific Theater and stateside units had been jungle warfare-trained in India and were ready for action. Stilwell put his friend Brig. Gen. Frank Merrill in command. "Merrill's Marauders" would be supported by troops from India, China and Burma as well as soldiers from Australia and New Zealand, Britain and their African colonies. Bill Tadlock's crew and C-47, assigned to the 10th Air Force, 443rd Group, 315th Troop Carrier Squadron would also be involved in this and other key engagements.

Over the next 14 months Bill and his crew would fly 123 missions over enemy territory. Half or more were night flights. He says, "Total missions were about 250, but that also includes flights over allied controlled skies."

On his missions he carried a few survival items in case his plane didn't make it back – a .45 pistol, a tin of opium about the size of a chewing tobacco container, money, and a double-sided silk map of his flight area.

"I also had a Tommy gun but seldom took it. I was given the opium and money before every mission and turned it in when I landed. The drugs and money would be used, if necessary, to help buy our continued freedom and get us to safety. I had the silk map sewn into the lining of my jacket and didn't remove it until I returned home."

The map, carefully folded, looks brand new. Unfortunately, when he was returning home the contents of his footlocker were stolen and his photos and keepsakes are forever lost.

Until capture by Merrill's Marauders mid-1944, the Myitkyina airfield in NW Burma included a contingent of Zero fighter planes. "The base was only 150 miles from the border with India, and just another 10 miles to Ledo, India. There were also enemy fighter squadrons in Mandalay, 250 miles south of Myitkyina. We'd fly 120-130 miles per hour, and would be easy pickings for the faster fighter planes if we weren't careful."

Bill continues, "In enemy territory we'd fly low over the jungle – 250 feet or less, including skimming the tops of the trees. There was not much a Zero could do at that altitude. They just didn't have enough time to do a shooting pass."

He adds, "While chased by the enemy a few times, we were never fired on." His plane did, however, take small arms fire from the ground and sustained minor damage on several missions.

"We were very good at aircraft identification. Until mid-1944 all American fighters in our territory had in-line engines. The Zero had a radial engine. If we ID'd a plane with a radial engine we'd fly very low and take evasive action as we thought necessary." He adds, "June 1944 a few 10th AAF squadrons were activated flying P-47 fighters. We'd be a lit-

tle nervous when we saw the radial engine until we realized
it was on our side."

For the first few months Bill's primary base was Ledo.
"Our job was to fly men, materials or both where needed.
Our very first flight was just across the Burma border into
Shingbwiyang. It was a very short gravel airstrip hastily
carved out of the jungle next to the newest stretch of the
Ledo Road. We did a short-field landing (steeper angle of
descent, flaps down to slow the plane, harder landing and
less field required to stop the plane), quickly off-loaded
cargo and were back in the air in a few minutes. As the road
progressed so did the hastily built airfields. Some of the
strips were just steel mesh laid down in a wet field."

Bill continues, "We also did many supply drops to roving patrols of General Merrill's men. We always flew with
the doors off, with aircrew in the cargo area tied off so they
couldn't fall out the door while dropping supplies. In the
cockpit we'd find the drop zone by radio, fire or light signals. We'd take it low enough for the chute to open, swing
once, then twice, then hit the ground. We didn't want men
on the ground chasing all over the jungle at night in enemy
territory."

He also towed gliders loaded with troops. "We made
three night trips with double tows – two separate cables behind our plane each pulling an individual glider. When we
were in position behind enemy lines we'd cut the gliders
loose for their landing.

Late March of 1944 Bill's squadron moved from Ledo
to Sylhet, India – several hundred miles to the south, to
support the Ledo Rd. effort and other operations in SW

Burma. Sylhet is set among terraced tea plantations and lush tropical forests with winding rivers. "There were no officer quarters on base; so three of us rented a bungalow. We hired a young man to do housekeeping and laundry. It was a comfortable setting."

After Merrill's Marauders captured the airfield at Myitkyina in May 1944, Bill's C-47 was the first to land. "I picked up six Japanese prisoners, guarded by Ghurka troops and took them to India for interrogation."

Bill recounts a night mission from Chittagong, India. "Chittagong was right on the Bay of Bengal about 175 miles south of Sylhet. The Japanese had cut the supply line for British troops in Burma. From Chittagong, as flight leader and assistant operations leader, that night I flew multiple missions with six planes to re-supply the soldiers. A reporter from a London newspaper was in my cockpit. He said he would be with us for all our missions that evening. The first run we needed our running lights on for the drop. The plane in front of me was taking tracer fire. The reporter asked what the light streaks were. I told him and he became very quiet as the tracer bullets swarmed around us on our pass. When we returned to Chittagong to load supplies for another drop he said he had enough material for his story and declined my invitation to take another trip over Burma."

He talks about hauling Chinese troops who helped guard jungle airfields and segments of the Ledo Road. "We'd haul 20-21 men at a time. In friendly airspace over India and western Burma I'd climb to 6-8,000 feet to cool things off, then as we approached our landing area we'd fly low, land and take off as soon as possible. After the fourth load I was asked how many troops I had carried each flight. While one of my crew had logged the troops onto the plane he didn't take a tally when they got off. We were in too big a hurry for head counts. None of my crew flew in the cargo area with the Chinese troops. Each of the flights had landed with two or three fewer men than we had loaded. Apparently as we climbed to cooler altitudes a few troops would cluster around the open double doors to get some fresh air. It only took one thermal, one bounce side-to-side to send a few soldiers earthward." He pauses, "Once we figured out what had happened, whenever we flew Chinese soldiers we put on the doors."

Bill explains a mission to China. "Late 1944 I was sent to a little airstrip on the southwest coast of China to pick up a photo officer from a B-29. His plane had made an emergency landing after a bombing run over Japan. I brought him back to my base and from there he was spirited off to Washington, D.C. to deliver his pictures for analysis."

Mid-1944 Bill was sent on a mission to Guilin, China, 250 miles NW of Hong Kong, to evacuate people from Yang Tong airbase, home to B-25, P-51 and Flying Tiger Squadrons. "I flew from Sylhet, India to Chengdu China, then 550 miles SE to Guilin. The base, the main American airfield in central China, was hectic in anticipation of the Japanese advance." Rather than letting it fall into enemy hands it would be destroyed.

On the tarmac Americans and Chinese were waiting to be evacuated. "I'll never forget a tiny old Chinese man with a wispy beard with his wife hoping to board my plane. I made sure he got on. I don't know why he was there or who he was." Shortly after Bill took off, twenty-two 1,000-pound bombs buried adjacent to the runways were exploded. Another thirty would be detonated when the last plane left. Buildings were being torched. There would be nothing left that the Japanese could use.

"Guilin is beautiful, the limestone peaks rising out the rice fields alongside the Li River." He was taking his passengers to safety in Luchow, SW of Guilin, away from the pending horrors of war.

"I flew low over a train also headed to safety. It was unbelievable – hundreds of people on top of the cars and hanging from the sides fleeing the Japanese."

Bill's last flight was transporting wounded soldiers from Mandalay to a hospital in eastern Burma.

For his 123 missions in enemy territory he was awarded an Air Medal with four clusters and the Distinguished Flying Cross with two clusters. He also received a Distinguished Unit Badge and the Asiatic Pacific Service medal. He left Burma as a Captain.

"January 1945 I was sent to instrument flight instructor training in Waco, then Minter Field in Bakersfield as an instructor. I was discharged from Camp Beale near Penn Valley, CA in 1946. After my discharge I was a civilian flight instructor at Chiem Field in Marysville, then I went into the insurance business."

He became a sales manager for Kemper Insurance in Sacramento and eventually the company's general manager for the Pacific Northwest, including British Columbia.

"I retired in 1984 and Ferne and I moved to Lake Wildwood in 1989."

Both enjoyed golf, and Bill was active in the men's club and environmental committees. They have three children, two boys and a girl, and four grandchildren.

Some historians claim the true heroes of the 10th AAF were the transport crews flying unescorted and unarmed over rugged terrain and in bad weather providing supplies and emergency services as required. Bill Tadlock says he and his crew were just doing their job.

Lew and Betty Lou

Chapter 15: Lew Connell –USN

"When American prisoners were released in Hanoi, I would send a Fleet Intelligence Officer to accompany each individual."

BACK IN 1914 Lewis Connell's father joined the Navy at age 16. Says Lew, "Dad spent the next 20 years serving our country and retired as a Chief Pharmacist's Mate during the Depression. He married in 1925 and the next year headed to Samoa, wife in tow, courtesy of our government. They lived in a thatched hut, and he became the 'doctor' because of his training, job title, supplies and uniform."

Lew continues, "Margaret Mead was in Samoa at the same time. In 1928 she published her best-selling book, *Coming of Age in Samoa*. Dad knew Miss Mead but didn't especially care for her – there were proper roles for men...

there were roles for women. She lived outside the lines from Dad's perspective – a bit too avant-garde."

Lew was the youngest of four children, born in 1930 in Minneapolis. "When dad retired in 1934 he went into law enforcement in San Diego. We moved around a bit, but by the time I was twelve he had settled into a government public health service job in a key management position in Fort Worth, Texas."

Lew was a good student in high school and played first-string football and basketball. In 1948, his freshman year at the University of Texas in Austin, he made the varsity football squad as a defensive tight end. That year Texas was in the top 20 teams in the nation. Texas football was as big-time then as it is now – one had to be a very talented athlete to play the game. His football career ended with a knee injury that first year. However, by the time he was an upper classman he had healed sufficiently to play semi-pro basketball. "Football was over, but I played hoops for the 7-Up Bottling Company team as a forward. We traveled the southwest, including Mexico, for twenty bucks or so a game." He also played intra-mural soccer. "Most of the soccer guys were well-to-do kids from South America. Soccer was a great experience from a number of perspectives."

With his bad knee, hopes for an athletic scholarship had disappeared. Lew worked his way through school and his parents helped with a little money each month. He waited tables for free meals.

He took up to 24 units a semester, and with summer sessions earned his degree in chemistry in three years. "I was accepted to medical school, but did the math in years on how long it would take to become a doctor. I decided I wanted to follow my dad with a career in the Navy."

After graduating university in 1951 Lew joined the Navy and attended Officer Candidate School, class #2, at Newport, RI. Following that, in 1952 he attended OCS for half a year in Jacksonville, FL.

"I was swimming at the junior base officer pool and met Betty Lou. She was going to Florida State. It was love at first sight." Her dad was commanding officer at the Jacksonville Naval Hospital. They married December 16, 1953 at the Submarine Chapel in Pearl Harbor.

It was not Betty Lou's first time in Hawaii. She says, "December 7, 1941 my Dad was captain of the sea plane tender *Tangier*, berthed next to the battleship, *Utah*. The *Tangier* was one of the few ships not hit during the attack. It left the next week for Midway and Wake Islands. While it made Midway, Wake fell to the Japanese before they got to it. My sister and I watched the Pearl Harbor inferno from the Waikiki apartment our parents had rented." A few weeks later the family, minus her father, headed stateside.

Lew continues, "After Jacksonville I spent a few months in San Francisco for specialized shipboard intelligence training. I spent 1952-55 as intelligence officer for the *USS Sicily, USS Point Cruz* – both Jeep Carriers – and VS-38, the Torpedo Bomber unit, the Fighting Red Griffins."

(Jeep Carriers are also known as escort carriers or "baby flat tops." Many were built on merchant ship hulls. Both carriers that Lew served on were nearly identical – 557 feet long, 19 knots cruise speed, built in 1944, a crew of 1,066 and about 30 planes assigned.)

He recounts an incident aboard the *Point Cruz* a few days after he reported for duty. "I went on deck when the squadron was returning from a mission. I wanted to see the landing safety officer in action. His job was to wave the flags to bring a plane safely on deck. He put me to work. 'Watch each plane through these binoculars as it comes in and yell to me when it has both wheels and flaps down. By the way, if you don't see me standing next to you, drop down the ladder... quick,' he said."

The LSO stood on a small platform next to the jeep carrier landing deck at the point where an aircraft would touchdown. The adjacent ladder descended to the ship's innards.

"I watched the first returning plane and yelled to the LSO, 'Flaps down... wheels down.' As the plane came in I lowered the binoculars, turned slightly to the left and watched the plane make a perfect landing. 'Number two,' the LSO shouted. I raised the binoculars and focused on the next plane. Through the binoculars it kept getting bigger and bigger. Instead of veering slightly to the left on the approach, it was headed my way. I turned towards the LSO. He wasn't there. I didn't use the ladder – I jumped into the hole. Seconds later the plane's tail-hook tore off the platform we had been standing on. The plane made another approach and landed safely."

Lew wasn't watching that second attempt.

When asked what he said to the LSO, who might have alerted him about imminent death, he only smiles. It's the smile a University of Texas defensive tight end might give to an opposing pass receiver in his territory.

The mid-'50s Lew attended photo interpretation school, then became an instructor at the Glenview, IL, naval training facility. From 1958-60 he was assigned to the special weapons employment group. It was an interesting time. From a nuclear weapons perspective each service picked its own targets. For example, the Strategic Air Command and Tactical Air Command had their targets, the Navy theirs, and the Army nothing because they lacked delivery systems. "There was a rule-of-thumb – the Navy would get enemy coastal sites, the Air Force places in-country."

Theoretically, were war declared, some places might be struck several times. In 1959 Lew became a key member in helping develop a single integrated operations plan for nuclear deployment.

"That 1958-60 period I helped build target folders for potential Western Pacific nuclear bomb targets. If war was declared, we were ready. I spent about a third of my time in Omaha at Strategic Air Command headquarters helping develop our national nuclear strategy and tactics." In 1959 he was promoted to Commander.

From 1960-63 he helped create and establish sophisticated shipboard intelligence centers for Forrestal class "Supercarriers" designed specifically for jet aircraft – CVA 60, the *Saratoga* and CVA 61, the *Ranger*.

The carrier intelligence center provides critical analysis, planning, control and coordination functions to ensure success of all missions.

"Electronic Data Processing and reconnaissance analysis were critical components of the intelligence center operation. Also under intelligence center management and aboard each carrier were six RA-5C Vigilante reconnaissance aircraft," Lew says.

The RA-5C was a mach 2+, two-man aircraft, capable of optical, electromagnetic and electronic reconnaissance. It could comfortably operate at altitudes above 50,000 feet, and in 1960 had set the world altitude record for its class at more than 91,000 feet.

In 1964 Lew took command of the intelligence center – one he had designed – for the *Saratoga.* "I had five intelligence officers and 30 or so enlisted men in my organization. Dotted line another dozen officers – the pilots and Reconnaissance Attack Navigators manning the RA-5C's – supported our intelligence center. We were assigned to the Atlantic Fleet, with much of our time spent in the eastern Mediterranean."

The *Saratoga* was more than 1000' long with an extreme width of 252'. It had a crew of more than 3,800 and could cruise at 33 knots (about 38 mph). It could handle 70-90 aircraft. The McDonnell-Douglas A-4 Skyhawk, a single-seat attack bomber, was the primary aircraft aboard the *Saratoga* and other Forrestal class carriers. The A-4 was sufficiently small to ascend/descend the carrier elevator without a requirement for having to fold the wings. The plane could carry up to 5,000 pounds of ordnance, including a Mk7 nuclear weapon. (The Mark 7 was 30 inches by 15-plus feet, with a 20-kiloton tactical nuclear bomb. It weighed only 1,680 pounds.)

"I enjoyed the intelligence officer job very much. From day one of my naval career almost everything I had done helped prepare me for the assignment."

He recounts an episode when the carrier was at Guantanamo Bay, Cuba in 1965. "We received an emergency sortie alert. The Haitian government needed some help. One of their DC-3's had crashed in the mountains and they wanted to find it. We launched an RA-5C. It quickly found the downed plane." He pauses. "We provided coordinates to the government and they asked if we could send a plane to pick-up any survivors. We had a C1-A on board, a small twin-engine propeller driven plane used for logistics, mail and cargo flights. Three of us – pilot, co-pilot and me – headed toward a western Haiti mountainous dirt airstrip as close to the crash site as possible. As soon as we landed, a jeep with two machine-gun carrying Haitian soldiers pulled alongside the plane.

"I exited the plane and got in the jeep. It was about a one-hour ride to a small hospital. The doctor had a .45 tucked into his waistband. He had two patients – one was a Haitian Army Colonel. I have no idea who the other one was. We helped them to the jeep and headed back to the C1-A. We circled Port-Au-Prince, the capital. There was smoke and many fires visible from the air.

"Our plane was met at the airport by the Haitian Ambassador, and the two passengers were unloaded. It was suggested we take off as quickly as possible as the city was in turmoil. That seemed a good idea."

In 1966 he left the *Saratoga* for Suitland, Maryland, headquarters for Naval Intelligence. He would be the executive officer for the Naval Reconnaissance Center.

"Much of the job involved photo interpretation. For example, when Cuba was deploying Soviet medium range ballistic missiles we provided considerable intelligence about their efforts. We supplied intelligence on Soviet subs and bases around the world, and information about other cold war adversaries. Vietnam, of course, was going full bore. Our info went to the Defense Intelligence Agency, responsible for sorting and collating information to send to the President for his daily briefing package."

In 1968-70 Lew moved to Hawaii as head of reconnaissance for the entire Pacific Fleet, including subs and aircraft. Again, a huge job because of Vietnam and the cold war. In 1970 he was promoted to Captain and left Hawaii for Newport, RI.

"I was appointed Chair of Intelligence at the Naval War College," Lew states. The college was founded in 1884 on Coasters Harbor Island in Newport. It has two primary missions – to educate tomorrow's leaders of our nation and Navy, and to define the future Navy. The NWC states they are "the leading educational institution for providing our nation's leaders a foundation on the principles of war and strategic thought. The curriculum is based on three cores of study: Strategy and Policy, National Security Decision Making, and Joint Military Operations."

Says Lew, "Each morning I would read and analyze message traffic on Vietnam and other hot-spots and review it with 400-500 surface naval commanders and senior naval aviators. In the afternoon I would work one-on-one with fifty or so students on issues related to intelligence."

In 1972 he returned to Hawaii as Commanding Officer – Fleet Intelligence – Pacific. "I also had an office at Subic Bay, Philippines. We assigned naval aviation targets for

Vietnam. We also built the nuclear target folders for the Pacific Region." Lew won't discuss specifics as much of what he was involved with is still classified. But a quick look at the globe, and China and Russia seem to be obvious candidates for Lew's attention.

"We coordinated very closely with the Air Force regarding targets. Costal, navy. Interior, them."

He continues, "When American prisoners were released in Hanoi I would send a Fleet Intelligence Officer there to accompany each individual. It was a one-on-one deal. They would stay with the former-POW for a month to six-weeks. Of the forty or so who were released during my term as Fleet Intelligence Commander about half were Navy pilots. It was gut-wrenching for the POW's and for my folks. We helped them through social and administrative problems. We tried to help them adjust to what had happened to them and how their lives had possibly changed related to friends and loved ones back home. I personally followed each case of each man. We owed so much to these wonderful patriots."

In 1976 he left Hawaii for Washington, D.C. He was appointed Director of NCIS, the Naval Criminal Investigative Service. "I had 1,200 civilian agents scattered around the globe – Yokuska, Naples, Subic Bay, Honolulu, London and other cities, large and small, with a major naval station or Marine base either abroad or in the states. I also had one agent on each big-deck carrier." The official NCIS website states, "NCIS is the primary law enforcement and counterintelligence arm of the United States Department of the Navy. It works closely with other local, state, federal and foreign agencies to counter and investigate the most serious crimes: terrorism, espionage, computer intrusion, homicide, rape, child abuse, arson, procurement fraud and more. NCIS is the Navy's primary source of security for the men, women, ships, planes, and resources of America's seagoing expeditionary forces worldwide... it is a unique, highly-trained and effective team of special agents, investigators, forensic experts, security specialists, analyst and support personnel."

Lew is asked if the hit TV program, *NCIS*, starring Mark Harmon is accurate. "Don't know," he offers, "never watched it." We move on. He recounts a real episode that took place in Subic Bay.

"We received intel from one of our paid informants, a local, that one of our 20- to 30-foot Navy launches would be stolen. The informant was right. A thief jumps in a launch and NCIS agents chase him, firing shots. We get him and turn him over to local authorities. He's just a kid – a teen-ager. One of my team looks at past cases involving stolen boats at Subic. Six years before the same informant had given us identical information. Our paid informant was interested in job security. He, through an intermediary, would hire a kid to steal a Navy boat and abandon it. We proved our case against our paid informant and referred him to the local authorities for prosecution and imprisonment."

He continues, "On a more serious note, we had a Naval Security Station in Algiers. A Soviet agent approached a Navy cryptologist on leave in Spain. The sailor did the right thing and reported the incident. The Russian had asked for a phone book of the base, ostensibly to look up some friends. We told the sailor to supply it. Next the agent asked for sensitive info, with the promise of payment. We asked the sailor to set up a meet in Madrid and requested the Spanish authorities, the Guardia Civil (Civil Guard), to make the arrest if appropriate. The sailor was paid and handed over the requested information. The Spanish police chase the agent, stop him and drag him from his vehicle. Turns out the Soviet agent was a colonel in the GRU – the Soviet intelligence agency. He had been in Spain just a month or so. A few days after his capture he was sent back to Russia to a likely unpleasant reception by his GRU superiors."

He pauses, "The sailor who reported the initial contact didn't do so by accident. That was part of the training in all branches of the military. When approached by enemy agents they helped us catch a lot of them." He continues, "During my time as NCIS Director I made many trips around the world meeting with my management team and agents. I guess I spent fifty percent of my time in the field, visiting each major site at least once a year."

Lew retired from the Navy in 1979. "In 1980 I went to work for Lockheed's Missile and Space Program. I was Deputy Director of their classified project programs. I retired from Lockheed in 1991. I worked on Tomahawk route planning – way point digitized pictures and was in charge of Tomahawk installation for battleships and cruisers."

We discussed his management style in the military and private sector. "Dig and find out what's going on. Make changes as required... take actions that will move the organization forward. Make objectives clear and hold people accountable. I never asked anyone to do something I wouldn't do myself. "

He and Betty Lou have three children, all successful in their careers. "We also have three grand-children. We moved to Lake Wildwood in 1990. I had a business meeting at a Lockheed site in the Sacramento area, and took time-out to visit our local area."

Betty Lou is active in Lake Wildwood's little theatre. "She's been a dancer in several productions and does a lot of costuming work for the organization," Lew states. "She's also active in the Women's Club, and was the president of the group. She does a lot of things for our community."

Lew is an avid and tough golfer and also restores VW's. "That's a carry-over from when I was a young officer in the Navy. At the time the VW van was the only one big enough for three kids." He has a van and bug in the garage. Both have been restored and are pristine. When his children earned their driver's licenses in high school he and Betty Lou bought them VW's.

Our community is a better place because of Lew and Betty Lou's contributions. Our community and nation are better and safer because of Lew Connell's outstanding service to our country.

Chapter 16: Tom Caswell – AAF

"...Tom and his fellow passengers spent the day ashore, wisely hidden in the jungle until nightfall."

IN 1938 a family friend invited Tom Caswell to go for a ride in his small plane. For a lad in his late teens living in Placerville the flight was an adventure that would change his life.

Not much later he left the foothills to attend San Francisco City College. Coincidentally, President Roosevelt inaugurated a program called "Civilian Pilot Training" which offered flight lessons as part of the curriculum in some colleges. By 1940 Tom had his license, learning to fly in a Piper Cub from Mills Field – the current location of San Francisco International Airport. Controlling his patch of the sky above the greater Bay Area was an exhilarating experience.

The flying bug had bitten. But it was expensive for a college student on a limited budget. He joined the Army Air

Corp as a flying cadet February 1941 so he could get more flight time. No longer did he have to rent a plane; the aircraft and fuel was gratis. He was also paid a modest stipend with the added bonus of free, great-looking officer uniforms. By the fall of 1941 he and 14 fellow pilots had volunteered to head for the Philippines to fly B-17's for the 19th Bombardment Group out of Clark Field near Manila. He shipped out on the *USS Bliss* October 14.

About the same time Tom joined the US Army Air Force, American dependents had been sent home from the Philippines. The military leadership at Clark Field had started to prepare for the possibility of war. B-17's and P-40's were widely dispersed around the field partially shielded by big earth revetments; personnel would be protected by slit trenches.

The informal buzz about war turned formal in late November. Tom and his fellow officers gathered around their commander and were told they were now on high alert. They, as pilots, were to do nothing to incite conflict – neither fighter planes nor bombers were to buzz Japanese ships. The annual big event of the radio broadcast of the Army-Navy football game was cancelled. Each officer was sent to Supply as soon as the meeting was over to get his WWI helmet, .45 pistol, canteen, gas mask and a web belt. "From now on," the Colonel concluded, "there will be six P-40's parked at the end of the runway ready to go 24 hours a day."

On the day of the attack on Pearl Harbor, Tom Caswell was not scheduled to fly. It was still dark when he was notified of the attack. There would be an interlude of less than eight hours until Clark Field was under assault by a large contingent of high-altitude bombers and straffing Zeros. More than once that day Tom praised the wisdom of his commanders for having the foresight to have the slit trenches dug. For him, they were a lifesaver. Of the 107 P-40's and 35 B-17's at Clark that day only 22 fighters and 17 bombers were left intact. A dozen B-17's had been flown to Mindinao days earlier. Tom was now a pilot without a plane and was told he and the rest of the 19th Bomb Group would have to hold out until help came. The Japanese were relentless in their attacks, bombing Clark Field two or three times a day until Christmas.

By December 22, the Japanese had made their main assault on the island of Luzon, landing large numbers of troops. By the next day they had attained naval and aerial superiority in the Philippines. That day, the 23rd, General MacArthur announced the decision to begin to withdraw American forces on Luzon to the Bataan Peninsula and declare Manila an open city. Late December the remnants of the USAAF 19th Bomb Group, some four hundred personnel, moved down the peninsula and on the 29th were ordered to sail from Marvailes, Bataan. It was hoped Tom and his comrades would get reacquainted with the air and be able to settle the score with the Japanese military.

Their ship, the *SS Mayon*, was a Philippine 305-foot long inter-island steamer built in 1923. She was not built for speed or comfort. Her objective was to sail almost 500 miles south from the tip of the Bataan Peninsula to Bugo Bay on Mindinao. The quoted odds for successfully completing the voyage were not favorable. The plan was to travel at night, and find safe harbor during the day to minimize encounters with Japanese air and sea forces. During the day, no passengers were allowed on deck; the ship was supposed to appear virtually deserted while at rest.

December 30, the *Mayon* was anchored in a cove off the Illin Strait near the coast of Mindoro. A Japanese seaplane bomber attacked the ship. The plane made five or six bombing runs, with one hitting close enough to raise the ship out of the water from the concussion. Some Americans panicked, dove into the water swimming for shore, and were killed by the shock of the bomb blasts. When the attack ended, the men who had gone overboard were picked up and the ship was underway by dusk.

The next morning, New Year's Eve, the ship anchored off Negros Island. This time Tom and his fellow passengers spent the day ashore, wisely hidden in the jungle until nightfall.

Jan. 1, 1942, the *SS Mayon* started the new year right by eluding a Japanese submarine shortly before dawn. At 6 a.m. the *Mayon* sailed into Bugo Bay, Mindinao. Tom and his fellow airmen were given five bullets for their newly issued rifles in case the enemy was waiting on shore. One man stood on the dock waving at the ship – the American manager for Del Monte Pineapple Co.

Tom was anxious to get back in the air... to return to the cockpit. He would have to wait. Every now and then an AAF bomber, having completed the long flight from Australia, would land at the plantation. With the pilot would be orders requesting by name more senior pilots from the 19th who would be flown to other assignments. Second Lieutenant Tom Caswell was a very junior pilot, and far down on the request list.

He, another officer and two enlisted men were assigned duty to guard and blow up, if necessary, a bridge near the community of Cagayen, some 30 miles from the plantation airfield. They were given cases of dynamite, 10-minute fuses, a plunger and orders to prepare the bridge for possible destruction. They were also directed to an abandoned bamboo hut to live in, and told food supplies would be delivered whenever possible. Tom was informed someone would notify him when it was his turn to leave. Meanwhile, he was to enjoy the rice, fish, molasses and cornmeal. Tom and his pals made many friends, including local Moro guerillas, civilians and an American priest from a nearby Jesuit school.

His turn came April 29, almost four months after he set foot at the Cagayen River Bridge. He was anxious to leave the Philippines and trade his rifle for flight controls. Tom boarded the B-24 and settled in for the long flight to Cloncurry, in N.E. Australia. His plane was the last one into and out of that Mindinao airstrip.

Three days later another bomber on a rescue mission tried to land at the plantation only to be shot at by the Japanese.

That initial night in Australia was especially sweet – it was the first time in months he had slept with his clothes off. That night he dreamt of flying – soaring – banking through the sky. Then he was flown to Melbourne, given his back pay, put up in a nice hotel, told the liquor laws, fed steak for breakfast, lunch and dinner and encouraged to enjoy himself – for one short week. The Battle of the Coral

Sea began May 7. Tom Caswell was told to report immediately to Townesville, Australia. He was about to become a B-26 Marauder pilot with the 2nd Squadron of the 22nd Bombardment Group – the "Red Raiders".

The B-26 was one of the most successful of WWII's warplanes. The plane was sometimes called the "Flying Prostitute" because it had no visible means of support – the wings were clipped for speed and particularly short with a span of 65 feet. It had a top speed of 340 mph and a range of 2400 miles. Its landing speed of 140 mph was higher than the cruising speed of the B-18, the previous bomber the 22nd had flown. It could carry 5,200 pounds of bombs.

Missions covered some 2,600 miles, with half of those carrying bombs. Planes would leave Townesville and head to Port Moresby, New Guinea where they would refuel, and head off to their target in groups of two-to-six planes. They were on their own, as fighter escorts were rarely available. Many times the planes were ordered to stay at Port Moresby for a week or so to avoid the long flight back to Australia and maximize their time over enemy targets.

The area surrounding the airstrip was malaria-infested and without accommodations. Tom and other pilots and crews had to bring their own mosquito netting and suspend it from the wings of their planes. There was no radar, and warnings of enemy planes about to begin strafing or bombing runs were signaled by red flags hoisted from the operations tower. After raising the flag, tower personnel had but a few minutes to scramble for cover.

There was little combat intelligence, maps were sketchy, weather was a factor (especially surrounding the

10,000-foot-plus peaks of New Guinea), and some New Guinea natives did not take kindly to strangers who might drop in. It was a far cry from flying a 40-hp Piper Cub in California, but it met Tom's "love of flying" criteria.

Tom Caswell flew 17 combat missions with the 22nd. Matter-of-factly he states, "I was doing what I had to do." He describes the tracer bullets that came toward him on some missions as, "looking like cigarettes that someone was flicking at you."

Of the 15 pilots that graduated with Tom's advanced USAAF flight school in Stockton, only five survived the war. Overall, the 22nd suffered forty-percent casualties. Tom came back to the United States May of 1943, and served until May of 1945 as a B-26 flight instructor at McDill AFB in FL, and Lake Charles, LA. By the end of the war he was a Captain, and upon his retirement from the reserves a Lieutenant Colonel.

May of 1943, while on his way to McDill AFB, a buddy introduced him to a beautiful blind date in Racine, Wisconsin. Her name is Myke. She, too, was a *PATRIOT*, a combat nurse in Burma, profiled in a *Wildwood Independent* article.

After the war in 1946 Tom returned to the Far East and flew for Philippine Airlines for eight years. Occasionally, and sometimes bittersweetly, he visited the places and local people he had known during WWII. He came home and worked for Pan Am as a flight instructor until his retirement Dec.31, 1979. That was the day he quit piloting planes. He and Myke do love to fly as passengers.

...And here's Tom and Myke

Chapter 17: Myke Caswell – Army

"Of the more than 900 officers listed as full-fledged members of the 'China-Burma-India Hump Pilots Association,' she is the only female."

MAY 30, 1943 Mydell (Myke) Pfanmiller would receive her BS in Nursing from Marquette University in Milwaukee. The day before, she would go on a blind date with Captain Tom Caswell (also in this book.) He had piloted 17 combat missions with the 22nd Bombardment Group, the "Red Raiders." Tom was a handsome young warrior -- seasoned and mature beyond his years.

He and a buddy were on their way from California to their new airbase in Florida, with a stopover in Racine, Wisconsin. His pal had a date scheduled with Myke's older sister. Tom and Myke went along for the ride.

Before the date she asked her mother if she might have a drink that evening since her older sister would be along. "I was very naive," Myke states. Permission was given. On the date she didn't know what to order. "Bourbon and water," said Tom. "If you mix it with soda pop you might get sick."

Tom was impressed with her degree and education but added, "You should join the service, it'll make you worldlier." Myke listened. A few days after their original date he was on his way to Florida. They wrote and occasionally chatted long distance. She took her state exams and earned the Registered Nurse designation. By October of 1943 she had enlisted in the military as a Second Lieutenant. After her basic training, Tom piloted a flight to where she was stationed. "I think it's great you're in the service," he said face-to-face, "but if you really want to broaden your horizons you should signup for overseas." She took his advice, was sent to Chief Nurse's training for three months, and by March of 1944, as a First Lieutenant, she was told to report for foreign duty.

Both she and Tom thought she would be assigned to Europe. One hour after lift-off from New York, and headed east toward Europe, she was told she could open her orders. She was being sent to a staging area in Karachi, India (now Pakistan), where she would receive further instructions. "Where is Karachi?" she inquired.

There were two other nurses on the flight along with 20 or so male officers. Her first stop was three days in Casablanca, the second a like number of days in Cairo, then on to Karachi. Her two female companions were sent to Calcutta. She was about to become, at age 22, the replacement Chief Nurse, 25th Field Hospital, near Lashio, in east central Burma some 75 miles from the Chinese border. The roving hospital was on the front lines astride the Burma Road and some 135 miles northeast of Japanese controlled Mandalay. The territory between them and Mandalay was also under enemy control. Myke's life experiences were, as promised by Tom, becoming more worldly; he had failed to mention the potential for other-worldly experiences.

The day Myke arrived, landing in a small single-engine plane at the short and narrow strip in Lashio, she was driven by jeep to the hospital. Her colonel asked her to sit. "The chief nurse you are replacing is gone because she was sick. The seven nurses who will report to you have all been here several years and are all past due to be replaced." He leaned forward and continued, "They will not like you... nothing personal. They have all been in Burma longer than you have been in the military. I'm working on getting you replacements as they leave... welcome to the 25th. You will report to me."

Myke says, "He took me under his wing. I think I reminded him of his grand-daughter."

The China-Burma-India Theater did not receive the coverage accorded other WWII fronts in Europe and the Pacific. Burma had fallen to the Japanese, and in 1942 they had cut the last land route to China. The flow of supplies to our Chinese allies depended on the airlift over the "Hump" -- the Himalayas -- from northeast India, across Burma to Kunming, China. The war on the ground was brutal to retake Burma and reopen the land routes to China. Allied ground forces included American, British and Chinese troops attacking the Japanese from several directions.

The 25th Field Hospital consisted of ten doctors, Myke as Chief Nurse, her seven nurses, 40 medics reporting to the nurses, four Veterinary officers responsible for snake control, water purity, and other safety/sanitation issues, and a contingent of soldiers to protect the hospital's staff and patients. Each nurse, including Myke, had two MP's assigned to them – one American, the other Chinese. They were their shadows.

There were up to eight portable ward tents, each housing about 40 patients. As the front lines advanced and receded, the 25th also moved. They moved everything -- patients, medicines, supplies, equipment -- several times a month. It was two steps forward, a step back. They were hospital nomads, a travelling circus of hope with their tents, skilled acts and medical magic dedicated to saving precious lives.

It took six months until the last of the original nurses was replaced. For Myke the short-term social isolation was difficult, but she had other things to worry about. At any given time there were as many as 320 patients to treat. The patient ratio averaged 60 percent Chinese, 40 percent American. Most were ground troops, although an occasional airman would be brought in.

More than half the patients died in the field hospital. Five percent would be sent back to the front, and the remainder transported to the more permanent station hospital in Bahmo, Burma for additional treatment. "Remember," says Myke, "penicillin wasn't introduced until 1941. Medicine wasn't as sophisticated as it is today, and the jungle and the enemy were difficult adversaries." The 40-plus percent of survivors would attest to the glass being almost half full. It was those who lived that kept the medics, nurses and doctors going.

"We didn't get to know the people," Myke states softly. "We had to push them through quickly. We knew more were coming, and we weren't set up for longer-term care."

Myke and her replacement nurses gained the trust of the doctors and medics. She and her team sometimes performed jobs normally reserved for physicians, including removing bullets and shrapnel. For each of them an average day was 10 or 12 hours long, seven days a week, month after month after month. There was no reason to take time off, as there was no place to go. Imagine the field hospital at the center of a bull's-eye with the total area within the inner perimeter ring no more than a few acres. One never left that ring. While Myke was there snipers shot ten people assigned to the hospital – none of them her nurses.

Hospital personnel often had to go light on rations as they were at the mercy of supply trucks and airdrops. If the airdrop missed their perimeter they did not venture out to find it because of the unseen, ubiquitous enemy.

There were days they ate reduced portions of the same food morning, noon and night. In 14 months Myke bargained for three chickens from the locals to be split evenly among her team. They also had an occasional wild pineapple.

When they went to eat, a medic was assigned to ensure each person took the anti-malaria pill Atabrine before proceeding in line. The fact that Atabrine gave the skin a sickly hue, sometimes caused headaches, nausea and vomiting, and, for some, an infrequent case of temporary psychosis, was irrelevant. "Take the pill or you don't eat."

Each nurse received a helmet full of water a day. The sequence of use was fairly important and obvious – brush the teeth, wash the face, hair and body, and then the clothes. They'd hang the clothes to dry on the tent lines.

Some of the more poisonous snakes in the world are in Burma. While none of her team was bitten, there were several close calls. She, personally, was not so lucky when it came to avoiding amoebic dysentery.

As the war wound down Myke was presented another challenge. The hospital began to deactivate and she was assigned to escort Chinese patients to Kunming, China via airplane. Of the more than 900 officers listed as full-fledged members of the "China-Burma-India Hump Pilots Association" she is the sole female. She flew eight C-46 missions over the Himalayas at high altitude using oxygen and wearing heavy clothing.

Infrequently, she was given leave for a few days between flights. On the Irrawaddy River she was introduced to being rope-pulled on a tiny disc by a small boat. She also rode an elephant. "Those were my first experiences of joy and fun in Burma."

She returned home around Christmas of 1945 after 20 months in Burma. Her mother told her to call that Tom Caswell; "He's telephoned every day."

"I'm leaving for the Philippines," Tom said. "I've got a job with their airlines. How long will it take you to come to the Philippines so we can get married?" They had dated perhaps a dozen times.

"Well, I would have to wait until my sister's wedding is over." July of 1946 she sailed out of San Francisco as a civilian on the SS *President Hoover* for a 31-day circuitous voyage to Manila. Before she left her father told her, "Honey, there's money to get you home if you get cold feet." She arrived on a Thursday and had a church wedding on Sunday, September 1, 1946. It was the right decision for someone who had, as Tom suggested years before, "broadened her horizons and become worldlier".

She retired from the Stanford University College of Medicine as Assistant Professor. For their 35th wedding anniversary in 1981 they went to Burma. "It had not changed," she says. Bourbon and water has been her cocktail of choice since May 29, 1943.

Chapter 18: Bergy Bergsma – USN

"Bergy pulled him aboard, this time under fire. The Army Ranger was grazed on the cheek by a bullet as Bergy lifted him."

EARL 'BERGY' BERGSMA, the youngest of three boys, was born May 5, 1924 in the northwest corner of Iowa. His parents lost their farm during the early stages of the Great Depression, and they moved into a home they owned in nearby Rock Valley. "It was a small town about equidistant between Sioux City and Sioux Falls. I spent twelve years at the same school, and in high school I played six-man football, basketball, and fall and spring baseball. I delivered the morning newspaper six days a week, the *Sioux City Journal*, to about 100 customers." He says he was, and still is, an avid game bird and waterfowl hunter.

"I left home with a buddy two weeks after I graduated high school in 1941. I'd had two years of high school woodworking and figured I could find a job building furniture in Grand Rapids, Michigan. It had a large Dutch population, and having that heritage, I thought I'd easily get work. We got as far as Chicago and I landed a job at 40 cents an hour making plastic radio knobs, then went with a printing ink company."

December 7, he was watching *Gone With The Wind*. "They interrupted the movie to announce the attack on Pearl Harbor." Soon after war broke out his company scaled back, and Bergy found work with the YMCA starting at $25 a week with room and board. He was promoted to a $75 a week job by the summer of 1942. Bergy also enrolled in junior college that fall. His two older brothers had joined the Navy as enlisted men. They advised him to enter their branch of service and try to become an officer.

Columbus Day, Bergy joined the Naval Reserve and was accepted into their officer flight training program. March 1, 1943 he was called to active duty.

He spent his first three months at Monmouth College in Illinois at flight preparatory school, splitting his time between studies and athletics. The next three months were in Prescott, AZ for flight training in Piper Cubs and Aeroncas. "We slept on folding cots on the basketball courts in the veterans building. About half the time we wore military clothing, the other half civilian."

Next stop was Monterey, CA for preflight training. They were quartered at the old Del Monte Hotel. He was appointed Cadet Battalion Commander, then Regimental

Commander with three Battalions and 600 young men. He explains his appointment, "I was 6'4", 230 pounds and had a booming voice. When I shouted commands, I could be heard by everyone." Bergy and his classmates went through ground school and navigation training. Sports and physical conditioning were also key components of the curriculum.

"I played a lot of football and was a heavyweight on the boxing team as well as the wrestling team."

January 1944 he went to Hutchinson, KS to fly open cockpit Stearmans. "We had to hand shovel runways and wear felt masks. It was bitter cold." After a few months he was transferred to Glenview, IL Naval Air Station for more flight training, then to Pensacola, FL for flight training in AT6 SNJ's and Vultee SNV-1 basic trainers. "There was a huge purge of fellows going through flight training mid-1944. It was decided the Navy wouldn't need as many pilots as originally estimated and thousands were let go. I made it through the cuts and was commissioned an Ensign and earned my wings the same day – November 16, 1944.

By January 1945 he was in Miami learning to fly the TBM Avenger Torpedo Bomber, the same aircraft flown by former President George H. W. Bush during WWII. He also qualified for Jeep Carrier takeoffs and landings.

In June he was at the Corpus Christy complex, Kingsville, with a new organization forming fighter and torpedo bomber night squadrons.

"Mid-July I was in the pattern for a landing. I got in the slipstream of another airplane, flipped over and went in hard. Luckily I was alone. The Avenger was destroyed. Only the aft section of the plane was partially intact. I was unconscious, with the top part of my scalp peeled back." The part peeled back had the shape of the shaved bald spot of an ancient monk. Ambulances were trying to get to him, but the mesquite trees were too thick.

"I came to, covered in blood, and in shock. I pulled the flap back in place, and took off running in the direction of the runway, brushing past the trees and cactus."

Thirty-five stitches and a day or so later he was ready to fly again.

September 1945 he was in Martha's Vineyard, MA with night torpedo bomber Squadron VTN 90. VJ day had been celebrated the month before – August 15th. The official surrender occurred aboard the Missouri September 2. He stayed involved in night flying with assignments in Key West. In early 1946 he shipped out to Hawaii.

"I joined VTN 53. It was strictly voluntary. Our job was to develop new principles of night flying. My best friend was killed doing night carrier landings. I re-volunteered for a new night attack combat training squadron." He pauses... "In all I volunteered three times. The fourth time I opted for a change of pace."

By the early summer of 1946, while others were being mustered out of the military, he was reassigned to the small atoll Ebeye, six miles from Kwajalein, in the Marshall Islands. He was involved in set-up activities for the Atomic Bomb Tests at Bikini Atoll.

After six months his status was changed from Reserves to Regular Navy and he was promoted to Lieutenant Junior Grade New Years day, 1947. He also assumed the role of executive officer. It was there he saw his first helicopter and logged time as copilot. When the initial bomb tests were over he went back to the states in the fall of 1947.

"I was interviewed by the Commander Fleet Air/ Commanding Officer NAS, Alameda. He said, 'I need a line coach for my football team.'" Bergy also played tackle for the team, the Alameda Hellcats. Their fullback was Joe "The Jet" Perry who signed with the San Francisco 49ers when he was discharged after his winning season with the Navy. "We beat a lot of good teams, including SF State and Stanford during scrimmage games. We beat the Hamilton Field team in Marin 108 to zip. We played in the All Navy Championship game in San Diego and lost by one touchdown. We had a heck of a squad."

During the summer of 1948 he received orders to attend University of California Berkeley as a student. According to Bergy this was required of officers who had transferred from the Naval Reserves to the Regular Navy. "We were sent to university for five semesters of study in English, math, physics and other subjects." He continues, "I was 24, had a new Pontiac convertible, drew regular officers pay plus flight pay, and lived in a hotel. Life was so sweet."

He had also found time to marry and, in January 1950, with wife and baby, he was sent to Connally Air Force Base, Waco, TX for training as a helicopter pilot. His ten man graduating class, May 5, 1950, consisted of two Army, three Navy and five from the Air Force. Bergy was sent to Helicopter Utility Squadron One (HU-1) at NAAS Miramar, near San Diego. (HU-1 was the first operational Navy helicopter squadron, commissioned April 1948. Bergy was on the ground floor of helicopter/military operations.) Imme-

diately he was assigned Officer-in-Charge of a small helicopter detachment aboard an icebreaker, the USS *Burton Island*
scheduled to depart for Alaska.

His first stop in Alaska was Point Barrow at latitude 71,
some 340 miles north of the Arctic Circle. The Korean War
had started while steaming north from San Diego.

"We flew around the clock in daylight. Between 2 and 4
a.m. the sun was below the horizon, but one could still read
a newspaper." He continues, "Our convoy was re-supplying
the Distant Early Warning (DEW) Line. Our icebreaker led
the way for the supply ships, and my helicopter led the way
scouting open water channels for the icebreaker." The flying conditions were difficult, with radio and radar reception
frequently blocked, so close to the Pole. Bergy was required
to wear a "Poopy Suit" similar to a diver's dry suit worn in
frigid waters.

"Wearing the suit we were told we could survive up to 20
minutes in the water; without it two or three. With that
thought in mind, I tried to keep ice floes within reach of my
copter." Poopy Suits did not come in 6'4" sizes... rather it
was like fitting a foot long hot dog in a six-inch bun. Inside
the helicopter the temperature was 15-20 degrees Fahrenheit. "I always wore a felt face mask and Lindy cap to keep
warm." He describes taking the oil out of the copter every
night and warming it on the stove before refilling. When
not operating, the rotor assembly had a rubber cover with
hot air pumped in to keep it from freezing.

He led the ship up to 76 degrees north latitude, before
they could go no further. The Arctic was harsh flying, but
Bergy had one more flight to make. "I wanted to pay trib-

ute to earlier aviators and flew to the 1935 site where Will Rogers and Wiley Post had died in their historic flight." He shows a photo of himself leaning against the monument, with his helicopter but a few feet away.

After a month in the far north, they headed back to San Diego and Miramar. He was soon to head to Korea and the combat he had trained for and missed as WWII ended. "I stayed at Miramar for the next several months performing a number of duties, including Legal Officer, Athletic Officer, Welfare and Recreation Officer, and more. As a junior officer I was still low on the totem pole." January 1951 he received orders. Bergy headed west mid-February for Japan and his final war destination, Korea.

(In the early 90's Bergy authored a book, *Chopper Pilots is the Craziest Peoples*. The title is a take-off on the weekly Movietone news clips shown in the theaters in the 40's/50's, *Monkeys is the Craziest Peoples*. Lew Lehr – no relation to Bert – would narrate this short with shots of chimps in costume doing something slightly goofy and offbeat... at least for chimps. Bergy's book is a wonderful piece of writing, unfortunately out of print. He has one well-thumbed yet near-pristine copy left, and another in mostly single sheets held together by a rubber band.)

The description of his arrival in Korea to the Baltimore Class Heavy Cruiser *USS St. Paul* is from his book:

"At 2325, on March 7, 1951, we logged aboard... I noticed Lieutenant Commander Bolt..." (the man Bergy was to replace) ..."standing off in the shadows. I went over to greet him. He said, 'Boy, am I glad to see you.' He hugged me and started to cry. To hide his embarrassment, he hurried me off... and showed me my bunk. I never saw him again. He and his crew departed for home at 0800 the next morning."

Bergy footnotes his book with the fact the man he replaced died in a training flight at Miramar later that year. "I did not get into combat during WWII. I had only gone as far west as Hawaii when the war ended. After witnessing Lt. Cmdr. Bolt's emotions I thought, 'What in hell am I getting into?'"

After Earl "Bergy" Bergsma's arrival at Inchon Harbor March 7, 1951 and a short boat ride to the *St. Paul*, he started flying the next day. "I was flying senior officers to Inchon and Suwon to top-brass planning conferences. I flew my first rescue mission the 12th. A boat carrying nine *St. Paul* men from Inchon to the ship had not arrived as planned. I made seven search flights over the next two days. A few bodies were recovered, and what happened to the boat remains a mystery." He rescued no one.

March 13, the ship left Inchon for Sasebo, Japan for resupply. They sailed back to Wonsan Harbor on the east coast of North Korea. Beginning the 23rd he flew daily gun-spotting missions for the next week.

March 25, the ship's Operations Officer, who wanted to assess the accuracy of his gun crews, accompanied him.

"My job that day was to help direct fire towards a railroad bridge. As we circled the area I noticed a strange vibration each time I flew over one particular hilltop."

He realized he was hearing and feeling the chatter of machine-guns.

For a while he continued to give coordinates, while changing altitude and location.

Quoting from Bergy's book, "...I yelled to the Commander, 'We're catching machine-gun fire. Let's get the hell out of here!' He wrote me a note suggesting we just change our position over the target area. I thought he was making with a funny, so I called the ship to cease fire and we were on our way home.

"When I landed aboard ship he proceeded to chew me out for coming back to the ship. I asked him, 'Didn't you hear me yell we were being shot at?' 'No!' he said.

"'You wrote me a note and I interpreted it to mean, Let's get out of here.'

"'B.S.!' he said, 'We weren't getting shot at.'"

They hadn't left the helicopter yet when the chief mechanic approached and told Bergy two rounds had entered the bottom of the chopper. The entry holes were six inches in front of the Commander, and 18 inches behind Bergy. They found the bullets had exited through the top of the cockpit. Bergy received an apology and a vote of confidence for his good judgment. The Commander had refused to wear a sidearm the first flight. He always wore one on subsequent take-offs.

March 31, the wind was coming from the south at near 40 mph, and there was snow the night before. Bergy was roused at 5 a.m. and briefed on a needed rescue mission. Four Army Rangers and 20 South Korean soldiers had been dropped behind enemy lines to destroy enemy targets. The men were on the top of a mountain surrounded by the enemy 38 miles south of Wonsan Harbor and 20 miles inland. There would be three helicopters involved: one from LST 799, piloted by Lt. (JG) Thornton; another from LST 0012 flown by Lt. Felten, and Bergy's chopper. Each pilot would fly alone, to keep the weight down, and also be responsible for lowering and raising the rescue sling.

They were expected to meet an Air Force C-47 south of the *St. Paul* and follow the plane to the site. Bergy's helicopter was the only one that could communicate with the airplane. Bergy would have the task of relaying info from the plane to the other two helicopter pilots.

During the briefing Bergy suggested the *St. Paul* begin heading south. With a 35 mph headwind and a cruising speed of only 65 mph, the further south they got, the more flight time he could have at the rescue site. The ship turned south as Bergy and the other rescue choppers took to the air. At the rendezvous point, Bergy was told the C-47 had made radio contact with the Rangers who had laid out an orange spotting panel. He radioed this info to the others.

Lt. (JG) Thornton spotted them first. The men were located in a Korean graveyard atop a 2,500-foot mountain. As Thornton tried to set down, his right wheel hit the top of a pile of rocks on a grave. The helicopter tipped, the rotor blades contacted the ground and it began to cartwheel down the mountain. The chopper came to rest 45 feet down the slope in some trees and began to burn. Luckily Thornton escaped and the fire went out. Bergy hovered over the site, began to descend, then observed tracer machine-gun fire coming at him from down slope. He moved out of the line of fire looking for a safer place to attempt a rescue. The winds were still 35-40 mph. The next spot he chose, the wind currents accelerating over the top of the mountain were so strong he could not hold the ship in a steady hover.

Lt. Felten made an approach in his helicopter to an adjacent site, and lowered his horse collar sling. The sling raising/lowering control was a button on top of the flight control stick, so in a pinch the pilot of the chopper could do everything. The anchor to the hoist cable was located halfway up the side of the chopper by the open door, and a rescued man could swing himself into the cabin after being successfully hoisted. One of the Rangers put on the horse collar. Felten radioed Bergy that he couldn't rewind his cable. It was like a dead and extended yo-yo, with the spindle twirling fruitlessly within the loop. Bergy told him to fly the rescued Ranger away suspended at the end of the cable, and ease him onto the ground at a safe spot. He also told him, to quote his book, "Get the hell out of here!"

On his third try, Bergy found a place to hover away from enemy fire and the very strong winds at the peak. Meanwhile, Thornton had scrambled back up the mountain dragging the horse collar sling out of his wrecked chopper and placed it around one of the soldiers. Thornton unhooked Bergy's sling from the cable and attached his. Bergy hoisted the Ranger to safety.

Bergy lowered his sling for the second time and motioned Thornton to put it on. He refused as he already had a second Ranger rigged to go. Bergy pulled him aboard, this time under fire. The Army Ranger was grazed on his cheek by a bullet as Bergy lifted him. Bergy attempted a third pickup. Again, from his book:

"I went into a hover over Lt. Thornton. I had applied maximum revolutions per minute to the rotors, and my collective pitch (which controls the angle of the rotor blades) was as high as it would go. Thornton shook his head with a 'No!' and waved me off. Perhaps he found the enemy soldiers were getting too close and I was sure to be hit by their gunfire. In any case, I couldn't wait around so I headed back to the ship."

The two helicopters were refueled, the hoist repaired on the one flown by Lt. Felten, and fresh pilots assigned. When they returned they encountered enemy fire.

Felten had piloted the rescued Ranger 20 miles dangling at the end of a 75-foot cable 5-6,000 feet above the ground in freezing weather. Because of the wind, the soldier and his weight acted like a pendulum, and when it reached the outer limit of its swing Felten thought his aircraft would roll over. The Ranger, nearly frozen and more frightened than anyone should ever have to endure, made it through the flight.

Thornton, the downed pilot, and the other Ranger survived three years as POW's. The South Korean soldiers were shot on the spot as spies.

(Bergy adds Lt. Thornton passed away late 2003. The two of them had "What Iffed" the problem for years.)

Bergy, Thornton and Felton were awarded the Legion of Merit with combat insignias for their heroism under fire.

The first week of April Bergy flew gun-spotting missions in North Korea preparatory to amphibious landings by the British Royal Marines. On the 8th he flew three flights totaling almost ten hours searching for an F4U Corsair pilot. He was not found. April 9th was another search and rescue flight inland from Wonsan City. He climbed to 6,000 feet, when two unfamiliar aircraft made a run by his helicopter. Bergy thought they were Russian YAK's. Instead, they were British.

From his book: "I say, Old Ace Tip Top, is that you? The *St. Paul's* call sign was Tip Top and mine was Ace Tip Top. He rogered affirmative.

'This is Dragon Fly One and my wingman is Dragon Fly Two. Shall we saunter inland? ...Tip Top old boy, you are catching ack-ack from seven different villages.'

'Dragon Fly One, this is Ace Tip Top, why don't you go down and try to stop those guns:'

'Righto...' 'I continued to climb. A little while later I heard, 'Tip Top old boy, where are you?'

'I'm at 12,000 feet and climbing,' I said.

'What in the world are you doing up thaar? The downed pilot is down haar.'

'Dragon Fly, I have no speed, no guns, no armor. You go down and find out if he is alive and I'll come down and try to rescue him.'

'Righto. Come on #2.'"

Ten minutes later Bergy is advised to head home as the plane is spread over the mountainside. His helicopter pals kid him, as they did not think his HO3S helicopter could climb to that altitude. He states it felt like 12,000 feet.

During his time in Korea Bergy personally rescued four men – the two Rangers at the end of March and two downed airmen. He followed one F4U Corsair that was in trouble, advised the pilot to leave his wheels up and do a soft flare into the water. As the plane landed the Marine pilot scrambled onto the wing.

"I picked him up before he even got his feet wet and dropped him on the deck of a destroyer."

Another sea rescue was not so easy. The downed pilot, paddling like crazy from his plane on his overturned life raft, was under fire from shore-based North Koreans. That meant, of course, that Bergy was under fire, too. Bergy hovered and successfully rescued the airman.

During his time in Korea he had 63 combat missions and almost 200 flights total. He earned three Air Medals, a DFC for his gun-spotting heroics and the already mentioned Legion of Merit. His Unit, HU-1, received a Presidential Citation, and his helicopter detachment received an award from then South Korean President Syngman Rhee.

He returned to the States September 1951. In 1955 he was sent as detachment Officer in Charge for six months with a Mediterranean Sixth Fleet unit, a time of conflict between Israel and Egypt. He watched through binoculars as Jewish tanks advanced across Gaza. He was promoted to Lieutenant Commander while on this assignment. He retired while stationed at Alameda NAS, April 1963, with more than 4,000 hours as pilot in command in fixed and rotary winged aircraft.

The year 1963 was also when he divorced.

"I went into the real estate business working for Jack Haley, the Tinman in *The Wizard of Oz*, selling land in Madera, California." He liked selling real estate, was good at it and quickly earned his broker's license and wended his way north. He remarried in 1965. "Gwendolyn was a wonderful, beautiful woman," he muses. "We bought a lot at Penn Valley's Lake Wildwood in 1979 and moved into our new home in 1980. We loved the area."

He describes a duck club that he formed. He leased property in the mid-'80s near Marysville. "It had seven blinds, and I got it up to 32 members, most from Lake Wildwood. We had a lot of fun for almost a decade during hunting season."

Bergy was president of the development's fishing club for four years in the mid/late '80s. Gwendolyn was also active in the community and was a Regent with the Daughters of the American Revolution. She passed away August 2000.

A total 33,741 Americans died during the Korean War; four less than might have were it not for the rescue efforts of Bergy Bergsma. During his time serving America with the United States Navy he was a tall, strong, brave, handsome, intelligent, good-sense-of-humor tough guy from the John Wayne mold.

He has the John Wayne hitch to his walk, but it's partly attributed to his new knees.

All the other attributes are intact.

Juanita and Russ

Chapter 19: Russ Bryant – Army

"I headed up a grade, running, and had my pipe and cigarette lighter smashed by a bullet."

IN 1937, after graduating from high school, 18-year-old Russ Bryant tried to join the Army Air Corps and the Navy. Both said they didn't need him right then.

"My family was dirt poor," says Russ. "There were six of us kids in the family – three boys, three girls. We lived in the small farming community of Ashland, IL, just west of Springfield. We were tenant farmers and didn't have much in the way of possessions." He pauses for a few seconds. "We did, however, have each other, but life was pretty tough.

"After the military turned me down I drove truck and worked in a local gas station. In 1941 my draft number came up. I took my physical and was declared 4-F – a minor thing with the heart and a bit of a hernia problem. I was very disappointed."

"In '43 I headed to California with a buddy and took a job with Douglas Aircraft in Long Beach building B-17's. Then, in mid-'44 I received another notice from the government to report for a physical." He chuckles, then continues, "There were 170 or so of us previously declared 4-F who turned up for examinations, and 168 of us were reclassified as fit for duty." By August he was back in Illinois and inducted into the infantry.

Russ Bryant had 16 weeks of basic training in Little Rock, Arkansas. "By New Year's Eve I'm in Fort Meade, Maryland sitting on the back of a truck waiting to go to Camp Miles Standish outside of Boston. A few days later I'm one of 12,000 men on the *Ile de France*."

At the outbreak of WWII in 1939 the French luxury liner *Ile de France* was berthed in NYC's harbor. The French loaned her to the British for the duration of the war as a troop transport. The attire changed from black tie and tails to olive drab, and the food from caviar to K-rations.

"We were supposed to go to Le Havre, but because of heavy U-boat activity we anchored near Glasgow where we were put ashore by small boat. The Scots were very surprised to see us. The Germans had been broadcasting they had sunk the *Ile de France*. I was immediately assigned guard duty. I had no ammo, but at 6'4' and 195 pounds was pretty good-size." He smiles, "None of the enemy got by me in Scotland."

By mid-January he was on a boat to Le Havre, then to Neufchateau, Belgium. "I still was not assigned to a unit. They loaded a bunch of us onto boxcars, each of them marked '40's and 8's'." While each car was originally designed to carry 40 men or 8 horses, fewer than 30 soldiers could be crammed in with their weapons and gear. It was abnormally cold and by some accounts, one of the worst winters in half a century, with the snow about two feet deep across most of Western Europe.

"When I got out of the boxcar I was in Metz, Germany. From there I was sent to Veckring, France. I was on one of 20 truckloads of replacement troops that day to the same location -- General Patton's 3rd Army. I became a part of the 94th Infantry Division, 376th Infantry regiment, 1st Battalion, Company B." He pauses, and his comments are measured, "The 94th had suffered great casualties. The reception the other replacements and I received was like the weather... chilly. People were civil but that's about it. The soldiers we were joining just didn't talk much. I think it was because of the loss of their comrades and their lack of trust in us, the new kids." Again he pauses, then concludes, "I never felt so alone... never.

"I saw my first combat around the 1st of February 1945 in the area around Sinz in the Saar region of Germany." This area was considered key to the defense of the Reich and was called the "Siegfried Switch" by the Americans. It was a triangle that started where the Saar and Moselle rivers met. The base of the line, on the high ground, was some 13 miles long and two miles deep with pillboxes, bunkers, anti-tank ditches and concrete dragon's teeth.

"All the villages were pretty much rubble. One day we'd advance a bit, then fall back a few days later. I think Sinz was taken and retaken a half-dozen times.

Mid-February was his first major engagement. The orders were to take the Bannholz Woods and eventually the high ground on Munzingen Ridge. "We went single-file to the edge of the woods, then two companies abreast firing indiscriminately at anything in front of us that moved. There's a feeling of isolation as you're running through the woods... your nearest comrade to the right is some 20 or 30 yards away, and the one to the left about the same."

"We drove the enemy to the edge of the forest and across the meadow to Munzingen Ridge where they had trenches and foxholes and other protection. Orders came to move out and take the ridge. We were crossing the meadow when three machine-guns and one German 88 began firing on us and our tanks."

(The German 88 was one of the most famous anti-tank and anti-aircraft guns of WWII. It had a shell weight of almost 21 pounds and a range of five miles.)

"Three of our four tanks were hit. My company was sent to knock out the three enemy machine-gun nests. My squad took out one of the nests. I headed up a grade, running, and had my pipe and cigarette lighter smashed by a bullet. A round caught my glasses right where the frame attaches to the piece that runs to the ear. My helmet was also knocked off. I tossed a grenade in the nest from about 20 feet and it became quiet... deathly quiet."

They had taken Munzingen Ridge. Russ looks at the glasses he had worn that day, now displayed in a glass-fronted shadow box. "The sun came out; we sat around thinking and talking of home. There was good-natured ribbing. My Lieutenant asked me to do something on my Harmonica. I gave it my best and played *Home, Sweet Home*."

"February 22nd we were milling around Ayl, Germany when General Patton pulled up in a Jeep with the rest of his entourage. He's talking with his various commanders about crossing the Saar River. Some 20 or 30 of us enlisted men were close enough to hear their discussion. Some of his direct subordinates were cautioning against a direct assault across the river."

Russ is emphatic and angry still with the words he attributes to Patton. "I heard him say loud enough for all to hear, 'I don't care if it takes a bushel basket full of dog tags, we're crossing the river right here.' There was a gasp from all us enlisted men. If Patton heard it he ignored it."

The time for debate was over. Russ and his comrades would attempt crossing the Saar River near their present location.

"The day of the 23rd, Companies C and L were the first to head out. They ran into heavy fire. About 10:30 that evening they called B Company. We loaded our eight-man squad and two engineers into a small flat-bottom boat and shoved off. The moon was bright and our smoke generators weren't working. The river was very high and several hundred yards across. When we were nearing mid-stream the Germans opened up with machine-guns and 20mm fire. I was hit in the arm by a 20mm shell."

(The entire 20mm shell and casing is about 7.5 inches long. The projectile is about 2.75 inches.)

"It was like being struck with a baseball bat and I was knocked to the bottom of the boat. The soldier to my left fell on me. He died never knowing what hit him. The man in front of me was also killed.

I felt something bump the boat. It was part of a bombed out bridge. The sarge ordered us to jump out of the boat. Everyone got out except me and my dead companions. To this day I don't know how many of them safely got back to shore."

Russ's voice is soft as he recounts floating down the Saar. "I tried to get up, but was fired on. I stayed on my back. I could see the trees and bluff on the high ground on the German side. I did not want them to get closer."

The boat turned occasionally like a slow-motion Tilt-A-Whirl. "I did not have to move my head to stay focused on the German side, just shift my eyes left or right, up or down as the boat twisted in the current. I think I drifted for about half an hour."

The boat headed back toward the allied side. "And then I heard American voices, and I yelled out. The boat was pulled to shore and a medic crawled over the side and gave me morphine."

They tried to make a litter out of oars, but couldn't, and they weren't able to bring a Jeep down because of enemy fire. With a soldier on each side they got Russ to a point where they could put him on a Jeep with a stretcher on the hood and get him to a first aid station. The medic cut off parts of his jacket and clothing and asked a question that would be repeated by at least one other during that long night, "What's holding that arm on?"

Some 2.5 hours after shoving off on his short voyage on the Saar he was on his way to a medical distribution center, then to a field hospital.

Another medic removed the rest of his field jacket, wool shirt, wool sweater and long underwear, and he repeated the question asked earlier. A doctor came in and examined Russ, then touched him reassuringly, "Son, I have to put you under now. You need to know I want to save your arm. I will only take it off if it's the best thing to do."

"I woke up about 5 p.m. on the 24th," Russ says. "I think I was in a horse barn. I looked down at my arm. It was in a solid cast...the whole arm. That same day they put me on an ambulance to Luxembourg, then to Paris and England. I wound up in a hospital in Salisbury west of London until the end of April; then Modesto, California via New York. By the time I got back to the States I had dropped 50 pounds. I was discharged from the Army near the end of November."

Russ returned to Ashland for a short time, then back to California and the Spear School of Broadcasting at Hollywood and Vine. He worked small-time radio for a little over a year, then earned a speech and education degree at Long Beach State college. He taught at Fullerton Junior College, where he met and wed Juanita, his wife since September 1948. They have two children and two grandchildren. They have lived in Lake Wildwood since 1988. Both retired as instructors at Cabrillo Junior College in Aptos.

Much of the muscle in his damaged forearm is gone. The arm and elbow won't straighten. The wrist won't bend. Juanita brightens as she says, "It still hugs good."

Also in the shadowbox with the glasses nicked by a bullet is a patch for the 94th, a 20mm shell, dog tags, and his Purple Heart and two Bronze Stars for gallantry. The harmonica is also there – in this, its "home, sweet home".

Jim in FH2 Banshee jet fighter cockpit

Chapter 20: Jim Manfrin – USN Pilot

"I knew I had also hit the Pilot"

IN JUNE 1942, Jim Manfrin graduated from high school in Clarendon Hills, IL, some 15 miles west of Chicago. He had been a good student and athlete and was ready to face his obligation to his country – military service. By September he had figured it out; he wanted to be a Navy pilot, and he enlisted.

December 1942, at age 18, he was sent by the Navy to Southern Methodist University for a concentrated program to get his private pilot's license, the University of Georgia for three months of intense physical conditioning, and another three months in Memphis for military flight training in Stearman biplanes.

Next stop was instrument and advanced flight training in Pensacola – a transition to the more powerful AT6 trainer. He graduated from their rigorous program in February 1944 and went to Daytona Beach to fly the F4F Wildcat fighter. It was a single-seat carrier-based fighter with a top speed of 320 mph and a ceiling of 35,000 feet. It would become his in-air home until near the end of the war.

Jim was a quick study and became proficient at close formation flying, simulated dogfights, and aerial gunnery. By May he was sent to Lake Michigan's Naval Air Station at Glenview for carrier training on the *USS Wolverine*, a converted lake cruiser with a tacked-on flight deck. By July of 1944 he was in Oahu for more carrier qualification on the *USS Ranger*. From there to fighter and torpedo bomber squadron, VC-27, and the Navy escort carrier the *USS Savo Island* (CVE-78). His squadron's logo was a stick figure with a halo, the adventure hero Simon Templar -- "The Saint".

On board the *Savo Island* he had one more obstacle... one more challenge... to be fully accepted as a Navy fighter pilot. He had to be wrung out by his peers. The "wring 'em out" process included intense air combat practice, aerobatics, fly close formations, 6-G turns and the testing of other key elements connected with becoming a master fighter pilot. While the process helped Jim become an even better pilot, it also gave his comrades the reassurance that he could be trusted to fly a few feet off their wingtips and perform his job with excellence when under pressure.

Jim Manfrin, at age 20, had made the grade. Years later he was told if it hadn't been for some bad weather that delayed his flight training and subsequent graduation that he, not George Bush, would have been the youngest WWII carrier-based fighter pilot.

The escort carriers (also called "Jeep carriers" or "baby flat tops") were smaller than the "fleet" carriers. The *USS Savo Island* was little more than 500 feet in length with a beam of 65 feet. Her top speed was 19 knots.

Jim made more than 200 carrier takeoffs (and landings), and 170 were from the *Savo Island*. "Every landing," says Jim, "required a great deal of attention. Not only is the carrier deck moving forward, but it may also be moving up and down. I never had an accident even though I had lots of opportunities."

His first combat assignment was air support for the landings on Peleliu Island. "Between the middle and end of September 1944 we operated with other Jeep carriers. We did pre-landing strafing and supported the troops during landings. We were looking for targets of opportunity."

In early October the carrier reported to the 7th Fleet at Manus, and by the 12th of October had joined with the Leyte invasion task force of cruisers, battleships and other carriers.

"Near the end of October all hell broke loose. The Japanese made a late afternoon assault on our forces at Leyte, including an attack on our carrier. We were in a big hurry to get in the air quickly," Jim says matter-of-factly.

"That was my first night landing. We were in the air some four hours protecting our air space and dangerously close to exhausting our fuel supply. It was dark, and the attack had died down. The carrier threw on the deck lights, angled down each side of the deck and the center."

He paused then continued, "I wanted to make the first pass good because I wasn't sure if I had fuel enough for another go-around. That night every one of us landed successfully."

"We were pretty cocky," Jim admits. "Young and well trained. We had some attitude, I guess you could say."

(It's been said Will Rogers never met a man he didn't like. One jealous wag jokingly said Rogers just hadn't met a carrier pilot – a case of pilot envy.)

"I was on the carrier for seven months. We'd be on the water for a month, then ten days ashore in the Solomon Islands, or Ulithi in Micronesia, for maintenance and resupply. During that time," he paused and did some verbal and silent calculations, "I probably had as many as 80 to 100 missions – maybe more."

He paused again. "And about 60 percent of those I engaged the enemy somehow – shooting at something or other... or being shot at.

"Our squadron was about half Wildcat fighters and half torpedo bombers – 25 of each. When on combat air patrols we were looking to destroy ships or subs at sea, planes in the air, and truck convoys and troop and gun emplacements ashore. Anything connected with the enemy was fair game."

Protecting the *Savo Island* was obviously important.

"It was early in 1945 and the 'Tony' was headed toward our ship. "My wingman and I knew we had to engage him."

(The Tony, the Kawasaki Ki-61-1b Hien, looked virtually identical to, and considered an improvement on, the famed German Messerschmitt 109 fighter. At 367 mph it was almost 50 mph faster than the Wildcat flown by Jim Manfrin and his peers. It was very maneuverable and a dangerous adversary.)

"We tried to bracket him. He was a good pilot. Eventually I was able to get the advantage and come in on him from the side." Jim reflected for a few seconds. "The plane did not explode when I hit it. I knew I had also hit the pilot. The plane veered off, fell into the sea and disappeared." He paused again. "My guns..." (four 50-caliber machine-guns with less than 400 rounds each) ..."were empty. I had used up my 30 seconds worth of firepower."

In describing his emotions he said he felt nothing – that he was doing what he had to do.

"I thought of it as shooting down an airplane... It was impersonal... fighter plane against fighter plane..."

The next day he had another opportunity to test his skills. A Japanese Nakajima type torpedo bomber (a Kate) was making a kamikaze run on an American ship. The suicide bomber was getting heavy fire from the ship and turned back to escape. Jim saw the departing aircraft and engaged it. The battle was short. This time he returned to the carrier with ammunition to spare.

"Our carrier was hit by one kamikaze in the Surigao Straits January 5, of '45." He reflects for a moment, then continues, "I was topside getting a little sun. He nosed over from about 5,000 feet; his wing hit our signal halyards then plunged into the sea."

By March of 1945 the *Savo Island* left the Leyte area and headed with an invasion force for Okinawa. The 27th of March, Jim's squadron joined the assault on Okinawa as well as flying antisubmarine and antiaircraft patrols. Jim's last combat action was near the end of April when the squadron flew strikes against Sakishima Gunto, halfway between

Formosa and Okinawa. On April 29, the *Savo Island* had finished her seven-month mission and headed for San Diego.

During the time Jim was with her, the *Savo Island* received four battle stars and a Presidential Unit Citation for service in the Western Carolines, Philippines and Okinawa.

For his two "kills" Ensign James Manfrin was awarded the Air Medal for "...his meritorious achievement in action against the enemy."

He was ordered to Otis Field and the Camp Edwards area of Cape Cod. "I was assigned to a newly formed Corsair Squadron that would be joining the *USS Midway* when she was commissioned in October. We were slated to head to the final assault on Japan.

The atom bomb was dropped on Hiroshima August 6, 1945. On Aug. 14, 1945 America celebrated V-J Day. The war was over.

"I was on board the *Midway* during her shakedown cruise out of Norfolk, Va., late October 1945. I was with her until February, then reassigned again to Guantanamo, Cuba until I completed active duty June '46."

Jim stayed in the reserves until retirement in 1962 as a Lt. Commander, and flew, among other planes, the F2H Banshee jet fighter. This was the plane immortalized by James Michener in *The Bridges of Toko-Ri*.

"I spent a year at Stanford, then graduated from Culver-Stockton College in Missouri, in 1949. I wanted to be a radio sports broadcaster and attended night school at the Columbia School of Broadcasting in Chicago." He grins, then continues, "That's where I met Carol. We married in 1950 and moved to Penn Valley's Lake Wildwood in 1996."

Woodie & Jean

Chapter 21: Woodie Humburg –AAF

"Saw three B-24's go down – 7-5 chutes out of two of them. We lost eleven planes over the area that day."

ABOUT 50 MILES due west of Penn Valley, CA as the crow flies, rests the tiny, quintessential farming community of Colusa. There, in 1915, Woodie Humburg was born – the 13th of 13 children.

Then, as now, distances were measured by how long it would take to get someplace else: a little over an hour south to Sacramento, two plus hours to the fringes of the bay area, a half hour east to Yuba City and Marysville. It was a great place to grow up. The schools were good, the folks in the community took a keen interest in their youth; there were sports and work and study to help a young man develop in body and mind.

Woodie took advantage of his opportunities. He lettered in football, basketball, baseball and track and was student body president. When he graduated high school in 1933 he decided he wanted to play baseball and study at Sacramento Junior College. Some of those Colusa folks who had kept their eye on him over the years had bigger ideas. They thought he might better belong in a four-year university, and they might be able to help. Woodie listened. Once he got to Berkeley the rest would be up to him.

In the fall of 1933 Woodie headed to University California Berkeley with instructions to talk with Clint Evans, the legendary coach of Cal's varsity baseball program. Evans sent him to see the boss at Golden State Creamery. For the next four years Woodie worked ten hours a day, majored in economics and accounting, played frosh ball his first year, then three years as varsity first baseman. University Cal Berkeley was the CIBA (California Intercollegiate Baseball Association) champ two of his four years.

"I never liked cottage cheese, but I ate more of it that came back from grocery stores than you can imagine. I used to drink whipping cream by the pint. Anything that came back on a delivery truck that wasn't spoiled was fair game." He flashes a broad "Got Milk?" smile.

"When I graduated, the creamery bumped me up to the accounting department, then made me office manager in Richmond. I also married my high school sweetheart, Marie, in 1938."

In 1939 Woodie decided to change career direction to something that might have a little more long-term opportunity. He went to work with Pacific Telephone in an entry-level non-management job digging ditches. By 1941 he was working at corporate headquarters in the recently formed War Activities Department. His job was to help coordinate the communications linkage among the 450 military designated airports, naval facilities, and other key locations in the eleven western states.

"It looked inevitable we were going to war, and I always had a love for aviation. I went to my boss. I told him I wanted to enlist in the Aviation Cadet Program for the Army Air Force. I also said my wife supported my decision."

"Woodrow," his VP said, "you have an exempt job with us. You've got a key position that makes a big contribution to our national defense. You don't have to join anything."

"I told him I appreciated his advice, but I wouldn't change my mind." He pauses, chuckles and continues. "My window was beginning to close. To get into the cadet program I had to be younger than 26.5 years. I made it by about two weeks. They sent me to pre-flight school in Santa Ana February of 1942. Most of my peers were 18 to 19. I was the old man of my 200 classmates."

From there Woodie went to Roswell, NM, for Navigator / Bombardier training. He was commissioned a Second Lieutenant, August 1943. "I got my first experience in vintage B-24's at Gowan Field, Boise, then down to Hammer Field in Fresno. We used to fly these long training missions up to Seattle, then down to Tucson and home. I remember Hammer was closed one day because of bad weather and we were diverted to Bakersfield about 100 miles south. We didn't think we could make it, and went way below the cloud cover. Visibility was near zero, then a runway was spotted. We landed and taxied about 100 feet and all four engines stopped." He pauses. "We were out of fuel. We'd made it about 30 miles south of Fresno to a recently abandoned P-61 training base in Visalia by sheer luck."

January 1944 his crew received the B-24H that would be assigned to them for the duration of their war. It was one of 1,780 built at Ford's Willow Run plant, and one of 3,100 total B-24H models. It had four supercharged 1,200 hp Pratt and Whitney engines. At 25,000 feet it had a top speed of 290 MPH. The plane could travel 2,100 miles with a 5,000-pound bomb load. Each plane had a 10-man crew including pilot, co-pilot, bombardier, navigator, engineer, radio operator and four gunners – nose, tail and two at the waist.

Woodie had found his in-air home with the 461st Heavy Bomb Group, 765th Squadron as bombardier with plane #37. When they flew from Fresno to Hamilton Field in Marin County awaiting assignment overseas, they christened her the "Upstairs Maid" – a sexy looking girl painted on the nose, poised to do a clean-up on the Axis enemy from on high.

Also in January Woodie started the first of two 3 x 4 -inch notebooks he could carry in his shirt pocket. The writing, in fountain pen, is neat, concise and often poignant. For Jan. 24-25, 1944, "Flew hi.alt.bombing & gunnery off coast of Fort Bragg. Golden Gate Bridge looked beautiful in early morning sunrise as we headed west toward the Farralone Islands. Heaters didn't work – cold – oh man - minus 35 degrees C at 25,000 ft. Finished acceptance checks on the 'Maid' – no more flying until we leave for Europe."

While at Hamilton Field, Woodie spent as much time off base as possible with wife, Marie. They were happy, but fleeting, times. He wrote: "Feb. 11, said goodbye to Marie and drove back to Hamilton knowing it would be an awfully long time before I would again see her. Can't explain feeling, but just like losing your insides. Flew to Sky Harbor at Phoenix." From there they headed east in their B-24 to Texas, Tennessee, Florida, then the southern route to Europe via Puerto Rico, Trinidad, Belize, Brazil, Senegal, Morocco and Tunisia.

By early March Woodie and his crew were at their base on the southeast coast of Italy, Torretta, almost due east of Naples and a few miles from the Adriatic Sea. His plane had had problems with the front gun turret hydraulics. As a consequence they arrived a week after the rest of their squadron. "We had the last tent, at the end of the line. We had no electricity. Our closest neighbor was 250 feet away. It was still winter, and it was cold."

Woodie laughs as he describes their in-tent engineering project, "We built a stove. The stove itself was a 50-gallon drum. The fuel was this low-octane German gas left behind in five-gallon cans. The chimney was a 105-mm shell with the bottom cut off. It usually worked okay. But sometimes it would start to spit, and that meant there was dirt in the tubing. We'd run like heck out of the tent and wait for the stove to either explode or sputter out. It was a real Rube-Goldberg design. It blew three or four times."

April 3, at 0300 his crew was briefed for a run to Yugoslavia. The highlight was no flak, no fighters. They dropped a load of 500-pound bombs. April 6 was the second bomb run. "We were assigned to bomb the marshalling yards at Zagreb. It was an assembly plant for Me-109 fighter planes. Our plane carried 180 frag bombs. The fragmentary bomb was designed to do maximum damage to anything that was above ground, and intelligence said there were a lot of new German fighter planes just waiting to go." He pauses for a moment, reflecting back almost 60 years.

"There was a very narrow catwalk over the bomb bays... about a foot wide." At 21,000 feet, looking over the edge of the catwalk would present an unobstructed four-mile view toward the ground below. "There on the walkway were three frag bombs. Somehow they'd not made it out of the plane." Each bomb had a small propeller. When the prop hit the wind it would turn and eventually arm the fuse that would detonate the bomb. The wind was buffered by the plane's fuselage, but slowly, ever so slowly, a prop began to rotate...

"I don't know how I did it... I don't know why the plane didn't blow, but I got on the catwalk. I grabbed the frag bombs one at a time, holding on to the vertical support adjacent to the walkway, holding the fuse propeller, then hurled them downward toward the ground below." One away from the plane, then two and then the final bomb out. UCB varsity first baseman -- and bombardier -- three bombs out, and the inning and the game, for that day, was over.

Two down, 48 missions to go... under his name. If you wink and don't tell anyone, he may do more than 50 missions – some incognito.

May 5 was Woodie's 24th mission, a raid on one of the key German oil refineries and marshalling yards, the heavily defended Ploesti, Rumania. Excerpts from his tiny notebook highlight the flight. "Over Yugoslavia we had trouble with #1 engine and had to drop out of our spot near the front of the formation. We were having a hell of a time staying up with them in #6 spot. Just out of the IP (Initial Point when the bomb run begins), we could see the intense flak barrage as another squadron went in ahead of us.

"We were still behind and way out of position but Roy (pilot) gunned us up into position. Target was really burning like the devil, smoke billowing up to about 10,000 ft.

"We started to get the flak while in the run and I could see it popping in front of us and all around. About two minutes out Roy lost the supercharger on engine #2, but we managed to stay reasonably in line. Plane got hit a couple of times before we dropped the bombs but no serious damage. Dropped bombs and could see the flashes of explosions in the oil tanks and in the rail yards. As we turned away, flak became more intense but we didn't seem to be getting hit. It was all around us though, so we were really lucky.

"We saw P-51's and P-38's circling outside of flak areas and it really looked good to see them up there when we were out of position. They were ready to get any German planes. We were in the flak for another 3-4 minutes pulling away from the target.

"As we got near the Rumania/Yugoslavia border, out of nowhere flak in bursts of six in a line exploding about 50' off our left wing – very accurate. We turned to right and it turned right. We turned left and it followed us. We got hit several times." The urgency of his writing intensifies. "Got quite a few bursts about 25-50' in front. Then the Messerschmitt's... they made a pass but didn't come in too close.

We couldn't stay up with the rest of the flight but we were okay. On the intercom the rest of the boys started talking about the ½ pint of bourbon we would break out when we got back."

The next day, May 6, this is the only entry in his notebook, "I traded two boxes of Walnetto's for a box of hard squares. Went to bed early."

May 18 was another run on Ploesti. "Two things went wrong," Woodie says, "the bomb door safety switch had been wired open and the bomb racks malfunctioned. Bombs fell out while we were closing the bomb bay doors. Robbie, the ball turret gunner, said the doors were swinging down all the way in the slipstream. I crawled back to see the damage – how to get those doors up? Flak was coming up through the undercast, and it was almost impossible to stay in formation with the added drag.

"We finally got over the Adriatic and fell out of formation. Robbie and I made loops out of arming wires and by hanging out in the bomb bay – we couldn't wear parachutes because the space was too confining – we managed to get all four doors wired up underneath the fuselage for a safe landing. I found I was sweating when I climbed back up on the flight deck to have a Camel.

June 6, reveille was at 1:00 a.m. Woodie and the crew were briefed for another run on Ploesti, for an 0440 takeoff. "As we were coming up to the IP we could see a sky full of flak. We dropped into our bomb run and the flak was really thick... We caught several bursts -- one in the left front bomb bay... nose turret had one glance off it. Three FW-190's shot rockets that burst in front of us. Plenty of FW-

190's and Me-109's around and started making passes. One was so close I could see the pilot clearly.

"I was sick due to no electric suit and it was −28 degrees C at 24,000 feet. Hands froze up over target even with heavy fleece mittens. Logged 8.5 hours and chalked up mission #30. When we got back I took a cold shower to freshen up."

June 11, they were up again one hour after midnight for a mission to bomb an oil port and a pump and storage facility on the Danube near the Bulgarian border. "We hit the target and saw big storage tanks really blow up. Fighters were aggressive and flak was heavy. Saw three B-24's go down − 7 to 5 chutes out of two of them. We lost 11 ships over the area that day."

Some 300 crews (3,000 men) served with the 461st Bomb Group. According to official records, 422 airmen became POW's. They are the ones who survived the loss of their plane. Many, of course, did not survive.

Planes went down for a variety of reasons: enemy fighters and flak, mid-air collisions, explosions from their own armaments, mechanical failure, weather-related causes or just out of gas.

July 7, and Woodie's 45th mission deep into Germany:

"Heavy red, white and black flak all over and Me-110's, 109's, FW-190's, Ju-88's, Me-210's. The good Lord was watching over us because we didn't get hit, or at least none that we could see."

That night Woodie concluded his entry for that day, "five more to go... please, dear God, watch over us as you have in the past."

July 16 and a 3 a.m. wake-up for a mission to an aircraft engine plant in Austria. "Flak was good and heavy but 100-300' too low. Had beautiful P-38 cover and a P-38 cripple came back with us on our wing." Woodie had completed his 50th mission. "We landed and I kissed the ground – no more flying – boy, oh boy."

He had flown missions to Rumania, Yugoslavia, Greece, Austria, France, Germany, Hungary and Czechoslovakia. While Woodie was with the Bomb Group, the 461st received two distinguished unit citations for missions to Budapest, Hungary and Ploesti, Rumania.

"It's amazing," Woodie recalls, "that not one person in our ten-man crew got wounded, especially when we had flak damage to the plane on about half of our missions, and there were only about ten flights where we encountered no enemy opposition." Woodie was awarded three air medals for his service with the 461st.

He had 50 official missions, and 3 - 4 unofficial ones. He explains the unofficial flights: "You form some pretty tight friendships in war. When a guy gets sick, he worries that he will be permanently replaced if he's on the ground too long. So I took a few flights on my rest days on different B-24's under the names of a few sick buddies." He says it matter-of-factly, as though he were going in to pinch-hit at a Cal baseball game.

By September 1944 Woodie was promoted to First Lieutenant and on his way home. When he returned to the West Coast he couldn't pass the hearing test to get back on flying status. His last 25 missions the base doctor had laid him on a cot, head tilted back, before each flight and pumped fluids into his sinuses for 15-20 minutes to clear them. The result was a loss of hearing of 70% in his right ear and 60% in the left.

Woodie was grounded. He was sent to Harvard for five months for a course of study in Air Force Statistical Control. He was then assigned to Fort Mason in San Francisco, and received radium/radiation treatments at Letterman Hospital to prevent further hearing loss. He asked for and received a waiver to get back on flying status. It was granted and he was given a date to report to Omaha and qualify for B-29's. "The week before I was to report we dropped the first A-bomb on Japan. I was discharged from active duty a month or so after V-J Day. I went back to Pacific Telephone in their marketing department. Then I was presented an opportunity I couldn't pass up in the refrigeration business with the Ray Winther Co., and the outfit that eventually bought them, Hussman Company."

Woodie spent 41 years, from 1946-87, with that organization. "I loved the business. I ran the Winther Co. from 1948 to '66, and was head of West Coast marketing and public relations for Hussman until I retired. We'd go in and design, build, or remodel refrigeration systems for almost all the major independent retail grocers in Northern California.

"I stayed in the reserves until 1960. I left as a captain."

Marie, his first wife, passed away in 1961. "I stayed single for a while, then fell in love with Jean. We were married in 1967. I had a daughter with Marie, and Jean came to me with her daughter. So, I have two beautiful children and two wonderful grandchildren.

"When I was overseas I never worried about not coming back... never. I was too busy to be afraid. I was a very lucky man back then." He reflects for a moment. "I have always been a very lucky man." He flashes that smile and there seems, for a few seconds, to be a faint hint of a milk mustache from long ago.

Woodie and Jean have lived in Lake Wildwood since April 1990. They are both active in the community.

Woodie is a modest guy, and consented reluctantly to the story interview. A few months after publication he called to say he was happy he had done the story. He received a call from one of his grandchildren, who had taken the article to school to share with classmates.

"Grandfather," the child told him, "you're a real hero. I'm very proud of you."

Jeanette & Maurice

Chapter 22: Maurice Emanuel – USN

"You haven't seen the President's dog have you?"
"Sure," I said, "he's under my desk."

BACK IN 1916 a number of Fort Collins' finest young men went to fight the war in Europe. Helping balance this out-migration, Maurice Emanuel came bounding into the world.

It was about this same time in Fort Collins that automobiles began sharing the streets with horse-drawn wagons and buggies, and a few of the main streets in town were paved: College and East and West Mountain Streets.

As Maurice grew up he didn't much care what took place in town. As the oldest of eleven children he was kept busy working the farm, school studies, and helping with his siblings. "The dairy cows were the worst," he declares, "getting up before dawn to milk them in freezing weather was miserable work."

By 1933 the economy of the United States was near collapse. Hundreds of thousands of farmers faced foreclosure, and more than 10 million people were out of work. That was the year Maurice went to work for a government paycheck. He was 17 years old, accepted by the Navy as an enlisted man, and knew a big part of his pay would help his family during the Depression.

"I had finished my junior year at Cache La Poudre High School when I enlisted. Joining the Navy seemed a great way to continue my education, learn some useful skills and earn some money for me and my family during very tough times. A few years later I earned my GED, and eventually wound up taking a number of university classes throughout my career."

Following boot camp Maurice was assigned to a Destroyer based halfway around the world, the *USS Smith Thompson*, DD-212. She had been launched mid-1919 and was three years younger than Maurice. The *Smith Thompson* was a four-stack Clemson-class warship ten times longer than wide − 314' x 31.7'. The ship, prior to Maurice joining it, had seen distinguished service in the Eastern Mediterranean, Adriatic, and Black Seas and Asian waters.

Maurice made his way from Denver to the West Coast, then by naval vessels to Hawaii and the Far East. "I joined up with the *Smith Thompson* in Manila. She was a beautiful fighting ship and I was proud to join her as a Radioman."

The Naval Radio Operator job of the 1930's required expertise in Morse code. "You need to be able to think of the code letters as patterns of sound, rather than dots and dashes on paper," Maurice explains. "It's the rhythm, the sound, and then you do it faster and faster and the better you get — fast at sending and fast at receiving." Dit-dit-dit-dah-dah, his index finger taps rapidly on the arm of his easy chair, a message to no one in particular, or someone in the recesses of his memory. His finger is a perfect beat...Gene Krupa, Woody Herman, Lionel Hampton... a master of rhythm. -- ..- ... .. -.-.

"The Navy had a standard of about 15 wpm after a month of training, with a requirement of perfect accuracy. I mean perfect," he emphasizes. "I was doing about 35 when I arrived in Manila, and 50 wpm before too long." He isn't bragging, just iterating the skill level that comes from long hours of transmit times and the quest for the required perfection. The ship and his comrades depended on his speed and accuracy.

The *Smith Thompson* and other destroyers in the Asiatic Fleet patrolled waters from Shanghai to Manila and were part of the Yangtze River and South China Patrols. April 14, 1936, the *Smith Thompson* was rammed amidships by another Clemson class destroyer, the *Whipple*, while steaming from Manila to Shanghai. She was towed back to Subic Bay by yet another destroyer, the *Barker*. "We didn't lose anyone," says Maurice, "and the messages I transmitted and received between us, the *Whipple*, and other nearby ships were generally polite." The emphasis is on the word "generally." The aftermath to doing mortal damage to an American destroyer may require language skills that a young radioman had yet to master.

An inspection of the damage showed the ship could not be economically repaired. The *Smith Thompson* was decommissioned May 15, 1936 and sunk at sea near Subic Bay a few months later.

"We were all sad at the loss. I was assigned another ship but don't recall much about her." Maurice explains his various assignments are recorded in documents now in storage due to his and Jeanette's move from the Bay Area to our foothills environs. He is a believer in the Albert Einstein philosophy related to remembering: "Never clutter your mind with facts and dates that can be looked up."

"Honestly," he says, "the most important aspects of my life are my family. I cherish my memories of them and have kind of shoved my military experiences to the back burners."

Maurice knocked around the Pacific on other ships. "I was good at my job, and when I could intercept a Japanese transmission, I recorded it and forwarded it to Naval Intelligence. The Japanese used a different code for telegraphic communications. The Japanese code had nearly twice as many dit-dah combinations as our Morse code." His right forefinger taps a rapid staccato on his chair. "We broke their code, the Kata Kana, but they encrypted it again so we had to start over."

The story of breaking the Japanese codes is a complicated one, but men with the radio-telegraph skills of Maurice Emanuel played a key role in American Pacific Theatre victories. "I had the equivalent of a Crypto clearance, but I didn't understand all of what I was asked to send or receive. Every message that came to or left the ship on

my watch went through me. I had a position of great trust."
His right forefinger does not move; he speaks the truth.
"My main issues were speed and accuracy. A few simple dots
and dashes could mean the difference between life and
death."

We skip ahead a few years.

"I stood on deck looking at the dependents -- women
and children -- of American servicemen being loaded onto
our transport ship Dec. 6, 1941, in Oahu. It was like every
other day in the islands... near perfect." Maurice's finger
moves much slower. The pace of the finger taps are more
like the swaying hips of an island dancer, measured and
rhythmic... dit...dah...dit and a slow dah as a tiny wave
breaks on the sand. Hips to the left, hips to the right... a
precursor to the fins of singer Jimmy Buffet, decades away
from 1941. It would be easier to tap in Morse, "No... Don...
Ho...!"

"We were maybe 250 miles out of Oahu. I got the message from Pearl Harbor, 'Japanese attack.' I sent it topside.
'Son,' the Captain asked, 'is your message accurate?'"

It was a rhetorical question. "Eight years of expertise,
and my answer was a definitive, 'Yes, Sir.'"

"Son, we have to protect our precious cargo. Radio silence for a while, if you please. We have no escort ships. We
are alone except for your radio." Again, Maurice ("Emme" to
his long-ago comrades,) taps his fingers on the arm of his
chair as if hundreds of American wives and children still depended on his movements. He says nothing for a minute or
more, and the precious cargo from some 60 years ago is still
safe. The fingers relax and caress the chair fabric.

"We made it home to San Francisco. We all cried when we went under the bridge." His living room window faces toward the Golden Gate more than one hundred miles westward.

"In 1941 I got leave and went home to Colorado. I'd had a girl friend when I left, and I went by her place in Fort Collins. She wasn't there. '*I'm* here,' I said to her roommate, 'and I'd like a date if you aren't real busy.' We went out."

"He was kind of pushy, but cute," says Jeanette, his wife for six decades. She leaves the room on an errand after patting his arm. She is very tall and still very beautiful.

"I really embarrassed her 'cause I said this is the girl I'm going to marry. I said that on our second date to my Mom. Also, it was a Catholic/non-Catholic kind of thing. But I loved her and, as you will note" – his right forefinger is tapping imaginary code very rapidly – "it all worked out.

"I was sent to the East Coast and was assigned Chief Radioman for a ship yet to be commissioned, the *USS Baltimore*." Jeanette has re-entered the room as he speaks.

"I was stationed back east, and she got a great job in Washington, D.C. working with the Dept. of Agriculture." He pauses. "We got married... me, her, a bridesmaid and a best man. That was it. We had a much bigger wedding 50 years later." They both smile.

Maurice pauses, and the fingers begin to count off the thumb, "In 1943, Gary, back east; Sharon, Denver, '45; John, Guam, '50; and Linda in Ft. Leavenworth, 1953. All of our children are fantastic and all our girls are beautiful. The girls take after Jeanette." He smiles. The listener nods agreement and the compliment about his lovely wife is not wasted.

The fifth American fighting ship to carry the name, the *USS Baltimore* was launched July, 1942. The main sailor on the radio key was Emme Emanuel. "After launch we sailed down the East Coast, through the canal and out to the Pacific." While Emme is matter-of-fact about their deployments, he cannot mask the fact that the *Baltimore* earned nine battle stars while he was on board.

The *Baltimore* provided fire support during the Makin Island landings, the Kwajalein invasion, Truk, Eniwetok and other Pacific hotspots including the Saipan Invasion, the Philippine Sea Battle, Iwo Jima and more. "Look, we were just doing our jobs." His thoughts seem to sail past the decades of military service.

"We returned to the States July of 1944 for a short period. President Roosevelt and his entourage boarded and we headed back to Hawaii. I guess he didn't go anywhere without his black Scottie, Fala." He chuckles and continues, "I was working at my post when FDR's dog enters the compartment. I reached down and petted him. He curled up under the desk at my feet. Much later, this officer shows up and asks, 'You haven't seen the President's dog, have you?' 'Sure,' I said, 'he's right here.' I pointed under the desk. 'Do you know what would happen to me if I lost that dog?'

"'Bad things, I'm sure.' The officer led Fala back toward Roosevelt's quarters."

After a meeting with Admiral Nimitz and General MacArthur, the *Baltimore* sailed north and FDR left the ship in Alaska in early August. Some of Roosevelt's political opponents accused him of leaving Fala on the Aleutian Islands during his time on the *Baltimore*. That prompted his famous

"Fala Speech" delivered the next month at a Teamsters Union convention.

"These Republican leaders," FDR said, "have not been content with attacks on me, or my wife, or on my sons. No, not content with that, they now include my little dog, Fala. ... When Fala learned the Republican fiction writers in Congress had concocted a story I had left him behind on the Aleutian Islands and sent a destroyer back to find him — at a cost to the taxpayers of... eight or twenty million dollars, his Scotch soul was furious. He has not been the same dog since... I think I have a right to resent, to object to libelous statements about my dog."

"That was quite a dog," Maurice chuckles.

"I retired as a Chief Petty Officer... a Chief Electronic Technician. The Navy was a superb career. I married a beautiful woman, had four wonderful children, fantastic grandkids and I love my country."

Recently he and Jeanette moved into a beautiful home in Grass Valley's Eskaton Village.

His right forefinger does not move. But it is poised... it is ready. There is a smile as he reflects back to milking cows in the cold. Back to his youth in Fort Collins, waves of foothill prairie grass surpassed only by the waves of the Pacific Ocean. He leans back in his chair. Nothing moves... not an eye or a finger or a wave in the ether.

The water ripples, the waves in the eastern Pacific Ocean move gently westward toward mid-ocean. Then they begin to generate a crescendo until they crash onto the California shore. He smiles and the finger taps away... wave after wave of tapping.

Joe and Marty

Chapter 23: Joe Lombardi – USMC

"Joe's voice is soft, 'My Company started with 247 men. We drew about 100 replacements. We had 87 men left when the battle for Iwo Jima was over.'"

JOE LOMBARDI in 1941 was about to graduate from UC Berkeley. He was in the College of Commerce, the business school, focusing on economics. He also knew he was facing military service and, when the Marine Corps came on campus offering qualified students the opportunity to take a shot at platoon leader class, he signed on.

Joe had also been dating the same young woman, Marjorie, since his days at Lowell High School in San Francisco. Life was good.

April of 1942, at age twenty-two, he was ordered to report to Quantico, Virginia, the hub for professional military education for the Corps. He spent ten weeks in Platoon Leader training as a PFC, followed by ten weeks of Reserve Officer class.

Joe successfully completed his training and became a platoon leader. By January, 1943 he was with the newly formed "I" Company, Third Battalion, Twenty-third Regiment, Fourth Marine Division headquartered at Camp Lejeune, NC.

He wrote and asked Marjorie to marry him. The engagement lasted the length of her train ride from San Francisco to North Carolina where they were wed May 28. A month later he was on his way to Camp Pendleton in Southern CA., for additional training. By January of 1944 the Fourth Marine Division was headed west to the Marshall Islands, Roi-Namur in the Kwajalein Atoll. Marjorie would spend the remainder of the war with her parents in San Francisco.

It would be the first combat action for Joe and the Division. They landed February 1, on Roi Island, and six hours later declared it as secured. Some twenty-four hours later Namur Island, connected to Roi by a narrow spit of sand and a causeway, was also under Marine Corps control. Each island was less than 1,000 yards across. This battle was the first to capture Japanese mandated territory in the Pacific Theater.

Joe's Third Battallion then moved on to other Kwajalein Atoll's. When it was over Joe had led his platoon well. For the Fourth Division 190 Marines had perished with 547 wounded. Almost 3,500 enemy troops were buried on the Roi-Namur Islands.

The Division headed back some 2500 miles to Maui. That would be their home base for the rest of the war. The beaches and terrain of Maui were excellent and challenging training grounds. The extinct Haleakala Volcano was a "super" obstacle course.

Joe was promoted to Captain, the Second-in-command Company Executive Officer for the 247 man "I" Company. Within months they were headed west again, this time 3,800 miles toward the Marianas Islands, and less than 1,500 miles from Tokyo. The Fourth Marine Division, almost 22,000 strong, landed on seventy-one square mile Saipan June 15, 1944. Joe's Company was assigned to go ashore on "Blue" Beach at 8:40 a.m. There was opposition, not so much from the immediate beach area, but from mortars, artillery and anti-boat guns. Shells poured in to the incoming troops on the water and on the beaches.

The enemy had positioned many heavy weapons around the island, and the terrain was amenable to their style of fighting. The Japanese plan was to smash the Americans on the beach. As the battle wore on "I" Company was met with almost point-blank fire.

"My job was to help each platoon achieve their objectives," Joe states matter-of-factly. "I communicated with platoon leaders either by radio or in person, sending them reinforcements, supplies and relaying changes in strategy and tactics... whatever I needed to do to move us toward our goal." The men called him "Captain Joe".

"Saipan was rough in many ways. Our job was made difficult because some of the enemy used the civilians, some 20,000 of Korean, Chamorro or Japanese heritage, as human shields." July 9, twenty-five days after landing on Saipan, the island was under American control. The Fourth Division lost almost 6,000 men – missing, wounded or dead. Four times that many Japanese perished.

The Fourth Marine Division written history published in 1946 summed up the victory, "Saipan was more than a mere stepping stone to Tokyo. It was a major intersection on the main highway."

Less than two weeks later, July 24, the Fourth Marine division began the invasion of Tinian, an island slightly less than fifty square miles, with slightly more than 9,000 Japanese defenders. Tinian was just three miles south of Saipan. This time a plan was put in place which seemed impossible to implement. It was hoped it would seem impossible to the enemy, too. The landing of the entire Fourth Division would occur on two beaches less than a combined 200 yards wide. The Division would sneak in the back door of Tinian Island. The strategy worked. By the end of the day an area 2.3 miles wide and more than a mile deep had been secured. It was that night that the major battle of Tinian occurred – the enemy counterattack.

It was a well-planned onslaught but by the next morning there were several thousand enemy dead. By August 12, more than thirteen thousand civilians were safely under Marine protection. On August 14, 1944 "I" Company and the rest of the Division boarded ships for Maui. The cost was

290 American dead, 1,515 wounded and 24 missing. Virtually every enemy defender had perished.

Back on Maui replacements came for those no longer with the Division. "They had to be trained. We eventually got the Division and Company "I" back to full strength. We made countless practice amphibious landings at Wailea and the Kihei area. We kept doing them until we got them right."

"I made a lot of friends on Maui," Joe reminisced. "It was there, in '44, I learned to play golf. The Maui Country Club offered us a membership at four dollars a month. Members would loan their clubs. We had to provide our own golf balls," Joe continued. "They were in short supply. I relished the packages from home, which usually had a dozen or so balls. I remember the PoDo golf ball," he chuckled. "It did the job."

Early in 1945 the Fourth Division sailed out again toward an island 747 miles beyond Saipan and about the same distance from Tokyo. Iwo Jima, one-ninth the size of Saipan, had some 23,000 defenders. At dawn on February 19, 1945 the men of "I" Company got their first glimpse of the island. Unlike their previous conquests there were no white beaches, no palm trees, no green fields covered in sugar cane. Instead they were confronted with an ugly, barren landscape. Mount Suribachi loomed at the south end of the island.

"I" Company went in on the sixth wave to hit the beach. According to Joe, "The beach was black sand and ash and traction was almost impossible. It was like trying to move on a deep coating of B-B's. We sank to our ankles."

He continued, "We didn't draw much fire the first two to three hours, but then they opened up." The Japanese machine guns in the dunes in front of them came to life, along with the guns at the edge of the airfield 300-400 yards away. Artillery came in from Mt Suribachi to the south and the hills to the north. While most pillboxes and blockhouses had physically been demolished many still contained enemy who were willing to fight to the end. The enemy trenches had not been thoroughly destroyed before the assault began.

Some twenty-six days and nine-hours later Iwo Jima had been secured. "My Company started with 247 men," Joe's voice is soft. "We drew about one-hundred replacements. We had 87 men left when the battle for Iwo Jima ended. I never even knew some of the replacements... they would join us in the evening and be gone by morning." Joe taps the table with his fingernails as he talks. "If you add it up – the 247, plus 100, minus 87 who remained – we had some 260 wounded, missing or dead in Company 'I'."

"We just kept going," he said as he traced "I" Company's advancement on the 2 X 3-foot canvas backed original map he used as Executive Officer. Daily progress was marked off like the weather maps in our newspapers that track storm fronts. "We had to keep going... we couldn't stop. There was no doubt we would win, and we did."

Joe earned the Purple Heart on Iwo Jima. One bullet made seven holes in his shirt, entering through the right sleeve, zinging across his chest, smashing his pipe and assaulting his notebook, and into the flesh of his left arm. He also earned the Bronze Star when the Japanese attacked him and a contingent of one hundred Company "I" Marines. By the next morning there were 250 enemy dead. "We were dropping mortar shells only forty yards or so in front of our own lines. Only one soldier made it through our lines, swinging his sword and slashing one marine. Our men did their job."

The Fourth Marine Division disbanded at the end of the war. Joe stayed on a little longer, as a Major, to help it close out its rich history. He has had a home in Penn Valley's Lake Wildwood for twenty-eight years, and has lived here full time for twenty. Eleven years ago, after fifty-three years of marriage, Marjorie passed away. Joe married Marty, a widowed friend, almost nine years ago. He has attended a number of 4th Division reunions.

Several years ago he began corresponding with the son of his Iwo Jima radioman. The man had questions about his dad. He had found Joe's signature on one of his father's liberty passes and tracked him down. "I remember his dad very well," Joe states. "He was a fine person, and I'm very happy to share my memories of him as a good man and a good Marine."

It takes one to know one.

Guy and Jean

Chapter 24: Guy Throner – USN

"...He was asked by the CIA to undertake a mission for them in Germany. He states, "My assignment was to find out if the German government was engaged in the development of an atomic bomb."

GUY THRONER was born in Minneapolis in 1919. By 1924 the family had moved to Oberlin, Ohio, about 30 miles west of Cleveland. His Dad, a psychologist by training, was with the physical education department of Oberlin College.

"My early years were near idyllic," says Guy. "I had the usual pets and hobbies, including building a go-cart in 1932 from a wrecked Harley Davidson. I used it for my paper route. My dog rode with me. In high school, I was a skinny kid until the PE teacher got me interested in gymnastics and parallel bars. I put on weight and added muscle."

His physique earned him money while he was a student at Oberlin College.

"I worked as a model for art students. I made $1.00 an hour which was pretty good money."

The winter of 1939 he met Jean Wellington Holt, a fellow student, at the ice rink. Says Guy, "By 1941 we were going steady. There was really little time for romance since the girls had to be in their dorms by 10 p.m. every day except Saturday, when they could stay out an hour later."

Guy has written a few key chapters on his life for his family. The military portion begins in May of 1943. The Navy was going full bore with its ship-building activities and new officers were in demand. Guy enrolled in the program that allowed college seniors to become officers in four months.

"Rather than wait for my graduation from Oberlin in June, the Navy called for me to attend the Midshipman school at Northwestern University in Chicago. Each of my college professors had to sign-off that I was likely to pass the course. Successful completion of the Navy program would also guarantee my college degree."

The first month was spent as an apprentice seaman. "It was tough, intended to weed out the misfits. We received $5.00 a week for spending money. Our liberty was from Saturday noon until 9:00 Sunday evening. The $5.00 wasn't much to cover expenses in downtown Chicago, but it was enough because people would pick up the tab for supper or drinks at the local restaurants and bars."

Guy was in the top 10-percent of his graduating Midshipman class. As a result he had a wide range of available duty choices.

"The Commander of the Bomb Disposal School was Lieutenant Commander Tom Boardman. He was a Rhodes Scholar and I had met him when he was affiliated with Oberlin. He convinced me bomb disposal was good duty, so off I went to their school in Washington, D.C. My parents were aghast."

The course at American University was intense. The other applicants were also from the top 1/10th of their Midshipman classes. About four-in-ten flunked out.

"Oberlin College is a difficult school, but this was far harder. There was only one grade acceptable and that was perfect on every test. Exams started at 8 a.m. and lasted about 15 hours. Any test mistake that would have resulted in the student being killed was cause for dismissal. We had to learn the essence of a hundred or so fuzes every two weeks, be able to draw them and describe how to disarm them."

(A *fuze* is a mechanical device that detonates a bomb, grenade, mine, torpedo, artillery shell or land mine. A fuse is a pyrotechnic detonator, often lit with a match, like a firecracker or stick of dynamite.)

"We had to learn the fuzes of all the projectiles used by the Allies as well as each Axis nation."

December 5, 1943, the weekend before his exam on Japanese ordnance, Guy and Jean wed. "We were married in Germantown, a suburb of Philadelphia, then rushed back to D.C. by train. We had supper at the Mayflower Hotel and took a cab to the house where we had rented a room for

$100 dollars a month. I got up at 3:00 a.m. on our wedding night to study for my ordnance exam... and passed it the next morning." Jean, who had already graduated from Oberlin, went to her temporary job at American University.

Guy finished the bomb disposal school a few weeks later and went to Underwater Demolition School (frogman training) in Florida, then other related courses on the East Coast including chemical warfare, ordnance reclamation, photography schools and more. Says Guy, "The great thing about this series of schools, I could take Jean along. I was on temporary additional duty status that paid $7.00 more a day, which covered her expenses. Essentially we were on a paid honeymoon."

Late February 1944 he boarded a convoy headed to Oran, Algeria near the eastern border of Morocco. "The Liberty ship had a top speed of 9 knots and we zigzagged the whole way. It took us 19 days." Oran was a temporary posting on the way to Cagliari, Sardinia via Palermo, Sicily then Naples and assignment to Admiral Moon's staff on the Flagship *USS Bayfield* for the August 15 Allied invasion of Southern France.

"I went ashore with the second wave with the 3rd Army Division," states Guy. "We came under German 88mm cannon fire. Their bombardment ended as quickly as it had started. I don't know if the Army put the 88's out of business or the gun crews, seeing 700 ships off shore, decided to get out while the getting was good."

He continues, "My first job was to investigate a hose laying on the road with one end buried in the dirt." The concern was it might be part of a buried mine. "It turned out to be a piece of surgical tubing. My second job was to get rid of a 100-pound unexploded bomb near the path of Army personnel coming ashore." He had it picked up and set on his lap while seated in a jeep. "My First Class Petty Officer, Miller, drove me to a remote spot where we stashed the bomb without detonating it."

Almost immediately he and Miller were requested to accompany an intelligence officer up a heavily mined hill to a German radar station. "Lucky for us the Germans had been so surprised by the landing they had left the path through the field marked with 'Achtung Minen' flags on short metal stakes. The intelligence task was to find the German code books used in radar work and to transmit radar findings to their command. Our search was successful."

Guy continues, "As we were finishing a German radar sergeant and twelve privates assigned to the facility surrendered to us. The sergeant told the intelligence officer, who spoke German, they had run to a gun emplacement when the sea bombardment had started. Hours later, after the landing, they had watched us search their radar tower. The sergeant kept his men from killing us. He said he had lived through WWI and was determined to live through WW II. He figured if we were killed, American soldiers would come and kill them, so he convinced his charges to surrender peacefully by keeping them covered with his 'burp gun'."

Guy continues, "The three of us marched the soldiers down to the beach... the first prisoners taken on the Southern France Invasion. I brought the sergeant's 'burp gun' back to the States, where it ended up at the Presidio Museum in San Francisco."

Guy Throner's job had three key components – ordnance intelligence, bomb disposal operations and underwater demolition. As a newly commissioned Ensign he was a qualified UDT expert – a frogman. "I never had to go underwater," he says. "My work mainly consisted of bomb disposal operations and ordnance intelligence. While we knew the inner workings of most enemy bombs, mines, torpedoes and the like, new weaponry was coming on board all the time."

He describes one of the tools in his kit. "If we found a new piece of unexploded enemy ordnance, I would use the radium camera. It consisted of a film holder tightly placed against the ordnance item. The radium was positioned on the opposite side. The thickness of the object would determine the x-ray exposure time, as the film was developed in the normal way. The resulting shadowgraph was analyzed to figure how the ordnance worked and how best to disassemble it." Once he had dismantled the object he immediately forwarded information about the weapon to headquarters.

"Around the world there were four Mobile Explosive Investigative Units (MEIUs) – one in England covering northern Europe, another in Pearl Harbor, and a third in the South Pacific that moved north as the war progressed. The fourth was our team in the Mediterranean. Info we gathered was shared with other MEIUs and the service training organizations."

After about four days on the beach across the bay from Cannes they were ordered to head to Marseilles.

"Our small team was the only Navy personnel in the city. We volunteered to help Army engineers clean up the port and harbor. The battle for this city was still going, and the harbor was littered with mines. The Germans had also wired the port with close to 1,000 demolition charges, each with about 2,000 pounds of high explosive. All were set to detonate with the closing of a single switch. Fortunately the Army shut off juice at the power station before detonation could occur."

Guy continues, "After about a week, a naval intelligence officer said there was a German Naval officer that wanted to talk with an ordnance officer. We met at the French POW camp outside Marseilles. He said he was responsible for placing 174 magnetic/acoustic mines in the port. I told him only 173 were left because one had detonated and sunk a ship. He said there was no map where the mines were placed but he knew exactly where they were and would tell us if we would get him and five men out of the French camp.

"The French would not release the prisoners to us but did allow us to use them during the day. Every morning the German officer and his men were delivered to my petty officer and me. I used his five men as my bomb disposal team. The POW's were well-fed and willing workers. They were out from under the control of the French during the day and very happy with the arrangement."

He continues, "We neutralized the mines by putting a diver down at the spot the German officer designated and would search in an ever-increasing circle until the mine was found. There were two ways to solve the problem -- put an explosive charge on it, bring the diver up and detonate the thing, or place a thermite charge on the mine and burn a hole through the case, ignite the explosive and let it burn until the case was empty of explosive. The mine had its own oxygen supply and would burn under water. We only used the detonation method once as the explosion was so violent we were afraid the port facilities would be damaged if other mines were exploded. All the mines were successfully destroyed."

Once the MEIU teams had cleared land and sea of bombs and mines, Guy's team went on with its basic mission – doing ordnance intelligence. "We were sent to a German airfield north of Lyon. We were the first Americans to visit the site. We found eight experimental aerial torpedoes. They were all different. We discovered a very strange device that none of us had ever seen hanging on the wings of one of the bombers. We packed up the device and the eight torpedoes and took them back to Marseilles for shipment to the States. The unusual item turned out to be an engine used for jet-assisted takeoff of the bomber."

Guy continues, "After the US Army had cleared Marseilles of German troops they were ordered away from the city so General Charles de Gaulle and his rag-tag bunch of French Resistance Fighters could march down the main boulevard. This gave the impression the French had liberated the city.

"I was there as the city was being liberated but never saw a single member of the resistance show himself. Furthermore I had not seen a member of the resistance during the landing or during our long drive to Marseilles. It is my impression the resistance force put up little if any resistance until they were sure the Germans were gone. At this point they paraded around firing their guns in the air. I caught one of them filling his gas tank from our truck and chased him away. I was not impressed with the French resistance fighters I encountered during the war." He adds, "On later trips, after the war, I found them to be great people."

Moving on, Guy says, "There was less and less work for us to do in Marseilles and it was decided we would let the French finish the minor ordnance disposal work that remained. We had cleared more than 600 tons of unexploded ordnance (261 tons of sea mines alone) in our three-month stay. The 12th of December 1944 I received orders to head back to Washington, D.C. By this time I had been promoted to Lieutenant Junior Grade." He expected to be sent to the South Pacific; instead he received orders to report to the Naval Ordnance Test Station, Inyokern, CA.

"I was told to report to Lieutenant Dave Carnahan. He had been my instructor when I studied for the exam in his Japanese Ordnance class my wedding night. He was now the senior bomb disposal officer at the facility and had requested I join his team."

The station was the premier rocket development facility in the nation. The California Institute of Technology was responsible for the development of a series of rockets for the Navy. They would also get involved in the Manhattan Project – the development of the Atomic Bomb.

After returning to D.C. from France, Guy and his wife Jean headed for his new duty station in California. Says Guy, "The Washington Naval personnel office issued me orders to Inyokern but didn't know where it was located. They knew it was in California, and maybe in the desert. Jean and I had the option to drive or take commercial transportation.

"We found a car we liked for a little more money than we planned to spend, but we bought it anyway. It was a 1937 black Packard sedan with a back-opening trunk. The spare tire hung on the back of the trunk, and the car had a radio. It proved to be very dependable, and it got decent gas mileage."

They started across the country with most of their possessions jammed in the car. From St. Louis they took Route 66. The Inyokern facility, now called China Lake Naval Weapons Station, is about 150 miles northeast of Los Angeles on the western edge of California's Mojave Desert and eastern slope of the Sierra on Highway 395. They didn't know it then but this is where they would spend the next eight and a half years of their lives.

The Navy had given the responsibility for their rockets to Caltech under the direction of Dr. Charles Lauretsen and his protégé – and subsequent Nobel Prize winner – Dr. William Fowler.

"There were hundreds of rockets fired on the ranges every month," says Guy. "My team had responsibility for recovery of the duds and clearing the firing ranges of fired ordnance." Shortly after his arrival he was assigned, as a bomb disposal officer, to a very secret program. "The project involved the development of a large free-fall bomb, a strange looking device that wasn't anything like the bombs one was used to seeing."

Guy continues, "The project was different in several ways – no station aircraft were involved in dropping the bomb and no one would tell you anything about the project. After dropping the bombs, the planes left for an undisclosed base. Later we would know we were involved in the development of Fat Man, the atom bomb dropped on Nagasaki August 9, 1945."

Japan offered to surrender the next day.

Says Guy, "The development of the implosion version of the atomic bomb, Fat Man, was assigned to Caltech by Gen. Leslie Groves and Dr. Robert Oppenheimer. Los Alamos was very busy with the development of the bomb intended for Hiroshima.

"The only part of the bomb not made at our facility was the Plutonium pit, which would be provided by the nuclear reactors at the Hanford Facility at Richland, WA. I was involved with the assembly process, the recovery of duds, and eventually with the testing of explosive lenses We later learned the test bombs dropped on our range were from modified B-29's based in Wendover, Nevada. Fat Man was so large that the bomb bay of the planes had to be enlarged.

"I received a call asking if it was okay to machine a key explosive component, the composition-B explosive blocks. I told them I wasn't sure, but would find out. I was told it was critical that I find out within the hour or the whole project would come to a screeching halt and molds would have to be modified. which would be a four-to-six-week task."

Guy pauses, then continues: "One of my men and I had dug up two unexploded prototypes on the range without a problem; so I was pretty sure the stuff could be machined. I used a brace and bit to drill a hole in the block and flooded the drill bit with water from a garden hose. Comp-B could indeed be machined, and it was. Fat Man was produced and dropped on schedule."

When the war was over Guy started the Explosive Ordnance Section at the test station. "We were engaged in warhead research and the development of explosive devices for missiles and wing removal charges for the U.S. version of the German V-1. I was a member of the Army-Navy Shaped Charge Steering Committee."

Guy left the active Navy in 1947 but stayed on at the test station as a GS-13 in charge of three sections. He eventually went to the UCLA Graduate School of Business Management and registered as a Professional Engineer.

Guy had the opportunity to know and work directly with Werner Von Braun and his close associates during the time they were in El Paso working on a second stage missile for the V-2. In 1953 he joined Aerojet and started their Industrial Ordnance Development Division. "Starting with me as the first employee it grew to the largest commercial ordnance operation in the country. There were 853 engineers in that division by the time I left the company in 1964."

While at Aerojet he was asked by the CIA to undertake a mission for them in Germany.

"My assignment was to find out if the German government was engaged in the development of an atomic bomb. I had made many technical contacts and friends with German and other European scientists and engineers in the weapons development business. To cover the spy mission, a tour of all European R & D labs was arranged. In a week's time in Germany I was able to determine that the instrumentation they were using was neither sophisticated nor fast enough to measure the explosive phenomena to design an atomic weapon. I was able to reassure the State Department that the Germans were not engaged in the design of an atom bomb.

He joined FMC, the chemical, research and manufacturing giant, as a VP and formed their ordnance development organization – the Defense Technology Division. He grew it to 1600 manufacturing employees and 350 engineers. After the Vietnam War FMC got out of the weapons business. Guy went to work for Battele, the largest commercial Research and Development Company in the world. He stayed there until his retirement in 1986. He and Jean moved to Lake Wildwood in 1989.

Two of their three children were born while Guy was stationed at the Inyokern station.

Guy and Jean both golf. He enjoys listening to loud classical music in the garage.

Some of his professional recognition includes making 21 editions of *Who's Who in America* and inclusion in *Who's Who in Aviation and Aerospace* and *Who's Who in Frontier Science and Technology*. He is a member of American Men and Women in Science and an original member of the American Institute of Aeronautics and Astronautics. He had very early membership in the American Rocket Society and was elected to the Research Society of America.

Guy has written 80 technical papers, been recognized for 400-plus inventions and had 27 U.S. Patents awarded.

Congress and numerous industry and professional organizations have also recognized Guy's outstanding contributions.

With a twinkle in his eye and a great smile he says, "It has been an exciting and interesting life."

A little more than two decades ago Guy sent a congratulatory letter to Professor William Fowler of Caltech. He had just won the Nobel Prize. He and Guy had worked together at Inyokern during and following the war. Guy's letter begins, "Dear Willy." A week later he received a response, a few sentences excerpted here:

"Guy, It was good to hear from you... We all did a great job during World War II and not even a Nobel Prize can eclipse that. Sincerely yours, William A. Fowler, Nobel Laureate for Physics 1983."

Jackie and Dick

Chapter 25: Dick Randal – Army

"Sometimes we would hear German soldiers talking on the other side of the hedgerow."

DICK RANDAL was born in Detroit in 1922 and raised about 30 miles west in the Ypsilanti area, a rural community of about 18,000. His father Percy was a real estate developer and owned grocery stores, fruit markets, and restaurants.

Says Dick, "During WWI Dad was a military test pilot, crashing more than one plane." He pulls out photos from 1917 – one snapped immediately after a crash showing his dad unconscious, but okay, in the crumpled open cockpit.

Dick grew up loving to fish and hunt. By his own admission he was also a bit of a hellion – Tom Sawyer / Huck

Finn stuff. "I brought some dynamite caps to school, set them off and got suspended." He continues, "Mom passed away when I was 15, and I really straightened up." He channeled his energy to sports and played guard and tackle for his high school football team. "I was also on the track and swim teams and did individual as well as relay events."

While Dick was relentless in his pursuit of excellence in sports, Germany, in 1940, was relentless in trying to bomb England into oblivion. American entry into WWII seemed inevitable, and the largest factory in the world at the time – 3.5 million square feet – was started April 1941 at Willow Run near Ypsilanti. Charles Lindbergh, after reviewing the Ford facility, dubbed it the "Grand Canyon of the mechanized world".

"I went to work there," Dick says, "putting motor mounts on B-24's, then I graduated to working out of the engineering department, ensuring production people were getting the correct revised plans.

He had also signed up for the Naval Air Corps June 1942. "I wanted to be a pilot like Dad, but I had not been called yet and received a draft notice to report to the Army." After induction he was sent to Camp McCain, MS. "I grew up around guns and was an expert marksman. After basic I was assigned to shoot a light machine-gun and sent to Tennessee for final maneuvers." The term light machine=gun is a misnomer as the gun was about 50 pounds without the tripod. He recalls a summer endurance training day in Mississippi. "There were 100 two-man crews. I carried the gun plus a 30- or 35-pound ammo box. My crewman carried two ammo boxes plus the tripod. Out of 200 men, 193 passed out. I was number 192 to bite the dust."

He continues, "We went to South Carolina for a few months to make final preparations to head to Europe, then embarked from New Jersey late October 1943 in a convoy aboard a converted British passenger ship." During the almost two-week crossing to Liverpool, several ships were torpedoed.

"I was assigned to the 9th Infantry Division, 47th Regiment, 3rd Battalion, Company M and sent to Winchester, England some fifty miles southwest of London. I was also made lead man and gunner on a five-man heavy machine-gun squad." The water-cooled Browning was capable of firing 600 rounds per minute, and the gun, tripod, water, and a box of ammo weighed 100-plus pounds. Dick continues, "I had an assistant gunner and three men assigned to carry ammunition."

Over the next months Dick and his team honed their skills as a gun squad as well as intense hand-to-hand combat training. They were preparing for the 1944 Normandy Invasion.

"The 9th Division did not participate June 6," says Dick. "We were part of the third wave and landed June 11." While most of his division landed at Utah Beach, the most westerly assault area, Dick's unit landed at the adjacent western end of Omaha beach, the second of the five Normandy landing areas. "The morning of June 11, we were anchored off shore. Landing craft came alongside and we scrambled down a net – me with my heavy machine-gun and field pack and the remainder of the squad with the rest of our equipment, ammo, and their individual gear."

The assault forces were still taking intense German fire. "It wasn't the heavy turret guns lining the shore, as they couldn't get an angle on us. Instead it was anti-tank guns, machine-guns and mortars. The landing craft opened its ramp about 150 yards from shore. The water was thigh-deep. There were dead and wounded all around me."

He pauses, clears his throat, then continues, "I lost two of my men going ashore."

Still under heavy fire, Dick and his comrades scrambled to cross Omaha beach. "Fortunately we didn't have to scale a cliff." Company M began climbing a ravine that would lead them to the top – an arduous 16-hour-plus trek, under fire, with Dick lugging his heavy machine-gun.

The numbers involved in the Normandy Invasion are staggering – 133,000 troops landed June 6. By the end of the month, 850,000 men had landed on Normandy beaches.

"We moved up the ravine a few yards at a time. Eventually we made high ground and looked over a landscape of hedgerows as far as we could see. Our job was to hook up with the bulk of the 47th Regiment that had landed to the west at Utah Beach." He continues, "Shortly after reaching the top with my two remaining squad members I was offered replacements for the men I'd lost coming ashore."

The hedgerows separated the property of one farmer or landowner from another and had been built up over many centuries – some since the Roman occupation of the area. Typically they are an embankment base of field rocks covered with soil, trees and hedges. They vary in height and width from 3 to 5 feet, plus foliage, and double that in some cases. In places there are double hedgerows with a road between them – trees arching gracefully and meeting in the center.

As the Germans consolidated, they defended their positions behind each row. Allied tanks could not climb the hedgerows without exposing their unarmored underbelly.

Says Dick, "Our tank men welded iron beams onto the front of some tanks. The beams were slightly above ground level, like the tines of a fork, and would plow through a hedgerow without exposing the tank's underside." Ironically, the iron beams came from the barriers the Germans had placed along the shoreline. The modified vehicle was called a Rhino tank.

"Sometimes we would hear German soldiers talking on the other side of a hedgerow. We would lob a grenade or take other appropriate action," Dick says. "It was very slow going. Almost every day we'd set up my heavy machine-gun atop a hedgerow and fire across the fields into real or suspected enemy concealments."

He continues, "Having the Rhino tanks helped immensely. They'd plow through the hedgerows like their namesake animal and create a path for ground troops to follow with significantly less exposure to enemy fire."

June 15, Dick's 3rd Battalion was given the job of crossing the Douve River on the Cherbourg Peninsula. His unit moved forward encountering major resistance and suffering significant casualties. He hesitates, then continues, "By June 20, nine days after landing, I was all that remained of my original squad."

Two days later, the 22nd, his Battalion would be awarded a Battle Honors Star for their heroism and outstanding performance.

During the entire Normandy Invasion there were 209,000 allied casualties – dead, wounded, captured or missing. Of that total more than 25 percent died. A typical Army division is 10,000 – 15,000 men. Dick's division, the 9th, suffered 30,000 casualties. Put another way, counting replacements, they lost at least two-times their number of authorized men.

Ernie Pyle, famed WWII correspondent, wrote about the Cherbourg Campaign, "The Ninth Division did something that we haven't always done in the past. It kept tenaciously on the enemy's neck. When the Germans would withdraw a little the Ninth was right on top of them. It never gave them a chance to reassemble or get their balance... I was based at the division command post and we struck our tents and moved forward six times in seven days."

Says Dick, "We met resistance from German concrete bunkers and self-propelled guns. Their firepower was very impressive." After Cherbourg's capture his unit was to push south and sever the St. Lo-Perriers Road. "It was thick trees, thick shrubs, and swampy. The second week in July our Battalion Command Post was overrun. July 11, we launched a counterattack." Within hours the German attack was repulsed and the regiment was back on offensive.

"You have to have 24-hour vigilance in a combat situation. No matter how tired, you have to protect yourself. You have to dig-in and hope the enemy doesn't have your name or number."

July 20, Dick was digging a slit trench when a round – mortar or artillery – came in. "The pain was excruciating." He pauses, "I'm sure I shouted out when I was hit."

Dick's thigh was punctured with several shards of shrapnel. One of his knees was separated from the socket – like a rag doll's joint held together by the outlying fabric. Dick, the last surviving member of his squad, was out of action.

After a short recuperation period he was back to work. "I couldn't manage a heavy machine-gun any longer, lacking the leg strength to carry the weapon. But I did know how to drive and shoot." He was reassigned as a 9th Division headquarters jeep driver.

"My new job was driving officers and NCO's from HQ's to the front and on recon missions. One day a German fighter plane strafed the road I was driving. There were several jeeps in our group, each with a machine-gun mounted on a pedestal behind the front seats. We all stopped and fired on the plane. I had him in the cross-hairs when I pulled the trigger. The plane was hit and we watched it crash in flames."

By August the division had crossed the Vesle River into Belgium, hot on the heels of the retreating Germans.

"We traveled fast," Dick offers. Whenever possible soldiers rode on whatever they could – half-tracks, tanks, trucks, jeeps."

September 14, they crossed the German border at Roetgen. The assault on the Siegfried Line had begun and within a week it was under 9th Division control. Sept. 22nd the Germans counterattacked, only to be repulsed. American supply lines were sparse, and it was decided to stay in place for the remainder of September and October.

"I was going up a narrow road one night, lights off, on a recon mission with an officer. To our left was an American tank, with another tank just across the road on our right. I slowed to about 10 MPH to pass between them. The next thing I knew the officer and I were being carried over the front seats. We hadn't seen that the tank on the left was pulling out the other one with a cable stretched across the road. My driverless jeep coasted another 10 or 20 yards up the road."

By mid-November the offensive was renewed and the division moved north to Bergrath, Germany. December saw them fighting to protect one flank from the German Battle of the Bulge offensive. By Christmas the Bulge was eliminated. On Feb. 28, the division crossed the Roer River, headed toward the Rhine.

"March 7, we were told we were moving to Remagen prior to crossing the Rhine," says Dick. "It's acknowledged that capturing the Ludendorff Bridge intact helped shorten the war by several months." He continues, "The fighting was very heavy for several days with many losses on each side." By the 18th of March the division left the Remagen area and pushed across the Autobahn.

"The closest we got to Berlin was Dessau, about 75 miles southwest of Berlin." May 9, 1945 Victory in Europe was declared.

"From May until I returned home I stood guard at a military and war crimes prison in Mooseberg, about 20 miles from Munich." He continues, "I also did training for the Third Army Track and Field Championships and participated in the 800-meter relay and threw the 16-pound shotput. At the time I weighed about 215 pounds. We took second in the relays." Sept. 1945 he was reassigned and came home with the 10th Armored Division.

Dick earned a Bronze Star for meritorious achievement in ground combat, the European Theater Medal with five stars, each representing a major campaign, and later received a Jubilee Liberation Medal from the President of France. Missing is his Purple Heart. While *The Wildwood Independent*, through Senator Dianne Feinstein, worked on getting Dick his medal, the claim was denied due to spotty records-keeping from that era.

His Dad and Stepmom drove from Michigan to Indian Gap, Pennsylvania to take him home. "Dad now lived in Mio, MI, a small town of about 1,000." Dick met his future wife about ten days after returning. "My brother knew a couple of local girls and suggested a double date. He didn't care which girl he dated; so I picked Jackie."

Dick bought a small sawmill. He and Jackie eloped in March 1946. "I also went back to school. We sold the sawmill and opened a dry-cleaning business in Mio. In 1964 we moved to Santa Cruz, CA and opened the same type of venture.

In 1970 Dick went into cleaning-related chemical sales until his retirement in 1984. "Jackie and I moved to Lake Wildwood in 2003." Dick plays golf with the Niners and carded a hole-in-one on #3 June 28, 2005. Jackie plays in three different bridge groups. They have six children and 23 grandchildren and great-grandchildren.

Ted and Barbara

Chapter 26: Ted Ross – USAF

"The SR-71 pitched up violently, almost reaching an uncontrollable attitude… In eleven seconds we lost 35,000 feet in altitude."

TED ROSS was born and raised in Twin Falls, Idaho in the south-central part of the state. In high school he ran the mile on the track team and recreationally skied at Sun Valley. After graduating high school in 1968, he attended the College of Southern Idaho, also in Twin Falls, where he majored in mathematics and was president of the ski club.

"I loved to ski," Ted says, "and sometimes worked menial jobs during ski season at Sun Valley about an hour and a half north of Twin Falls." It was at Sun Valley during spring break in 1969 that he met Barbara Kinsell from Weiser, Idaho located about midway down the state's western edge. They started dating.

After graduating with an Associate Arts degree in 1970, Ted enlisted in the Air Force. He spent a year as a statistician and was selected for the Air Force Institute of Technology's commissioning program. He was promoted to staff sergeant 13 months after joining and was sent to Colorado State University in Fort Collins.

Meanwhile, Barbara was attending the University of Idaho in Moscow. She was selected Miss Washington County for 1971-72, with piano playing as her talent, and was a Miss Idaho contestant in 1972.

"She would have won, I think," Ted offers with a grin, "had she not admitted she had an Air Force guy as a boy friend." He continues, "She was – and still is – beautiful and switched to organ and played *Lady of Spain* superbly during the talent portion of the contest. In fact," Ted says, "she taught piano in Lake Wildwood from 1982-87 and was a member of the local Piano Instructors Guild." They were married December 1972.

Ted graduated from CSU with a degree in Management Information Systems mid-1973. "Attending CSU was a great opportunity – it gave me the chance to get my Management Information Systems BS degree, a second major in skiing, and two minor degrees – sky- and scuba-diving. I worked hard on my studies and sports." He adds, "Actually, a condition of marriage was retiring from sky-diving. Barb said scuba, skiing, and motorcycle riding were all okay. But not dropping out of airplanes."

Barbara chimes in, "He promised to give up dangerous activities like sky-diving, then replaced them with flying in a spacesuit at Mach 3 or more and getting shot at during his flights." She pats his hand and smiles. (We are ahead of ourselves in this story.)

Ted was commissioned in September through Officers Training School. By June 1974 he had completed navigator training at Mather Air Force Base then became a distinguished graduate of KC-135 Combat Crew Training School at Castle AFB near Merced. By November he was a First Lieutenant and assigned to Plattsburg AFB, NY. He served as a Navigator Instructor.

In 1978 Ted completed the FB-111A (fighter bomber) combat crew-training course, then was selected for early upgrade to Instructor Radar Navigator. Ultimately he was responsible for all training of FB-111 radar navigators with experience in other models of the F-111. He also found time during 1979 to earn an MBA from the prestigious Rensselaer Polytechnic Institute in Troy, NY.

"The FB-111 was the most exciting aircraft," Ted says. "We would set the altitude at 200' AGL (Above Ground Level) and scream across the countryside on a path with cliffs, canyons, and rock formations towering hundreds of feet high." He describes approaching buttes at high-speed level flight, then a jolt as the plane turns skyward and perpendicular to the ground; level flight while a butte is crossed; and downward as a cliff edge is passed. "Some days my shoulders would be bruised by the jolts from the safety harnesses. But what a ride... what a ride."

In 1982 Ted was appointed SR-71 Reconnaissance Systems Officer and was assigned to the 9th Strategic Recon Wing at Beale Air Force Base near Marysville and 15 miles or so from his home in Penn Valley, CA. He broke the Mach 3+

barrier for the first time July 1, 1983. At the end of that flight he presented Barbara with a beautiful SR-71 gold pendant and necklace he had carried on the flight. During his almost five years at Beale he flew 173 SR-71 sorties, and logged 610 hours. He had eleven temporary duty tours with 470 days away from home and family. Not counting landing pattern miles, he flew 568,554 nautical miles (653,837 statute miles) in the SR-71.

In the book *Deep Black – Space Espionage and National Security* by William Burrows, there is an excerpt about one of Ted's flights. The author is addressing the esthetics of flying an SR-71. Ted and Pilot Jerry Glasser, a Lake Wildwood resident at the time, were flying from Beale AFB to Kadena AFB in Okinawa.

It was a night flight, and somewhere over the Pacific they caught up with the sun. The sun moves about 1,000 mph. The SR-71 is more than twice as fast. From the book: "Lt. Col. Glasser and Capt. Ted Ross... overtook the sun just after it had set." (They were flying due west.) "Then the SR turned south for a while, allowing the sun to disappear once again under the horizon. Several minutes later the SR swung back onto the two-seven-zero heading. Slowly, the sun returned." There was a spreading indigo arc from behind the helmet visor. Said Glasser, "Aside from going around in the space shuttle I don't think there is anyone who has seen two sunrises in the west."

"It was incredibly beautiful," Ted confirms decades later. He shows me photos. The black / deep blue / purple / lavender / pale blue color, blended with the curvature of the earth, is breathtaking.

Late October 1984 there was a brewing crisis in Central America. Intelligence stated there were six MiG-21 fighters on a ship heading from Cuba to Nicaragua. When/if they arrived they would be the first jet fighters in the region.

Two Majors, Stormy Boudreaux and Ted Ross, donned their pressure suits, identical to those worn by astronauts, and headed south at Mach 3. "We had flown from Beale to Cuba, then imaged the entire Gulf of Mexico, including Cuba and the Nicaraguan coastline, looking for the ship. We were the first to fly in the Nicaragua surge. We did not find the ship."

He continues, "The next day another team flew from Beale. Their imaging found the ship and also made an over-flight of Nicaragua. There was a Sandinistas rally in Mana-gua, the capitol, being led by Ortega. When the SR-71 flew over there was a very loud sonic boom, and the crowd thought they were being bombed and headed for cover."

That day the ship with the MiGs turned around and headed back to Cuba. "I believe our flights helped the Nica-raguan leadership understand that having Russian fighter planes in their country was a very bad idea." Ted continues, "To this day the entire Central America region remains more stable because of the SR-71 and its ability to wave the American flag anywhere in the world."

June 1985 Stormy Boudreaux and Ted were flying a clas-sified mission at 80,000 feet at speeds greater than Mach 3. Ted picks up the story: "Honeywell was in the process of converting the SR's from analog to digital automatic flight and inlet control systems. The ship we were flying had been converted. The systems had triple redundancy – back-up to the back-up. All three systems failed simultaneously." He pauses. "The SR pitched up violently, almost reaching an uncontrollable attitude. Stormy suggested we get ready to eject. In eleven seconds we lost 35,000 feet of altitude. We restored one computer and headed back to our departure base." A write-up of the incident in a Strategic Air Command publication states, "Maj. Boudreaux's exceptional flying ability and quick reflexes, combined with Maj. Ross' cool professionalism, quickly put the aircraft into a safe flying regime. Their outstanding flying skills – while encumbered by bulky full-pressure suits, at speeds and altitudes unknown to other jet aircraft – undoubtedly averted the loss of a valuable national resource."

In a 1987 write-up when Ted left the SR-71 program, it was noted he had had a total of 32 in-flight emergencies, "including an engine failure requiring landing at an unanticipated AFB, an engine fire that required landing in Norway and a rear cockpit overheat which melted gauges, the communications kit and a burnt lip from a water bottle/food probe."

"Jim Jiggens was the pilot on the mission where we had an emergency landing in Norway, March 6, 1987," Ted offers. "Our right engine caught fire and we had to land. We selected a combined military and civilian airport in Norway and made a safe touchdown." He chuckles, "The next day we were the headline in the Norwegian Press. We landed 30 minutes before the first scheduled landing of the Concorde in Norwegian airspace. The Concorde folks were a little miffed that their story was just a few inches long while we took a major part of the front page."

He chuckles, "Actually I knew a number of Concorde pilots and crew. We needled them and vice-versa. We called them slow-pokes... they chided us for having to use afterburners as we passed them. We said, 'Eat my dust.'"

He continues, "The burnt lip was a more serious problem. February 5, 1987 the rear cockpit air-conditioning failed at 80,000 feet. The temperature immediately surrounding me rose to 4-500 degrees. I sweated a lot of weight that day. When we landed, my boots were literally full of water – my perspiration."

In 1985 Ted was on temporary duty at Mildenhall, England some 65 miles northeast of London. Mildenhall and Kadena, Okinawa were the two primary bases handling SR-71 overseas operations.

"I was partnered with Major Bob Behler. We flew the only SR-71 flight during 1985 that was a prelude to Operation Eldorado Canyon, the F-111 bombing raid in Libya that was in response to terrorist activities supported by Muammar Qaddafi." They flew down the west coast of Spain and Portugal and took a left turn past Gibraltar flying almost the entire Mediterranean, made a loop heading southwest and entered Libya on its eastern border where it meets the sea. "Over Libya we had a hydraulics system failure and had to slow down while over their airspace. There were a few tense minutes." It was a long flight. "While some nations, such as France, denied overflight rights because of the potential of revenge terrorism, sometimes we just flew around them because we didn't want them to know where we were going. It all worked out."

He describes an incident at the Mildenhall, England Air Show, early March 1987. "Major Jim Jiggens and I were to make a low-level pass the length of the runway for the crowd's enjoyment." He shows me a color photo of the SR-71 at its ebb over the runway. "Jim wanted to impress the crowd. We were in level flight about 500 mph barely ten feet off the ground. Then Jim pulled hard on the stick to begin a steep climb." When they landed it was discovered a combination of speed and severe G-Forces caused the fuselage to separate. Ted laughs, "Jim was about ready to get out of the AF anyway, so he didn't get into too much trouble, but that SR was out of service for a lo-o-o-n-ng time."

Ted was on the only successful SR-71 joint flight activity with the Space Shuttle Challenger 41-G mission, for which he was commended by NASA. The mission objectives are still classified.

July 1987 he joined the B-1B long-range Bomber program working on various projects to optimize aircraft survival and mission accomplishment. From July 1990 to June 1992 he was assigned to Offutt AFB, Nebraska where he developed, coordinated, directed and integrated the implementation of offensive avionics subsystems for the B-2 Advanced Technology Bomber Program.

June 1992 to September 1996 he was reassigned to Beale managing the execution of all worldwide U-2 and SR-71 computerized mission planning. October 1996 until his AF retirement as Lt. Col., May 1998, he managed all U-2 and SR-71 operational issues and was technical consultant to all future high-altitude Unmanned Air Vehicle reconnaissance programs (UAV) and was the unit UAV project manager.

During his career he earned 22 medals and commendations, including four Air Medals, five Meritorious Service Medals, a Republic of Vietnam Gallantry Cross, and Expeditionary Medals for Saudi Arabia, Grenada and Lebanon. The wording on his award certificates and commendations matter-of-factly state his contributions, often while in harm's way, to our efforts for world peace. Connected, they describe a man who loves his wife, family, job and country. He logged close to 2,500 hours of flight time in nine different military aircraft, with almost 25 percent of it in the fastest plane ever built – the SR-71.

Following retirement he entered the private sector, holding key management and executive positions. After 9/11 the AF asked him to return to Beale in a critical U-2 program. (As a harbinger of things to come, he also coordinated activities for the future Global Hawk program.) He was responsible for the U-2 Extended Tether Program. It is a modular communications package mounted on the back of separate U-2's allowing them to link directly with ground stations outside their theater of operations rather than having to rely on first going through an in-theater station. It was and is a key component of Operation Enduring Freedom and Operation Iraqi Freedom. Beginning June 2003 he was the Northrop Grumman site manager for the Global Hawk program.

Ted and Barbara have two daughters – Heather, a Computer Information Systems grad of the University of Nevada-Reno; and Hillary, a University of Arizona grad in

Architecture. She is now Hillary Griegel, having married a fellow U of A architect graduate.

Barbara says, "While the girls were in college we visited them frequently. Ted serviced their cars, their computers and other Daddy fix-its. He is such an incredibly generous and thoughtful person... mowing Lake Wildwood neighbor lawns and helping them with chores, a member of our church Host Team and so much more." (Top Secret Clearance revelation – they are in love.)

Barbara managed the Wildwood Center for Bob Nix mid-1999 until November 2000. That same month she became the District Scholarship Coordinator for Nevada Joint Union High School District, which includes Nevada Union and Bear River schools. She is active in the community and on the board of directors of Penn Valley Rotary. At public gatherings where birthdays are celebrated she will occasionally offer a Marilyn Monroe impersonation singing "Happy Birthday" as Marilyn/Norma Jean Baker did for JFK. The recipient, of course, donates to the organization or charity. Some members of Rotary claim multiple birthdays a year. One member, born 40 years ago, is now 97.

Our nation and the world are safer because of Ted Ross and his efforts during his military and civilian career. As of mid-2011 Ted is the lead intelligence analyst at the office of infrastructure protection for the State of California Emergency Management Agency. He leads a team of prior and current military officers responsible for identifying, prioritizing and recommending protection security measures for key state resources. Dams and bridges are just two examples of assets under their purview.

Joe and Betty   Bob

Chapter 27: Joe Feld, Bob Katen – USN

Feld – "Every table had a body on it, some dead, some alive. All had been burned."

Katen – "The water was covered with a thick coating of ebony goo; in places the surface was on fire."

THE FIRST WEEK of December, 2001, Joe Feld and Bob Katen began a trip that would take them thousands of miles from Penn Valley CA's Lake Wildwood and sixty years into their past. With Joe was his wife, Betty. At Bob's side was his spouse, Lu.

Flying westward toward Hawaii late afternoon in December the sun sits low on the horizon. It seems to hover forever above the port side wing tip, jiggling like one of those bouncing balls that were part of movie theater sing-alongs so long ago. The miles and years fall away and the ball seems to jump in time to tunes young sailors hummed and whistled in 1941. As the plane banks and begins a descent to Honolulu International Airport the sun disappears from the wing tip and the music fades.

At 6:00 AM the morning of December 7, the Japanese battle group was assembling hundreds of miles north of Hawaii in an aerial armada of fighter planes, torpedo, dive and high-level bombers. Eventually 181 first wave attack aircraft were aloft and joined in formation. By 7:55 the attack had begun with the first bombs and bullets falling on Wheeler Field, and almost simultaneous assaults at Hickham Field, "Battleship Row" and Ford Island.

Seaman Bob Katen, from Petaluma, had joined the Navy February 1941, and was assigned to the *USS Hulbert* (DD-342). The ship, launched in 1918, was one year younger than Bob, and served as a seaplane tender. It was one of 145 American vessels in the waters of Oahu Dec.7.

At 7:58 the Hulbert sounded general quarters. Bob did not finish his breakfast. The ship was berthed at the submarine base near the southeast corner of Pearl Harbor. Less than a mile to the northwest, up a narrow channel, is "Battleship Row", and just beyond that, Ford Island. One tactic of the Japanese torpedo planes was to approach from the southeast, fly down the East Loch channel and fan out to attack the battleships. The preferred altitude of Japanese torpedo planes on final approach to their target was less than ten meters. A pilot knew he was too low if the spray from the released torpedo splashed the wing.

Almost immediately after the alarm the *Hulbert's* anti-aircraft batteries opened fire and shot down one torpedo bomber (one of the first American kills of the war) and damaged several others. Minutes later and in the distance more than a million pounds of gunpowder was ignited when an armor-piercing bomb sliced through the forward deck of the USS *Arizona*. 1,177 men perished. Parts of the *Arizona* flew a hundred yards into the air and were easily visible from the *Hulbert*.

Bob Katen was ordered to help ready the ship to get underway.

In 1939 at age seventeen Joe Feld joined the Navy in St. Louis. After bootcamp he was assigned to the USS *Enterprise* (CV-6). Joe and a few of his *Enterprise* shipmates had been assigned temporary duty to Ford Island. He had been scheduled to report back to the ship when it returned to Pearl from Wake Island December 6. The carrier, thankfully, was late.

At 7:30 a.m. December 7, Joe and some of his pals were returning to their Ford Island barracks from a short liberty in Honolulu. Less than a half-hour later he was on the floor, with bullets overhead shattering windows and shredding the barracks walls. A liberty buddy wisecracked, "I'm glad we went to Honolulu last night 'cause the party's over now!" The planes kept coming, one after another. "Meatballs, they got meatballs on their wings," shouted a sailor near one of the windows.

After a while the first wave receded.

Joe Feld was issued a rifle, five bullets and told he would help recover sailors from the waters near the *Arizona*.

From Joe's memoirs, dedicated to his grandson, we read, "Someone had managed to secure a lot of blankets and we were assigned, four men to a blanket, to bring up injured or dead men from the burning battleships. The water from around these ships was ablaze from the oil that had been spewed out. This was by far the toughest job I ever did in my whole life. I think we made about four trips back and forth to the mess hall. Every table had a body on it, some dead, some alive. All had been burned."

At 8:50 the second wave of 167 planes – 54 high-altitude bombers, 78 dive-bombers and 35 fighters – began their assault. It lasted until almost 10:00.

Elated Japanese flyers pushed for a third assault. Their leaders opted not to pursue another attack, including as a reason that they did not know the location of the United States aircraft carriers.

On board the *Hulbert*, preparing the ship for departure continued while boats were simultaneously launched to also help recover personnel from the "Battleship Row" area. Bob Katen was reassigned to one of the rescue boats headed to the devastation.

Said Bob, "The water was covered with a thick coating of ebony goo, and in places the surface was on fire." Each man went about the task of the recovery of comrades – alive or dead.

The death toll ultimately reached 2,403. It would likely have been more without the efforts of Joe and Bob. Twenty-one ships of the United States Pacific Fleet were damaged or sunk. 347 aircraft were damaged or destroyed. Only twenty-nine Japanese planes failed to return.

Days after the attack military personnel were allowed to send a postcard home to let their loved ones know their status. The card, provided by the government, would arrive without a postmark. The sender had to choose from three preprinted options and line through the two that did not apply, "I am well, I am sick, I have been admitted to the hospital." Joe still has the one he sent. He was "well". Bob sent the identical message.

After Pearl Harbor the *USS Hulbert* made supply runs to Palmyra, then sailed north to the often stormy Bering Sea. The Japanese had occupied U.S. territory in the Aleutians -- Attu and Kisa -- as a part of the Midway Offensive. The *Hulbert* was assigned to tend seaplanes during recon and bombing raids on those islands. Late in 1942 Bob Katen was assigned a new job with Fighter Squadron VC20. In late November 1943, he landed with the second wave of Marines on Tarawa. By the end of the battle 990 Marines had been killed and another 2,296 wounded. Among the casualties were 76 sailors, corpsmen and doctors assigned to the Marines. The Japanese losses numbered 4,690.

His job on Tarawa was to help set up facilities for the F6F Hellcats and TBF Avengers that would be using the airfield. After Tarawa was under U.S. control Bob and a buddy were working side-by-side on an aircraft engine near the runway. His friend was killed by a sniper's bullet.

Early January 1942, Joe Feld was back with the *USS Enterprise*, and a part of the crew until late 1943. He did not know, of course, that he would be serving on the most decorated ship of the Second World War during many of its most memorable moments.

"In 1942 alone, the *Enterprise* was hit six times by Japanese bombs, and more than 300 of our crew were wounded or killed." Says Joe, "I served at the battle of Midway, Santa Cruz, Guadalcanal and a host of other engagements. They were harrowing times." He was on board October 26, 1942 when the *Enterprise* became the last operational US carrier in the Pacific. During 1942 the other carriers, *Yorktown*, *Lexington*, *Wasp*, *Saratoga* and *Hornet* were sunk or sidelined. Not until the repaired *Saratoga* arrived at Noumea December 5, 1942, would the *Enterprise* see another American carrier.

The *USS Enterprise* earned ten of its twenty Battle Stars while Joe was on board.

One example of the danger happened during the Guadalcanal assault. Bob and the Chief Metal smith were on the hanger deck. A bomb glanced off the arm of Chief Melsted on its way down to the third deck where it exploded. Bob states in his memoirs, "I imagine it missed me by about three or four feet. In all the confusion during this attack I don't know what happened to Melsted. I don't remember ever seeing him again. The concussion was so great that the hangar deck started to bow. It was a very eerie feeling to be lying on this heavy steel deck and feel it bowing."

In 1943 Bob Katen met Lu in Susanville, California, while on leave. They married in 1944. Joe Feld met Betty following his transfer to Alameda in 1944. They also married that year.

Dec. 2001, Joe Feld sat resting outside the *USS Arizona* Memorial Visitor Center. Nearby, oil still seeps drop by drop from the *Arizona's* hull. It is the same vintage that he and Bob encountered when they helped recover their comrades so many years before. Joe was wearing a ball cap that identified him as an *Enterprise* crewman. First one, then another teen approached him. They were respectful and solemn. They asked him for his autograph, and thanked him for his service to our country and his signature. He isn't exactly sure, but thinks he signed some twenty-five times.

At another venue Bob Katen, in his *USS Hulbert* cap, was stopped by a young couple he did not know. They asked if he would do them a big favor – they presented him with a sheet of paper with twenty or so questions and a stamped envelope. They requested he mail it at his convenience to their home on the mainland. The questions sought information about his military experiences and career. They thanked him for his service and contribution to America. Bob completed and mailed it to them just before Christmas

The list of official events for the 60th anniversary ceremonies at and near Pearl Harbor is three pages long. December 7, 2001, former First Class Petty Officer Joe Feld and Betty, and retired Chief Petty Officer Bob Katen and Lu attended the Pearl Harbor Survivors Association Ceremony at the National Cemetery of the Pacific – solemn Punchbowl.

The ceremony lasted ninety minutes in serene, peaceful, somber surroundings. Those who died were remembered and honored. And those in the audience – including Joe, Bob and other veterans who had participated in the chaos, violence and horror of sixty years before – were recognized and venerated for their contributions, their bravery and their sacrifices.

Back home they were asked about the inevitable comparisons to Sept. 11. "Vigilance...as a nation... a people. We need to be very vigilant," Joe stated firmly, yet softly, "so there is never another December 7... another September 11."

Bob nodded in agreement.

Beth and Dick

Chapter 28: Dick Landis – AAF

"Dick celebrated the end of hostility by doing a low level snap roll in his P-51 over Frankfurt airport. For the next ten days he could only watch others fly."

IN APRIL 1920 the wind had not yet started its rampage across the midwestern states; the term "dust bowl" had not yet been coined. From the distant western shores the clouds still brought the rain that nourished the crops. The air was fresh and clean and clear the day Dick Landis was born, the grandson of one of the earliest settlers in this part of Oklahoma – Davenport.

Dick was still a toddler when his folks moved a few miles down the road to Bristow, near the heart of the state between Tulsa and Oklahoma City. It was an agricultural area well suited for growing cotton, and in the 1920's it participated in the oil boom.

Dick's father was a successful business owner. But in 1929 he saw the potential for a better life in California.

Dick writes, "We were middle-class Oklahomans. Unlike Steinbeck's hardscrabble Joads, our family was not traveling to California in a ramshackle truck, but in a new 1929 Model 'A' touring car. Dad, Mom and baby Jack were in front. In the back were three older boys: John Jr., 12; myself, 9; and Georgie, 6."

Listening to Dick describe the two-week adventure, one starts mind-humming the Bobby Troupe classic, *Route 66*, as that is the road they traveled from Bristow to its western terminus in Southern California, then north up the Central Valley to Marysville. It was a grand and happy adventure, and John Landis, Sr., was right – it did lead to a better life for the family.

Dick's dad had operated a beauty shop and barbershop in Oklahoma, and he stayed with his winning formula, running the Landis Barber and Beauty shop in the downtown center of Marysville. Writes Dick in a wonderful book, *Making a Difference,* co-authored by he and wife Beth, he writes, "While Dad forged ahead providing for his family Mom was the anchor. She insisted on regular church attendance (even when we lived in Yuba City and the church was in Live Oak, ten miles away). She and my father were good partners."

At age 13, Dick started his first paying job, a paper route with 150 subscribers. By 15, he made money picking prunes and also started working at the Calpak plant during free time and summer vacations. He progressed from 37 cents an hour to more than $100 a week when he became the plant's youngest foreman at age 17. Also at age 15 he landed a job selling men's suits and shoes at Penney's and still found time to excel in his studies and high school sports – baseball and basketball. Dick writes, "My work during high school allowed me to save about $3,000, which I wanted to use to help with college expenses. I didn't want to ask my parents for too much assistance as there were six of us who wanted to pursue higher education." The writing continues, "Our parents miraculously put six children (Bill and Beverley were born in CA) in college, and all of us would have graduated had George not entered the Army Air Corps and Jack dropped out to get married and go to work." All the other children graduated from university.

His senior year Dick was elected high school student-body president as well as president of the Church of the Brethren's Young People of Northern California, a large youth group representing communities from Bakersfield to Shasta.

Dick applied to the College of La Verne, in Southern California near Pomona, and was awarded a scholarship for the fall, 1938 semester. Members of the Church of the Brethren founded the college in 1891. (Eventually the Board of Trustees became independent of church control, and it reorganized as the University of La Verne. Today it is one of the most highly respected small universities in America, offering bachelors and masters degrees as well as four doctorates within its six schools and colleges. Almost 50 percent of its nearly 5,000 full-time-equivalent students are pursuing graduate, doctoral and/or law degrees.)

Dick worked a variety of jobs on and near the campus. His grades were decent and he played football for the La

Verne Leopards – fullback on offense and end on defense. A knee injury in Fresno's Raisin Bowl ended not only his football career, but basketball and baseball as well.

Beth (nee Throne) Landis writes, "I enrolled at the College of La Verne in fall 1941. The second day of school there was a big campus gathering... One student, a tall, dark-haired, handsome senior, sang in a deep voice in a vocal quartet... It was love at first sight.. I was hooked." A mutual friend introduced them later that evening, and eventually Dick asked her for a date. She didn't accept until the third request. By late fall 1941 there was a budding courtship.

December 7, 1941 Dick and Beth were running an errand in his Plymouth auto. He writes, "We turned the car radio on. That's when we heard the announcement... I was 21, and Beth 18. I made up my mind almost immediately that I would enter the military as soon as I graduated that coming spring. I was so close to graduation I wanted to finish my degree. I knew the war would carry on for years, and I would be in it."

That was not a popular position with many at the college. Along with the Quakers and Mennonites, the Church of the Brethren considers war an unacceptable option for Christians. Their young people are encouraged to perform alternate service rather than take up arms.

Dick states, "Most of my peers on campus declared as conscientious objectors or entered a non-combat role such as medic. I listened to their positions about not fighting, but my mind was made up." He reflects back more than six decades, and there is silence for a moment. "Late January, 1942, the president of the college, a mentor to me, tried to dissuade me from joining the military. I had to tell him I had joined the Navy as an aviation cadet earlier that month. This war, in my opinion, was a fight to the death... a fight between good and evil, and I had no choice. He, like my classmates, said he respected my decision. We all agreed to disagree and continued to hold one another in high esteem."

In his book, Dick writes, "I'd grown up around crop dusters in California and shared my generation's rapture with aviation, triggered by Lindbergh's transatlantic solo flight. I entertained no other scenario for my military service than being a fighter pilot. I wanted to be in a one-seater fighter, responsible only for myself... I wanted to depend solely upon myself as master of my destiny."

A month after joining the Navy, he walked by an Army Air Corps recruiting station in Pomona. Out of curiosity he went inside. The sergeant asked if he were considering joining the service. Dick told him he had already joined the Naval air force.

The book picks up the dialogue: "You don't want to do that!"

"I asked why."

"Most of the flights run off carrier decks. I don't think anyone in his right mind would want to fly off a carrier deck as a matter of choice. If I were you, I would take a 5,000-foot runway anytime in my life, or even a shorter one than that if necessary, because you know you're going to land on it. Even if you don't make the end of the runway, you'll hit dry land. And in my judgment, the Army Air Corps has the best aircraft in the world."

In the book the discussion continues until Dick asks the recruiter the softball question about what he can do about his already having enlisted in the Navy. The sergeant reassured him he could take care of everything including an extension for a few months while he finished school.

As Dick writes, "I decided to jump ship right then and there."

May 2, 1942 he also decided to jump the ship of bachelorhood by proposing to Beth on her 19th birthday. She accepted. After graduation he went home awaiting orders, and returned to work as a general foreman for Calpak. He was ordered to report to active duty October 1942.

"My being called up to military duty was an emotional time for my parents. I was the third of what would be four males in our family to enter the service during WWII. My older brother, John, already a college graduate, married man and father of two, was serving in the South Pacific as a naval officer on a destroyer. George had dropped out of La Verne and was a tail-gunner in a B-17 in the European Theater. My Uncle Vernie, dad's half-brother living with my parents in Marysville, would enlist after me – becoming a Seabee, building landing strips and other structures for our invading forces in the South Pacific... My parents' home was the only one in Marysville with a four-star flag (designating four men from the household serving) flying in the window."

He reported to San Francisco, then Washington State College in Pullman for four months of classroom education and flight theory. From there he went to eight weeks of boot camp in Santa Ana.

By July 1943, Dick was learning to fly a Stearman in Dos Palos, California.

Dick writes, "I was allowed to solo after about six hours... My first solo flight was absolutely exhilarating." It was while he was in Dos Palos learning to fly Stearmans that he went down a different type of runway and had another exhilarating experience. Beth and Dick were married November 6, 1943 in Visalia – 105 miles southeast of Dos Palos. His commanding officer was less than enthusiastic about the marriage. "We're through here Friday at 1700. You're due back, as everyone is, Sunday at 1600 hours. And you be here on time."

Dick's advanced flight training was in P-39's and P-63's in Williams, AZ. Of 200 cadets who had started out together in San Francisco, Dick was one of 65 who had completed advanced flight training. Dick requested and received orders to become a P-38 fighter pilot. The training base was in Chico, less than 50 miles from Marysville.

While training, Dick Landis could fly his P-38 from his Chico base any time he wanted, day or night. He would fly from Chico to Los Angeles and back at 1500 feet. He writes, "I flew all over California at 500 feet. I scared more duck-blind hunters in the Sacramento Valley than I could count."

The writing continues, "One Sunday morning I led a training mission of eight planes. We flew down to Yosemite and back through the central valley to base. Our state looked just beautiful below us... I zoomed in and out of the cotton mattress-like banks, testing stalling speeds, feeling like I was on top of the world. Everything was hush; even the plane engines grow quiet above the heavenly clouds at

30,000 feet. The sensation was like touching the face of God. It was as close as a human being could ever come to a feeling of infinity, and the Earth, and one's relationship to a superpower. I felt at peace with everything."

He successfully completed P-38 training. He writes, "As the time drew nearer for me to be sent overseas, I did not grow nervous... I was the opposite of fatalistic. I felt better prepared than any pilot I knew. I left for Europe on November 8, 1944."

Beth writes, "I never entertained any qualms but that my husband would be coming home. I can't explain it. I just knew he would. Shortly before Dick left for overseas service, I became pregnant."

Dick was a replacement pilot for those who had finished their tour of duty or been brought down. He was assigned to the 9th Air Force, 71st Fighter Wing, 370th Fighter Group, 402nd Fighter Squadron based near Southampton in S.E. England. "Our planes were twin-engine P-38 J and L Lightning models, the very latest available. They could do 420 mph at 26,500 feet and had a range of nearly 2,300 miles. The luftwaffe called them 'Fork-Tailed Devils', and we did nothing to dispel that designation." He points to his squadron insignia, a red circle with a blue shield. Superimposed is a bright yellow P-38 coming at the viewer from one-o'clock. Where the cockpit should be, there is an angry yellow skull wearing a top hat. Its mouth is spewing lightning bolts. It is an attention getter. The insignia alone makes one want to surrender.

He writes, "About a week after I arrived at the airbase I was ready for combat. I'd gotten aligned with the 'flight' –

the 12 planes – within the squadron I was assigned to. My
first few missions were demolition-and-destruction raids...
We'd fly at 6,000 - 7,000 feet, heading for a quick drop
right across the Rhine River in Germany. As we got closer
on our two- to two-and-a half hour flight to the target, we'd
begin to encounter flak from the ground."

After a few missions Dick was assigned wingman to the
flight commander and usually flew to his right side. The P-
38 had four 50-caliber machine-guns, a 20-mm cannon and
typically carried two 500-lb. bombs.

He describes a bomb run early in his combat experience:

"The commander would say over the radio to us, 'I'll go
in first. Dick, you follow me second...' and he'd name the
order of planes. 'I'll take the train,' he'd say. 'I'll take the
forward building,' I'd say, and so on. He'd peel off and dive.
I'd be 3-4 seconds behind him, feeling the acceleration from
350 to 450 mph as I descended at an angle. He'd drop his
bomb at 300 feet or so then peel off and away. I'd drop my
bomb a little bit later, then turn in the opposite direction of
the flight leader. I'd hear the explosion, and if I scored a direct hit on a big target I'd see the flash of building parts flying in the air. Sometimes I'd feel a shock wave.

"...Our squadron would re-form overhead at a location
radioed by the flight leader away from the target. Then we'd
make another pass at it, strafing the whole area... Finally,
we'd go after the antiaircraft batteries on the periphery of
the target. If I managed to destroy a target such as an ammunition dump, I'd feel as if I'd made a giant step forward
in shortening the war."

After a tour of duty a pilot was eligible to go home. Dick served two-and-a-half tours with his squadron. He is asked about why he stayed. "My mission was to fly. I knew I was making a contribution toward getting the war over. I knew I was making a positive difference. I had to keep going." His voice is soft yet resolute.

"Besides," he says with a grin, "I had great self confidence. I'd trained hard to be the best that I could be. And, I'd say a prayer. It helped me focus on having a successful mission and getting safely back to base." He describes the small bible his mother had given him just before leaving for active duty. He carried it throughout the war.

He was flight leader (four planes within a squadron) or squadron leader (12 planes) for 60-70 percent of his 45 missions. Because he'd worked at Calpak, famous for peaches, he got the nickname "Peaches" – a nickname that stayed in Europe (and must remain there, according to Dick).

He says, "I was only based in England for about three weeks before my squadron relocated to France. After I'd flown some 27 missions, our squadron switched to P-51's. My last 18 missions were in P-51D's. I had six 50-caliber machine-guns and could pack 2,000 pounds of bombs. So, between the P-38 and P-51, I had the opportunity to fly two of the greatest piston-driven fighter planes the world has known."

He talks about never having a mechanical problem that was not enemy induced. "My ground crew chief and his team did such a fantastic job keeping me in the air. They were with me on every flight, and I let them know that.

"We were family, and I literally trusted the ground crew with my life, and they never let me down. My triumphs in the air were their triumphs, too, and I can't say enough about them.

"In December 1944," Dick writes, "the Germans rallied one more time and tried to break through the American and British lines in France to slow the Allies' advance and buy time for another military buildup. This offensive became known as the Battle of the Bulge and was the largest land battle of the war involving U.S. troops. More than one million men fought in it from both sides." Dick's longest day of combat came the day before the Battle of the Bulge ended.

He writes, "As soon as the clouds lifted and the sun shone over Bastogne, revealing the German army surrounding the city, our squadrons began attacking nonstop." Their airbase was only 8-10 miles away. He talks about the action. "We started at dawn. For this day, I was a flight leader – my plane and three others – a third of the squadron. We took off with bombs and ammo, looking for targets of opportunity. We knew if we couldn't stop the Germans we'd not be able to land at our base – they would have it. All in my flight kept a sharp eye out for enemy targets... convoys, tanks, encampments, artillery... anything we could effectively go after. We'd spot something and I'd assign the targets, then head in first and drop bombs or strafe, and we'd form up, and go in again. The Germans were trying to engage our Ninth and Third Armies, but we helped ensure that they were forced to keep their heads down." He pauses for a moment as he reflects back on that day, then verbally takes wing again. "You can't have different flights of four planes from one squadron, let alone different flights from different squadrons, all trying to land at the same time and put a refueling and rearming burden on the ground crews. Plus, if something was a little screwy with the plane, it had to be fixed quickly. It was pretty frenetic that day."

He continues, "My flight team had five missions from day's dawn to day's dusk. We did a good job. We had made a difference... I had made a difference. We helped break the back of our enemy... we helped end the war in Europe."

Dick had close calls on three different flights from flak hits during his 45 missions. His plane was in jeopardy from loss of fluids and/or other problems. "Again, I had confidence in my skill as a pilot and knew if I had to crash land I could bring it down safely if given half a chance. Again, a prayer was helpful." He gives the Clift Notes version: "I know I'm capable of getting back safely, just help me find a safe place if I need it." In each of the three cases of serious damage he landed safely at military or small civilian airfields. Once the engine froze solid, seconds before he touched down. "I had holes in my planes many times," he adds, "it came with the territory."

Germany surrendered May 8, 1945. Dick Landis would fly no more combat missions. The first baby was born a few months later. He was in Frankfurt. His father-in-law sent the following cablegram: "With respect to your new child born July 24, mother fine, baby fine. Features hers, fixture's yours." A bit later his father sent him five boxes of fine Cuban cigars.

Dick Landis earned an air medal with four oak leaf clusters and a number of battle ribbons. In early August the war in the Pacific also ended. Dick celebrated the end of hostility by doing a low-level complete snap-roll in his P-51 over the Frankfurt airport. For the next ten days he could only watch others fly... he was temporarily grounded.

He sailed home from England October 1945 on the *Queen Elizabeth* and served another six months at Camp Beale (now Beale AFB) helping discharge returning airmen. When he left for Europe, Calpak had told him they would credit his military service as time worked, and they did. They had also guaranteed him a return job. Calpak subsequently changed its name to Del Monte, the preeminent leader in the food distribution industry.

Dick Landis eventually became chairman and CEO of Del Monte. When it was acquired by R.J. Reynolds Industries he became President of the Western U.S. and Pacific Rim region. "The lessons I learned in the military served me well in civilian life."

Upon his corporate retirement he served as Chancellor of the University of La Verne and helped position it for 21st century success. He and Beth continue to be Trustees Emeritus of the university. The Venna and John W. Landis, Sr., Scholarship (honoring his parents) established by Dick and Beth in 1983 has provided 1,048 scholarships. Presently the scholarship is valued at almost $10,000 annually for every current recipient. All proceeds from the sale of their book, *Making a Difference*, benefit deserving young men and women.

Dick's brothers and uncle returned home safely from their WWII service. Gary, the son with the right features and fixtures described in the cablegram, was the first of three. Dennis followed, with daughter Kay four years later. Dick and Beth have lived in Penn Valley, CA's Lake Wildwood since 1996. They continue to make a difference to those they touch... as *PATRIOTS* are wont to do.

'George' and Nancy

Chapter 29: Richard J. ("George") Washington – USN

"We were told to abandon ship.
We were dead in the water."

MARCH OF 1940, on his seventeenth birthday, Richard Joseph "George" Washington enlisted in the Navy with his parent's permission. "No one knows me as Richard… I've always been called by my nickname, George." As a lad in Spencer, Iowa he was a long way from the ocean, but a magazine ad with the young, proud sailor standing at the bow of a ship at sea helped inspire him to join.

He was called to duty January 1941 and after boot camp was assigned to the carrier *Lexington* based at Pearl Harbor.

Friday, December 5, 1941 he received reassignment orders to the *USS Pope*, an old four-stack destroyer stationed near Shanghai, China. That day the *Lexington* sailed out of Pearl, with George on temporary shore duty until he could hitch a ride on a ship to China.

Two days later he and a buddy finished breakfast and were strolling near the area where the battleship *Pennsylvania* was in dry dock across from battleship row. George heard, then saw, the planes screaming down the East Loch channel toward them and the vulnerable battleships and remarked on how many there were. "Those aren't ours!" his pal shouted. They started to run for shelter as the bullets flew. George made it to safety. His friend was killed.

As the first wave of attack planes subsided George joined a band of rescuers aboard a 50-foot motor launch to pull battleship row survivors (and non-survivors) from the water. They worked feverishly for an hour or so until 10 a.m., the start of the second wave of attacks. "I was cotton picking scared...oh, was I scared."

At eight or nine that evening they stopped their rescue effort. "We had canned beans and some kind of meat, and then an officer asked if any of us knew how to shoot a rifle?"

"Yes, me." Twenty or so of us were given rifles, bandoleers, shovels and WWI type helmets and transported to the North side of Oahu. We were told to dig in on the beach and repel any invaders that might try to land. The area is now a surfer paradise – the Banzai Pipeline. "I was too frightened to sleep that night, but at least I was alive."

His orders to join the USS Pope were changed. His skills as a "hot shell man" would be needed on the Lexington. Simply, his job was to catch hot shell casings, each a potential careening cylindrical pinball, when they were ejected from his 5.38-inch gun. A missed catch could prove disastrous to the other six men on the gun crew. When the ship sailed back into Pearl December 13, he rejoined his old team on starboard aft gun number seven.

Mid-February, 1942, the *Lexington* was headed toward Rabaul, New Britain. The *Lexington* came under fire by several waves of Japanese attack planes. Seventeen of the enemy aircraft were destroyed either by the carrier's planes or anti-aircraft fire. "I saw these dark dots coming at me as I looked down the gun barrel," George recalls. "It didn't click that they were incoming tracers. I could see the two pilots in the cockpit... and the guy in the nose shooting at us. One of the 1.1 guns on the flight deck got them in the left engine. The bomber veered into the sea about 75 feet from our gun." He was in the middle of the battle of Lae. During that attack *Lexington* Pilot "Butch" O'Hare won the Medal of Honor by destroying five enemy planes.

The *Lexington* spent more than a month on other missions in the Western Pacific before returning to Pearl Harbor, refitting and heading out again. May 7, contact was made with an enemy carrier task force. Planes from the *Lexington* sank the carrier *Shoho*. Later that day planes from the *Lexington* and *Yorktown* shot down nine planes from the Japanese carriers *Zuikoku* and *Shokaku*.

May 8, a recon plane from the *Lexington* spotted the *Shokaku* and her escorts. The Japanese carrier was heavily damaged during a subsequent strike. The battle of the Coral Sea was well underway. At 11:20 A.M. the enemy struck back and a torpedo hit the *Lexington* on the port side. Within seconds, dive-bombers had scored three bomb hits along with another torpedo mid-ship. Fires were raging and the ship was listing seven degrees to port. By 1:00 P.M. the fires were under control and the ship was back to level. She was ready to recover the planes aloft, when there was a huge explosion caused by fuel vapors below deck.

"The whole time I was so scared... so tight... waiting for another bomb or torpedo. And then I'd have another hot shell to catch and I'd forget how afraid I was."

About 5 P.M. Capt. Frederick Sherman gave the order to abandon ship. The crew began an orderly descent to the water below, to be picked up by nearby destroyers and cruisers. The gun crews were ordered to stay on board; their job to protect the ship and those in the water in case of subsequent attack.

"We had our own torpedoes on board close to where we were. They were heating up from the fires. We moved to the port side guns in case the torpedoes exploded." George pauses while he remembers. "The port side guns weren't working."

"We were then told to abandon ship. We were dead in the water. When we got into the water the wave action kept us from swimming away from the ship. We had no life jackets, no boats or rafts."

"We were ordered to climb up a rope ladder to an area just below the flight deck. There was no one left except us gunners, Captain Sherman, his Marine escort, his cocker spaniel, 'Admiral Wags', and the Chief Warrant Boatswain." The Bosun took an ax to the lock on the PX door. George remembers him saying, "Let's have some ice cream." There, afloat on the Coral Sea on a dying carrier, a small cadre of American fighting men, including the ship's Captain, shared vanilla, strawberry and chocolate ice cream.

Again, George and his comrades abandoned ship. After some 25-30 minutes they found a balsa life raft with a net bottom. An hour later, and 1,000 feet from the ship, it began to blow. The destroyer *Phelps* fired two torpedoes into her hull and she sank a little before 8:00 P.M. By the end of the day 216 of the *Lexington's* crew had perished.

The destroyer *Dewey* had rescued George and his comrades. An hour later the *Dewey* was dead in the water with a fire raging in the engine room. The order was given to get ready to abandon ship. "Again?" George wondered aloud. The fire was extinguished, the engine restarted and they arrived in New Caledonia the next day.

By June 1942, George was back in the states where he was assigned to the *USS Altama*, a Jeep Carrier - or baby flat top - that carried twelve aircraft. George went back to the New Caledonia/New Hebrides area.

By the end of 1943 George returned to the states and stayed there until hostilities ended. He had decided to make the military his career. After the war he signed up for demolition and dive school, an intense yearlong program. After graduation in 1948 he was assigned to the *USS Partridge*, a wooden hulled auxiliary mine sweeper. His new job was a dangerous one -- dive to 20-30 feet in the inland strait waters of Japan to cut mine cables and/or deactivate mines that might get hung up in the mine sweeper mechanism. "My deepest dive is about 180 feet," he says matter-of-factly.

During the Korean War George was assigned to the *USS Bayonne* as the shipboard dive and demolition man. Jan 5, 1951 some 1500 miles east of Yokosuka, Japan the ship was straining against the remnants of a typhoon and 60-70 foot waves. Boatswain's Mate 1st Class R.J. "George" Washington was topside with one of his peers checking items in need of repair. The two of them had opted not to wear life jackets, as they were difficult to get to in the storm. George had a clipboard in hand, back to the wind and spray, near the bow. "Duck, it's a big one," his pal Nick shouted. George was thrown to the deck and skidded aft. A second wave finished the job and he sailed over the side, doubling up into a ball during the fall to cushion his landing.

"I screamed, 'man overboard!' The wind was howling. The ship passed and then turned toward me. I could see the lookouts on the stern but they were watching something on the other side of the ship. I pulled off my boots, undid my belt and struggled out of my foul weather jacket. I rolled it into a ball, draped myself over it, and started to kick and yell."

"I did not know Captain Clark had seen me go over. I saw the ship each time I came to the top of one of those 60-foot swells. I was in the water more than a half hour."

George continues, his voice softer. "I did not think I could be rescued. Then, a sailor in a life jacket with a rope tied to him splashed into the water nearby. He grabbed me, and I grabbed him." The ship was now dead in the water, rolling from side to side. A cargo net was lowered over the side and several shipmates climbed down with a stretcher. George was too weak to climb the net. Halfway up, and in the stretcher, the ship rolled violently and George was dumped. Again, he was loaded onto the stretcher and again, this time closer to the top, was ejected into the sea. The third try, a lieutenant clad only in polka-dotted shorts came over the side and helped guide the stretcher to the deck.

George's only injury, other than barnacle scrapes from the side of the ship, was a broken finger received when a rescuer stepped on his hand while unloading him from the stretcher.

George eventually retired from the navy. He had a home built along the shore of Lake Wildwood, in Penn Valley in the mid-seventies, where he lives with his wife, Nancy.

"George" in WWII

Dick and Shirley

Chapter 30: Dick Mallman - Army

"As we watched we could see parachutes catching fire and dropping like moths around a flame."

DICK MALLMAN was born in Bakersfield, CA in 1921. His Dad was an engineer and worked with the Army Corps of Engineers building dams north and south of the Tehachapi's. "We moved to Alhambra when I was about three and that's where I was raised." He graduated at age 16 from Alhambra HS, at the time one of the largest in California. "I played 'B' team basketball and football. It wasn't JV and it wasn't varsity – it was an intermediate level for mega-size schools."

He attended Pasadena Junior College and signed up for their boxing program. "I went there for three semesters and really took to boxing. I was a 5'11" welterweight (140-147 pounds) at the bottom end of the weight range. Then I transferred to San Francisco Junior college, which had no boxing program. I boxed the San Francisco Golden Gloves tournament in 1939, then joined the Olympic Club stable as a welterweight. They had a great sports program." (San Francisco's Olympic Club has also been the site of four U.S. Open Golf Tournaments – 1955, '66, '87 and '98.) "We boxed against San Jose State, University California Berkeley, the Athens Club based in Oakland and other organizations with significant fighting programs." His boxing-pose 8 x 10 photo hung in the lobby of the Olympic Club for years. Of his thirty fights he won twenty-eight.

Dick moved back to the south state in 1940. "I was playing a DeMolay football game December 7, 1941 in Alhambra. At half-time the announcer told us about Pearl Harbor. Six or seven of us decided to go down and enlist the next day. I tried to join the Marines and they said there was something wrong with my right eye. The Army Air Force turned me down for the same reason. I didn't want the Navy. The Army took me. My pals also joined a service that same day – the one of their choice. DeMolay was a committed group. I was proud of myself and my buddies the day after Pearl Harbor." DeMolay, sponsored by the Masons, is a top-notch youth organization dedicated to helping young men be better people and leaders. It is still going strong.

"I wasn't called up until March 2, 1942. I reported to Fort MacArthur then went to Camp Roberts, near Paso Robles." Dick is silent for a few seconds. "I guess I wasn't cut out to be a soldier, take the discipline and follow orders. I volunteered because I wanted to fight the enemy and knock them out."

As a preview of the main event overseas, Dick was willing to fight anyone who got in his way or upset him. He describes an incident at the induction reception center. "I asked a fellow soldier to pass me a piece of pie. He already had a piece, but he flicked the one I had asked for on his dish, laughed and passed me the empty plate. I stood up and knocked him off his bench. I had KP for the next week." He laughs then pauses, "I was busted three or four times." His wartime rank graph is a decent model for a junior roller coaster — up a rank, down a rank, up a rank, up a rank, down a rank...

At Camp Roberts Dick was trained as a message center chief. He received additional communications-related training and duty assignments at a number of other California bases and Camp Rucker, Alabama. October 1943 he was assigned to Camp Crowder, Missouri. (Fifty years after the war Dick wrote an autobiographical novelette with a soldier named Rick McGuire as the hero, a young man from Alhambra and a former Olympic Club welterweight. The story starts with his assignment to Camp Crowder. Says Dick, "The characters were actual people, but I changed the names to protect their privacy and that of their families. While my privacy doesn't need protecting, I kind of liked the name Rick McGuire, so I used it for myself. The people and events described are from my wartime diary and as factual as I could make it." (While never published it's a good read. Dick loaned me his only copy, and if you promise to take good care of it, he might loan it to you.)

Here's how it starts: "We all assembled at Camp Crowder, a cadre of men from many different military groups around the country... I, along with about 20 other soldiers from Camp Rucker's 35th Division had been chosen as a part of this new unit. We were there to form a special Army organization — the 592nd Joint Assault Signal Company, JASCO, patterned after the same type of organization the Marines had successfully used in the Pacific. The responsibility of a JASCO unit was to ensure there would be real-time accurate communications from the beach among all involved groups of any combined operation — Army, Navy, Marines and AAF."

Back to the real world, just prior to reporting to Camp Crowder he had fought an inter-unit match against a professional heavyweight boxer from New York. Says Dick, "I was still a welterweight. This guy was my height, 5'11", but about 40 pounds heavier." Quoting from Dick's novelette, "The word got around I had done some boxing. And his unit and mine wanted to set up a bout. I had little worry because this guy really wasn't any bigger than me, he just weighed more. He was also a real boozehound, getting soused every night and showing up at morning roll call with a hangover, so I accepted the challenge. We were using 14-ounce gloves. He was really confident and who could blame him? He was a legitimate professional heavyweight meeting an amateur welterweight so he didn't train at all except on PX beer while I was very religious in my training and in excellent shape.

"Right from the opening bell I set a fast pace, peppering him with left jabs, an occasional left hook and once in a while a right cross just to keep him off balance. By the end of the first round he was furious. I worked in and out on him and had him chasing me all over the ring, really tiring himself out. To my knowledge he hadn't laid a glove on me."

The second round Dick could hit his opponent at will and opened a cut over his eye. "The third round was a copy of the second and his face became a bloody mess. With about 30 seconds left in the round, the referee stepped in and I was the winner by a TKO. What an uproar. Since there had been a lot of betting between my signal company and his recon troop, and since the recon man, a sergeant, was the pro and a heavyweight, they had to give odds and lost pretty heavily.

"So they were screaming for a rematch, and every morning when we turned out for reveille, if I looked across the parade ground I could see my opponent doing road work getting in shape for a rematch. I was not a complete idiot so I dodged that guy all the rest of the time I was in Camp Rucker. He never did get his rematch as I was reassigned to Camp Crowder."

The newly formed 592nd Joint Assault Signal Company (JASCO) that Corporal Dick Mallman was assigned to October 1943 was relentless in its training program. Says Dick, "We were to furnish communications for amphibious landings along the beachheads. We had ten combat teams. Each had several key sections -- message center, radio and telephone with a switchboard. We also had other sections, including naval, air force, artillery and a group of army scouts whose duty was to move forward with the infantry. They carried 'walkie-talkie' radios and would contact the Beachmaster with any problems that might hinder forward pro-gress." As an example, Dick cites using post-attack air strikes.

"Sometimes there was a choice. It was up to us to rec-ommend appropriate air power – army planes if they had been put ashore on a captured airfield or navy planes from a nearby carrier if available. Or we might use our naval signal section to call shipboard gunfire on an enemy strongpoint or use army artillery if it had been put ashore. In short, my JASCO team was designed to expedite all types of commu-nications and assistance that might be needed for a success-ful amphibious landing and assault during the early stages of a battle."

The 592nd saw a number of stateside postings and on D-Day in Europe, June 6, 1944, Dick's unit embarked for Hawaii.

"We reached Honolulu on June 16 and made our way to Schofield Barracks in Honolulu. I took advantage of some spare time to go to the local boxing arena and found I could sign up for a couple of fights each amateur night. The fights helped me stay in shape and earn pocket money because we were paid expenses, despite the fact we weren't pros.

"We made several practice amphibious landings on Maui. Early July we left Schofield and went to the other side of the island. We were introduced to jungle training. This meant traveling along jungle trails, running various obstacle courses usually in driving rain, exploding land mines and hidden machine-gun fire simulating actual battle conditions. Other than being soaking wet all the time the training was bearable."

While in Hawaii Dick was part of a "Guard of Honor" which stood by while President Roosevelt, General MacArthur and Admiral Nimitz met for a war strategy meeting. "This was especially interesting to my father when I wrote him because he had been part of an honor guard for General Pershing in WWI."

August 10, 1944 Dick boarded the *USS Herald* and proceeded by convoy to Guadalcanal in the Solomons. "We arrived two-weeks later and were assigned to the First Marine Division, which had taken the island two years earlier. We practiced assault landings with both the Marines and Army 81st Division. We left September 8, with the Marines and Army. We were headed for Peleliu and Anguar Islands in the Palau group. It would be my unit's baptism of fire. As it turned out the Marines took the brunt of the fighting on Peleliu and the 81st had an easier time on Anguar. I was assigned to stay aboard our transport and monitor by radio how the battles were going on both islands. My lieutenant went ashore with the third wave. He was the 592nd's first death."

Dick continues, "The 1st Marine Division had its own JASCO attachment, but they went in on the third wave in Ducks – big, cumbersome vehicles that floated and had wheels so they could roll up on land like a truck. Landing craft were used by the Army. Their third wave, Marine JASCO, came under heavy mortar fire and seven Ducks were burning.

"The last Marine message we heard before their radio went dead was, 'I'm getting the hell out of here.' I knew then we were going ashore on Peleliu to relieve the Marine

JASCO. That is exactly what happened, and our Army JASCO successfully landed and did its job."

He continues, "Shortly, both the Marines and Army were making progress on their respective islands. At the Beachmaster's headquarters we were monitoring the progress on both fronts." According to Dick, "The two forces, Marine and Army, approached problems with contrasting styles.

"The marines reported to their HQ they had reached a machine-gun manned pillbox and were going to take it by direct assault. We heard, 'Roger! Good luck, marines.' And they did take the pillbox at the expense of significant casualties to their own troops.

"Then we heard the army on Anguar saying they had come upon a Japanese tank dug in at certain grid coordinates and it was blocking their advance. They told their headquarters they were falling back 100 yards and asked for an artillery attack on the tank. They received the necessary fire which took out the tank, and they continued their advance with no casualties. I know the army's way took a little longer but it was safer and made me glad I was part of their outfit. Of course, I was very proud of both organizations."

September 20, Dick and several combat teams headed to the Ulithi Atoll hear Yap. "After terrific artillery and bombing runs of the beach area we made our landing on the Island of Mogug. The first two waves worked their way inland and were not challenged by the enemy. Eight days later we moved to Falalop and set up another company area."

It was there he saw a single Kamikaze make an attack. "From the shore we watched him climb higher and higher and wondered which ship in anchorage he had selected as a target. The ships were all camouflaged and it was hard to make things out as daylight was fading fast. All the ships were firing their anti-aircraft guns. Finally he came to the top of his climb, leveled off and started his dive. Down and down he came until he finally crashed into his selected target. He had mistaken a very small uninhabited island for a large ship. As best we could tell he hadn't been hit by our gunfire. One G.I. remarked, 'That poor, dumb SOB tried to sink an Island.' I had not worked up any hatred for the Japanese. They were the enemy and had killed lots of people at Pearl Harbor, the Philippines and other places but the idea of killing them was just a job... not personal."

Early October the 592nd moved to another island, Asor. Then a week later back to Peleliu where the rest of the 81st and Marines were still fighting. "As we pulled out of our Ulithi anchorage I looked across the water and saw ships for as far as I could see. I had never before seen so many ships. This was Admiral Halsey's Third Fleet that was assembling to begin the assault on the Philippines. I was proud to be a part of it

"We arrived back at Peleliu Oct. 18, 1944. This time we got ashore without any opposition. The Army and Marines had forced the enemy into pockets of resistance among the intertwining caves along the few remaining hills of Bloody Nose Ridge still under their control. We were billeted not too far from the ridge and every night, all night long, we could hear and see flares lighting up the area from the artillery star shells and hear our 50-caliber machine guns going off sporadically. At night anything that moved was considered enemy. None of us went out after dark. A few days after we arrived, the Japanese soldiers came out of their caves in a banzai charge. Our guns cut them down. They never broke through and only managed to get annihilated."

Dick is respectful of the enemy, just as he is respectful of the 28 opponents he defeated in the boxing ring before joining the Army.

"Thanksgiving of 1944 we were aboard a transport in a huge convoy headed for a landing on the Island of Leyte in the Philippines. It was a Navy transport which meant we would eat a lot better than on an Army transport. The Navy had better food. For Thanksgiving dinner we had a hot turkey dinner. The convoy was very slow and we didn't arrive in Leyte until two days before Christmas, 1944. That was two weeks after the initial assault landings. We spent a full month following the 81st Division. Meanwhile, it was the rainy season and I developed a mild case of malaria, dengue fever and jungle rot. I was able to ride it out.

"The end of January, 1945 we landed on the beach at Luzon. We were unopposed, and the next day our troops captured Clark Field."

By mid-February Dick was on the Bataan peninsula at the edge of Manila Bay. An assault on the island fortress of Corregidor was imminent. It was one of the last Japanese strongholds. A land force would hit the beach while elements of the 503rd Parachute Regiment would drop topside of the island. On top of the island was a golf course and this would be the parachute team's target.

"On the night of February 16 our artillery proceeded to pound the island all night long. I laid down between two big guns and feel asleep. The next morning I couldn't hear a blessed thing.

"The first battalion of assault troops was assembled in preparation to board the landing craft. I was in the third wave and though the 155's were still firing and pounding Corregidor, our signal to attack was when a group of B-24's flew over and plastered the topside with bombs. We saw them overhead and shoved off.

"By the time our third wave arrived at the beach, the first two waves were still crowded on the beach and hadn't been able to break out.

"The paratroopers had it worse. When the bombers dropped their load they must have hit a fuel or ammo dump topside that was sending flames hundreds of feet in the air. As we watched we could see parachutes catching fire and dropping like moths around a flame. Then a wind came up, and some paratroopers who had already landed had their chutes filled before they could collapse them, and they were carried over the cliffs to a death on the rocks below.

"We had our own troubles. Our lieutenant was cut down by a burst of gunfire. We exited our landing craft and sought any cover we could. I was in our radio jeep and hustled it across the beach. A mine took off a tire and a wheel. I careened into a huge shell hole the size of a house. We finally got our communications post established and dug in around the edge of the shell hole. The first wave assault force scaled the cliffs, then the second made the top. A few days later a boat came across the bay and unloaded a Red Cross trailer with their personnel. Their intent was to furnish G.I.'s with coffee and donuts. They fulfilled their mission throughout that and the next day. The Japanese must have thought this was some kind of headquarters, so the third day a squad of their suicide Kamikazi troops worked their way through our lines to the trailer. They carried black powder taped along the sides of their trousers connected to grenades. They crept to the side of the trailer and blew themselves up. The trailer was knocked over, no Americans were killed, and that was enough for the Red Cross. They headed back to the Philippine mainland."

Dick participated in 15 landings with the 592nd JASCO unit. After the war he sailed November 4, 1945 from Jin Sin, Korea to Tacoma, WA aboard the *USS General Gordon*. He arrived two weeks later. His rank at discharge was Staff Sergeant. He had kept his nose clean long enough to hold a promotion.

"I was discharged November 30, 1945. I headed home to Alhambra as quickly as I could. Christmas of 1945 I met Shirley at the USO Canteen in the Los Angeles Union Station. She went there almost every evening to dance with military personnel. This is complicated, but my current brother-in-law had gone with Shirley's sister in high school. He introduced me to her.

"Anyway, she was beautiful then and is beautiful now." (Dick is a master of under statement. He offers their wedding album - he is handsome, she is magazine-cover gorgeous. In boxing terms, a real "Knockout"!)

"When the atom bombs were dropped we were training for the invasion of Japan. I think millions of lives, including mine, were saved by that action. When I got home I went to work for the post office for awhile. Then I joined

Dairy Gold, a statewide dairy products distributor. I started as a driver and progressed to route manager, salesman, and sales manager. In 1979 I became General Manager for the organization. We retired to the Carmel Valley in 1986."

Dick continues, "Shirley and I have five wonderful kids – four girls and a boy. The son was a varsity football player at Chico State. The girls take after Mom in the looks department."

Shirley and two daughters opened an upscale dress shop in Carmel in 1989, Jane Archer. It was sold just prior to their move to Lake Wildwood almost five years ago. She was the Queen Mother of the Classy Hatters Red Hat Society based in Lake Wildwood. Both are avid golfers and travelers.

Mallmans' Wedding Day

Ione and Bill

Chapter 31: Bill Bacheler – USMC

**"Who's in (Corsair) number 17? I asked.
A voice answered 'Lindbergh.'**

AUGUST 14, 1919 the first airmail delivery at sea was made by a U.S. Aeromarine flying boat. Near that same day, in the Queen Anne Hill section of Seattle, Bill Bacheler was also delivered. The Queen Anne Hill area, just north and slightly west of downtown, sits between and some 450 feet above Lake Union and Elliot Bay. It took its name from the stylish Victorian homes that were built on its slopes during the 1890's.

"I trace my love of airplanes and flying back to when I was a child. I was seven when Charles Lindbergh made his historic flight May 20-21, 1927 from New York to Paris." The years peel back as Bill continues, "Imagine my excitement when it was announced he was coming to Seattle in the Spirit of St. Louis later that year."

September 13, 1927 Lindbergh came to the Seattle area during a three-month tour of America to promote aviation. "Before he landed he flew over downtown and my Queen Anne Hill area, but I didn't see him. I remember my folks, sister and me chasing all over town to catch a glimpse of him. I was crushed when we failed." But just having him in town was heady stuff for a boy who had turned eight the month before.

"I think that's when I knew I wanted to be a pilot."

Growing up Bill enjoyed both sports and study, and graduated from Queen Anne High School, situated on the crest of its namesake hill. His next academic stop was the University of Washington, little more than three miles from his home. In 1916 Boeing Company had donated a wind tunnel to the university and established a chair in aeronautics. By 1930 there was a full-fledged Dept. of Aeronautics and Astronautics on campus. Bill graduated with a degree in Aeronautical Engineering in 1940 at the age of twenty. "I skipped a few grades along the way," he says modestly.

Bill had also joined the Marine Reserves. "My folks let me enlist as a buck private when I was seventeen. I had my sights set on being a Marine Corps pilot." His reserve outfit was headquartered at Sand Point Naval Air Station, the site where Lindbergh had landed in 1927. "After I graduated I spent summer at home, then headed east on a train in September to Pensacola, FL for flight training in Stearman open cockpit biplanes. I graduated May 1941 as a Second Lieutenant and was assigned to the Grosse Ile Naval Air Station near Detroit as a flight instructor. I spent until November learning to be a teacher. My students were from the British Royal Air Force and Fleet Air Arm. We used three different, but similar biplanes – the Stearman, Spartan NP-1 and the Naval Aircraft Factory's N3N.

"It was fun teaching the English to fly. But it was cold flying in an open cockpit in the winter, and frostbite was an issue. About the only times we didn't go up was when it was snowing, or too cold to start the hand-cranked engines. Flying at ten degrees below was not unusual." Bill smiles, then continues. "Mid-December 1941, shortly after I'd started teaching, I had British Cadet Longmuir at the controls. The NP-1's engine stopped because of carburetor icing. I took over and looked for a place to land, but it was all wooded. I brought the plane down in the trees, and we flipped over. It was heavily damaged but I was unhurt and Longmuir only had black eyes. From then on about half the students wanted to learn from me... an instructor who knew how to survive a crash."

While in Grosse Ile, Bill began dating a very attractive young woman – Ione Rounds. May 1943, and now a major, he was ordered to the Marine Corps Air Station in Santa Barbara as executive officer for Corsair Squadron VMF-115. His commander, and direct boss, was Marine Corps Ace, Joe Foss. Earlier in the month President Roosevelt had awarded Major Foss the Medal of Honor. His 26 aerial victories against the Japanese equaled the record set by Eddie Rickenbacker during WWI. (Joe Foss died Jan.1, 2003 at age 87.)

"A few days after arriving in Santa Barbara I met Charles Lindbergh. He was a field rep for Chance Vought, the builder of the F4U Corsair. It was quite a thrill to meet my boyhood idol."

From May to December 1943, the squadron's 40 pilots trained in Corsairs and Wildcats. "We lost eleven men during training exercises; one just disappeared over the ocean during a night-flying exercise, two were killed when colliding during a mid-air dog fight, one in a landing fire, and the remainder in a number of other mostly pilot-error mishaps."

Bill is silent. "Some of them were married and their spouses lived off base in Santa Barbara. Joe Foss, the squadron doctor and I would visit to tell them about their husband's death. It was tough."

He changes the subject. "One day I was leading a practice gunnery flight. Lindbergh, unannounced, joined the squadron in his Corsair. He didn't know anything about gunnery and I had to give him orders to close up just before we did a roll and dive toward the tow plane's trailing target. I got quite a kidding about giving orders to Lindbergh."

January 1944 the squadron bussed down to San Pedro and boarded the seaplane tender *Pocomoke* headed to Espiritu Santos in the New Hebrides. "The planes we had trained in stayed behind. We would get 16 new Corsairs for our 40 pilots at our destination. We arrived in February, and a month or so later we headed northwest to the small island of Emirau in the St. Matthias group." The Marines had captured it from the Japanese March 20, 1944.

"My very first combat mission, out of Emirau, I was also the leader for our 16-plane squadron. Joe Foss was quite sick with malaria and couldn't lead the flight. We were headed to a Japanese naval base on Rabaul, some 250 miles away, in the New Ireland chain. Rabaul had a reputation for being very heavily defended against air attack. Each of our planes carried a 500-lb. bomb.

On the way I liked to count my planes to ensure everyone was okay. When the count was done, it was 17 instead of sixteen.

'Who's in number 17?' I asked. A voice answered, 'Lindbergh.' There was a rumor that the Japanese had forced down a Corsair in earlier engagements, and now were flying it, joining squadrons, and shooting down our planes."

He states that story was likely the equivalent of today's urban legends. "But I did have a real concern. If the Japanese knew Lindbergh was in the air they'd do everything they could to destroy his plane. I didn't ask the pilot any more questions. Instead, I dropped down, back and then up to his side to verify his identity. It was Lindbergh. I gave him a thumbs up and I went back to the lead position.

"As squadron leader I went in first. The ack-ack was heavy as I was jinking (dodging) and strafing after I had picked out the target for my bomb. I continued firing after the bomb drop, then gained altitude and circled the area away from the action to watch my men on their runs. The last plane to go in often gets the heaviest fire and is in a tough position." Lindbergh was in that slot, and, Bill emphasizes, "He did a good job.

"When we all got safely back to base Lindbergh didn't show up for the debriefing, and I never saw him again. May 1945 our squadron was split up, and I wound up with VMF-

251 – again as executive officer. Our base was on Bougainville, about 150 miles SE of Rabaul.

"As squadron exec I should have known better," he says with a wry smile. "In a combat zone it was a good idea to keep your eyes open, your mouth shut and not to volunteer. One Sunday a buddy and I were relaxing on the beach and I opened my mouth. 'Let's you and I take a little bomb run to Rabaul. The Japanese won't expect us on a Sunday and we might do a little damage.' Somehow he agreed, and we headed out, me in 'Little Onie Bug'." That was the nickname of Bill's girlfriend, Ione, painted on his Corsair.

"We were approaching a mountain range on New Ireland, just west of New Britain's Rabaul. We were flying at about 7,000 feet. I had a bomb and a full 120-gallon belly tank. The engine ran rough and the nose started going down. I fooled with the fuel mixture and the engine quit. I had about a 2:1 or 3:1 glide ratio – a foot drop for every two to three feet forward." He also had an instantaneous fuse on the bomb.

"I got the engine restarted at about 4,000 feet and it ran okay. I climbed back to 7,000 feet and it died again."

Bill briefly pauses. "I thought I was going to die, and that feeling got worse as I nosed over."

Again, the engine restarted at about 4,000 feet. "My pal and I continued on to Rabaul and dropped our bombs, and I kept it under 7,000 feet. When we returned a tech rep from Pratt & Whitney found a hole in a carburetor diaphragm that regulated the air/fuel mixture depending on altitude. The next day, every carburetor on every Corsair was checked for this problem."

When VMF-251 was reassigned from Bougainville to Samar, Philippines, it had a new squadron commander – Bill "Batch" Bachelor. His final assignment was supporting MacArthur's invasion of the Lingayen Gulf. "I was on a bomb run and somehow my bomb hit my belly tank and knocked it off. There was an explosion of bomb and belly tank slightly below the plane." The blast lifted the tail up and over vertical, with the nose of the plane pointed back and upside down. "I got the plane under control, but it could have been disastrous."

April 1945, Bill returned to Seattle. He had flown 83 combat missions. "While in Santa Barbara and overseas one of the things I looked forward to was receiving mail from Ione. She wrote me two letters a week after I left Grosse Ile, MI." He is quick to add, "I also think I did a good job of writing letters to her." They were married June 1945 in Fenton, MI, then headed to Seattle. Bill was hired as a pilot by Pan Am.

Bill was reactivated for the Korean War and was promoted to Lieutenant Colonel July 1, 1951. He spent 1½ years on active duty flying USMC DC-4's (the same model he flew for the airlines) from Moffett Field in California to Korea. "In 1953 I applied for the astronaut program, but received a very nice rejection letter stating I was a little too old. I was very disappointed."

After the war Bill held a number of key positions with Pan Am, including heading up their navigation section. He helped develop the free gyro steering process for polar route navigation that became an industry standard, and was Air Safety Chair for Pan Am pilots.

In 1966 Bill became a Pan Am 707 Captain. On his first round-the-world as captain Ione rode in the jump seat the entire flight. In 1976 Bill became a 747 Captain. "I would make two round-the-world trips a month, each a week long. Pan Am One circled the earth heading west; Pan Am Two headed east."

Bill and Ione moved to Lake Wildwood in 1977, some two years before his retirement. He commuted to SFO and his aircraft. He has more than 22,000 hours in airplane cockpits.

He and Ione have two daughters and a son. "When our boy was in the Navy as a pilot, he was aircraft carrier qualified. We are very proud of his service to our country."

Bill earned two Distinguished Flying Crosses and an Air Medal with some 16 oak leaf clusters. During a Nov. 11, 2002 ceremony in Grass Valley he was issued a medal from the Korean government, the Korean War Service Medal. Previously, the U.S. had prohibited the wearing of medals issued by foreign governments.

Norm and Eloise

Chapter 32: Norm Traverso--AAF/USAF

"We all felt it as a branch from the main trunk ripped into the plane's belly."

NORM TRAVERSO was born in Akron, OH the end of September 1922. His parents had immigrated to America years earlier − his mother from the toe of the boot of Italy, the Calabria region − his father from the top front of the boot, the Piedmont area. They had met after coming to the United States. Norm was the third child, and the only boy.

His dad worked at the Goodyear plant, while his mom devoted her time to the children. Three or four years after his birth the family moved to Brooklyn to be closer to relatives.

"Brooklyn was a great place to grow up," Norm reflects. "And I guess being the youngest child, and the only boy, I was a little spoiled." A smile flashes across his face as wide as the center span of the city's namesake Bridge. It continues as he describes Currier and Ives childhood scenes of winter sledding in Prospect Park – not far from his Avenue U flat.

"One of my most vivid memories is with my parents and sisters watching an air show from lower Manhattan's Battery Park. There were all kinds of planes, and I'll never forget watching a formation of military aircraft fly over the park and head toward the Statue of Liberty."

The planes pulled the small boy's imagination along as they headed across the water. "I was sure I would fly one day." He was a little guy, with big boy dreams.

Shortly after the Battery Park wonderment, his father took flight and his parents divorced. "I didn't see much of my dad after that. And times were tough for my mom, having to raise three children."

He explains that his mother was an accomplished seamstress and toiled at home and for others on the outside. His two older sisters helped support the family and Norm also went to work at an early age without losing focus on his education.

"I worked at the local A&P doing all kinds of jobs, from washing the produce, to stocking shelves and cleaning – just about anything they asked. Sometimes," he adds, "I'd even get a call at home from the store that someone needed groceries delivered, and could I do it? I don't think I ever turned them down."

Norm attended PS 206 and Brooklyn's Madison H.S., then moved with his mother and sisters to Long Island. "I graduated from Newton High School in 1940."

Looking at his yearbook, among other accomplishments, it is noted he was a member of both the Spanish and German language honor societies. The fall of 1940 he started at St. John's University studying accounting, then to CCNY the following year.

"I know the day Pearl Harbor was bombed was the day I decided to join the military." His opportunity came in early January. "I saw an announcement in the paper that the Army Air Corps would be giving exams for those interested in becoming aviation cadets."

Again he smiles as he recounts the location for the testing. "They were going to test applicants down at the Battery." He passed his exams and was put on the enlisted reserve list to be called up in the near future.

"I had to provide my birth certificate, and got a big surprise. I had only known my name to be Norman Harry Travers... the same as in my graduation yearbook. My two sisters had lobbied my mother years before to anglicize our surname, and she had dropped the 'o' from Traverso. Plus, my name was officially listed as Normand, instead of Norman. Besides that my parents had wanted my middle name to be Henry... the English version of Enrico. Harry was just a mistake the hospital records clerk had made. I might add, my confirmation name was Anthony, or Antonio, in Italian." Norm continues. "So my correct name in Italian was Normando Enrico Antonio Traverso." He waits for a reaction, then the bada-bing... N-E-A-T. Would he have had more dates... been more popular with that acronym? In the 2003 phone book it is listed as Normand Traverso, just as it was on his enlistment papers.

October of 1942 Norm boarded a train at Penn Station headed to Nashville via Chicago. He was wearing a nice gabardine suit for his two-day train ride.

"We picked up other aviation cadets along the way. When we arrived in Nashville we were immediately taken to our base and put up in bunks."

The next morning they were awakened early, and in formation by seven. "I put on my suit to make a good impression. The first words out of the sergeant in charge were soft spoken. 'Boys, you don't have to do one Gosh Darn thing in this army you don't want to,' and we all kind of breathed a sigh of relief as he continued... 'but I'll make you wish you had.'" There were no questions.

Early on they had a number of assessments to determine their training direction. Some went to pilot training, some to navigator or bombardier and some went to non-flying assignments. "I had an interview with a psychologist. 'Why do you want to fly?' he asked, and I told him about my visit to the air show years before, and my desire to become a pilot. I laid it all out." This time the smile is as wide as the gap between the Brooklyn Dodgers 1920 National League Pennant win and their next one in 1941. "One of the guys in my barracks said he had pulled a good one on the psychologist. When the doc asked him why he wanted to fly, he said because he didn't want to walk. He became a navigator."

A few days before Christmas of 1942, Norm and the rest of the recruits were given a leave. He went home to Long Island. "I was there for two or three days and received a telegram to immediately return to Nashville."

From there he went to Santa Ana for pre-flight, then Visalia for basic in the Ryan PT22 low-wing, single-engine trainer. Next, to Bakersfield and Yuma for more flight training, including the twin-engine Cessna UC-78 Bobcat, known as the "Bamboo Bomber" because of its light wood construction in the fuselage and wings.

"Oh, we were pretty cocky in Yuma. On long flights there was no such thing as radio contact with FAA stations because they didn't exist. At strategic points there would be light-line stations flashing a letter in Morse code. You'd leave the base on a certain heading... say 270 degrees. You knew when you reached the signal you needed to change to a different compass heading. You kept following the light stations until you got to your destination."

Radio silence between planes was critical. "We left at different intervals, and the instructors wanted each pilot to find his way on his own. 'Bugs Bunny to Snow White,' a pilot transmitted, 'about 5 minutes behind you on heading 270. Have you seen the light station?'

"'Negative, Snow White, how 'bout you Red Riding Hood?'"

And so it went, until a voice boomed, "This is Base, please ID yourself.' 'Snow White,' came the reply, then silence. 'Dumbo,'" said another. Then nothing save static.

"The next day we ran and ran and ran and ran and ran through the desert until we could run no more. I, of course," Norm states, "was not involved." He looks and sounds so smooth, verbally displaying an imaginary "For Sale" deed for "THE" Bridge on the East River.

"Let me tell you how good we were... when we were in the air and approaching rail lines crossing AZ, CA, NM, NV, CO we'd warn one another to look down the tracks to the right and left before crossing to make sure we didn't hit a navy plane using the rails as their navigation aid."

Another rim shot... the put is on. Brooklyn guys even in Lake Wildwood like to stir the pot.

October of 1943 he received his wings, a second lieutenant.

"From Yuma I went to Sacramento's Mather Field for nine weeks of B-25 instruction, then to Columbia, SC for combat flight training. It was there I met my future bride, Bobbie." He was given orders to head west in a new B-25. "Once again I wound up at Mather Base near Sacramento and was outfitted with a 'Tokyo Tank' (– a long-distance fuel tank fitted into the bomb bay). "A special navigator was brought on board. We were told our departure point would be the Golden Gate Bridge and what our heading would be."

It was a Horace Greeley moment. "We spent a day in Hawaii, then to the Christmas Islands, Guam and Guadalcanal."

Norm recalls the landing at Guam. "I was very close... my flaps and wheels were down and I was almost in the flare position where landing was imminent." He pauses then continues, "The tower ordered me to 'Take it around!' I poured it on and did as ordered. There was risk involved, but a tower order had to be obeyed."

He continues, "After we landed I radioed and said I hadn't seen anything that would warrant their order. 'We have one pet on this island... our dog... and he was on the runway... welcome to Guam.'"

When they arrived in Guadalcanal the B-25 they had ferried was reassigned. "My time as a Pilot-in-Command was short-lived for a brief time. I was assigned to the 13th Air Force, 42nd Bomb Group, 390th Bomb Squadron as a co-pilot for a few missions.

"My first mission was to Kabanga Bay 6/29/44. I was in the assist seat. It was fairly uneventful. We landed at Kabanga. A pygmy male came running to the plane, followed by 4-5 women. The pilot chatted in Pidgin English. The little guy watched me puff down a cigarette and made gestures that he wanted one. First I gave him my still lit smoke, then I gave him a few out of the pack, and finally an unopened batch of 20 from my flight jacket. 'Today's your lucky day,' the pilot said. 'Your first mission and already you have the pick of any wife he has.' The women buzzed with excitement, giggling and chattering as best they could."

Norm continues, "The pilot said, 'We could probably fit one in the plane, but we'd have to carry 75-100 pounds less of bombs on future missions. What do you think?'"

Norm looked at the women and smiled, "A wonderful offer, but not today – maybe later."

The North American B-25 Mitchell was a medium bomber first flown in early 1939. It had two 1700-hp 14-cylinder radial engines with a speed of 275 mph, a ceiling of more than 24,000 feet and a range of almost 1,400 miles without auxiliary fuel tanks. It could carry up to 5,000 pounds in bombs, had five .50 caliber machine-guns and hosted a crew of six.

Norm Traverso, Brooklyn lad from PS 206, could fly a B-25 like Dodger Lefty O'Doul could field and hit... with skill, finesse, strength, daring, determination and a love of the game.

"Of my 59 missions slightly more than half were low-level runs." He is pressed on the definition. "Low is low," he emphasizes, and one nods that there is finally understanding that low is low. "It's skimming the trees, literally." Imagine a line drive hit toward Dodger's legendary Pee Wee Reese and having him scramble to get out of the way... out of the way so a knee doesn't get obliterated. That was a B-25 at tree-top height. "We came in low for two main reasons – the element of surprise and we had less of a chance of getting hit by enemy fire."

He gives an example of a low-level mission. "It was near the end of the war, and we were making a run on an island in the Philippines. We had bombed it before, but needed to do some cleanup. Where we were attacking, the greenery was gone. Maybe I was 200-225 (mph) and very low on a skip-bombing mission." He pauses, then continues, "And there was the trunk of a big tree right in front of me. I put the left wing down, and went perpendicular to the ground. We all felt it as a branch from the main trunk ripped into the plane's belly." His engaging smile is fluid yet tight, like pushing through a subway system turnstile.

"It was a little tougher flight coming home. After we landed, the crew chief came to me with one of his guys dragging a tree branch that had lodged in our bomb bay.

The whiplash of the trunk had also knocked off part of our twin tail assembly."

"Welcome back," he said, "and thanks for the lumber."

We look at his "Short-Snorter." Take a dollar bill with an imprint designated for use in Hawaii. Hold it vertical, Washington's side facing you, and use clear tape to attach an Australian bill, then a New Zealand bill, and to that one from Dutch New Guinea, followed by a Japanese ten-peso bill used in the Philippines during their occupation. On the face side of the currency, neatly jot down each of your 59 combat missions in the South Pacific – date, target and territory. On the backside, it's like signing a high school yearbook – Norm Traverso with crews from other planes, squadrons, allies and new and old pals writing their names. The colors of the currency... the different shades of inks used in signatures and mission documentation, the circle from a damp bottle or glass now empty for six decades, blend words and names into Rorschach's and help make the long, thin, poignant and remarkable work of art and history – the "Short-Snorter."

(I make a note to buy Norman some clean white gloves – the kind worn in museums by those who handle irreplaceable things of great value.)

Norman had flown about 50 combat missions. His crew decided it was time he also learned to drive.

"We'd returned from a mission and some of the guys were having refreshments and one of them said, 'C'mon, boss, let's take the Jeep and drive around the island.'

"I said I'd driven once in Brooklyn for a few minutes when I was a kid and smashed a garbage can, and that was the end of it." He asks rhetorically, "Who needs a car in NYC?

"They took me out in the Jeep and I learned about the clutch, shifting, steering, brakes, horn, lights, cornering, digging out from soft sand, tipping a Jeep back to right-side-up and other key items associated with driving on land." He is kidding on some of the details. His men were happy they had made a good start with teaching him a new skill.

Norm is quick to point out when he took instruction on that South Pacific island his crew team mentors had set their refreshments aside before getting in the vehicle... as had he.

The missions from June 29, 1944 to April 14, 1945 follow our nation's progress to victory across the South Pacific. The "Short-Snorter" details the places where some of the key battles occurred during his 59 combat missions– Rabaul, Haroenoe, Battan, Hatebako, Liang, Cebo.

"We were on a heckler mission one night... we wanted to bomb six islands with Japanese airfields very quickly to keep the enemy nervous. It was just my plane. One bomb for each airfield. We completed the first five and were approaching the sixth. It was pitch black on a moonless night. My gunner tells me to look out the right side. My co-pilot and I could see a cockpit light keeping pace with us, but could not make out the markings. We made the approach for the Japanese airfield and got a green light. That meant we were approved to land. We knew it had to be for the plane to our right. I sometimes wonder if our bomb hit the field as that poor SOB was touching down." His words are respectful of a likely fallen enemy.

"Were we hit... of course, but nothing like the guys in Europe." He pauses as he reflects back on wounds to his plane. "Soon after I joined the 390th I was given my own plane." He still has his leather flight jacket. On the back is an exact replica of the painting on the nose of the aircraft. "We were called 'The Battle Babies' because at age 22 I was the oldest member of the crew." It is a painting of a stork carrying four babies in a diaper. One is facing forward with what looks likes a gun barrel out of his mouth (front gunner). Another is about ready to drop a bomb. The third tyke is scanning the sky (engineer or navigator), while the fourth looks toward the rear (rear gunner). "Maybe my co-pilot and I were the stork." Much of the nose-art for individual planes is the Vargas type voluptuous beauties. Their plane is an exception.

"We had ack-ack damage to the plane's structure on some missions, and on one flight my front glass crystallized and the co-pilot had to bring it down, but we lost no one. One flight where we came in low, the trees began to blow... the enemy had put explosives in the palms and were detonating them from the ground."

He describes a near perfect run. "We had a new squadron leader from the states who, on his first mission, suggested our 12 planes head into the target at 500 feet. I was leading the rear group of three planes. I thought we should go in low and told my team to follow me. The squadron leader took nine planes in at his recommended altitude." The flak arched upward from both sides of the target like a dual line of cadets holding their swords aloft in a ceremony. Norm took his three planes through that arch near ground level like a groom, bride and ring-bearer marching down the aisle. He is silent as he revisits the bomb run. "It was beautiful... It was near-perfect." The bombs they dropped fell like rice on a departing wedding party.

May of 1945 Norm headed home. Later that month, the 29th, he married Bobbie, the woman he had met while in Columbia, SC.

Norm stayed in the AAF and did flight instruction right after the war. "It's somewhat ironic," he states, "that a number of the Chinese I put through B-25 flight training in Texas in 1946 likely flew against us in Korea.

"Our daughter, Karen, was born Oct. 11, 1948 not long after I went into the PR arena for the Air Force." He continues, "I went to Korea as a Public Information Officer. They stationed me in Pusan. My job was to take care of dignitaries and prepare press releases from the front. I liked James Michener when he visited... he was truly interested in what the war was all about." He talks about the P-51 pilot from Texas who feared his buddies from back home would kick his rear for shooting so many beautiful horses being ridden by Chinese cavalry men. That story made it in hundreds of papers. Only the men riding the horses were the enemy. The horses were unfortunate casualties.

Norm loved to fly, and to keep current he had to have so many hours in the air. He asked to fly the A20 of WWII. It had two 2000-hp engines, a three-man crew, eight .50 caliber machine-guns and could carry 4000 pounds of bombs plus a napalm bomb and up to seven rockets.

He flew eleven combat missions in Korea, and still kept the press releases flowing and the dignitaries informed. "I was flying at the far north of Korea, down a canyon separating North Korea from China. The lead plane said there were steel cables strung from peak to peak to bring down aircraft. I dropped a photo bomb to illuminate the night area as though it were daylight. There were Chinese on their side of the border, and we gained altitude to miss the cables."

After Korea he returned to the states and to the inspector general office in the Pentagon. He was then sent to Spain to help set up American air bases. "My family and I lived in an apartment complex in Madrid with five other officers and their families. A close neighbor was AF officer Bill Mayo and his wife Eloise. We became good friends. Our three years in Spain were a wonderful experience."

Norm recounts spending a month on the road with the American ambassador to Spain's PR man, meeting key people in critical locations to sell the need for our presence in their country.

When he returned to the states in 1958 Norm was made squadron commander for an AWAC (Airborne Warning And Control) unit out of McClellan AFB in Sacramento. He spent a brief period with NORAD, and in 1960 was assigned the job of Chief of the Summer White House for President Kennedy. In 1963 he wanted to fly again and commanded another C-121 AWAC squadron out of Otis AFB in MA, then was reassigned to Hamilton AFB in Marin County, CA.

(Norm's home office has wonderful commendations; including his Air Medals, Jt. Service Commendations and other recognition from his Air Force career. There is also a wall with civilian recognition and plaques with gavels ready to slam down to help one recount past, significant personal accomplishments.

"I retired in 1965 as a Lt. Colonel and went to work as CEO for the Redwood Region Conservation Council – an organization representing the timber industry. Then I went into property management in Marin." A few years later he and Bobbie moved to Truckee. "Coincidentally, our friends from Spain, Eloise and Bill Mayo, had moved to Lake Wildwood in the early '80's, and we stayed in touch."

Bobbie passed away in 1985. Eloise's husband passed in 1988. Eloise and Norm married August 1990, and Norm wisely moved down the hill. Between them they have six children, ten grandchildren and enough great-grandchildren to keep the memory cells working overtime.

Some 75 years ago he watched the planes cross NYC's Battery Park and wing toward the Statue of Liberty – a little guy with big boy dreams. The dreams were fulfilled.

Of his crew in the South Pacific, Norm brought them all safely back to America and their loved ones. NEAT, don't you think, for someone without a license to drive a car during WWII?

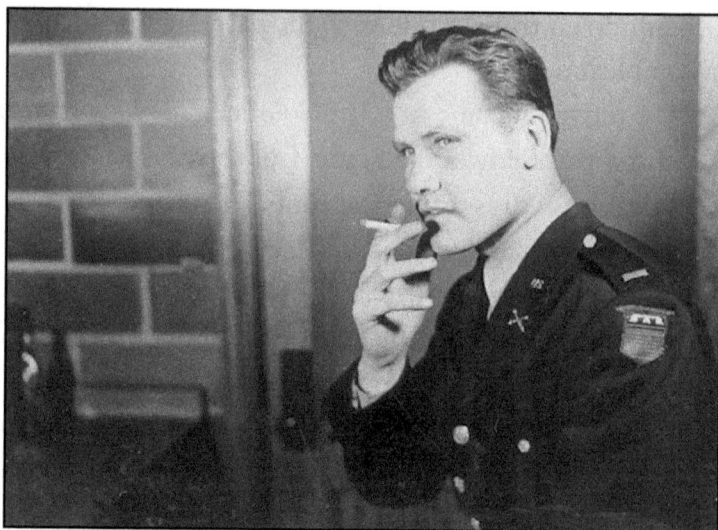

Chapter 33: Bill Barger –Army

"We were six-to-eight feet apart. My sergeant died and so did the man who had shot him."

FOR THE 1920 census the town of Leon, Iowa had a population of 2,009. Some 80 years later it's still the same size, just a slightly different cast. A year after that 1920 tally, the population grew by one with the birth of Bill Barger. By 1939 he was 90 miles due north at Iowa State University majoring in economics. He was also a starting right tackle on the football team, and working on a road crew when school wasn't in session.

"They didn't have football scholarships back then," states Bill. "The job the coach got me was the closest they came, and it was hard, physical labor that helped me get in better shape for football." His senior year he was 6'2" and well over 200 pounds.

"I guess I was pretty good, because the Philadelphia Eagles suggested I try out for the team, but I had another obligation that was more important." While at Iowa State Bill had also taken ROTC, and in June 1943, upon graduation, he started infantry basic training at Fort Riley, Kansas.

"From there I went to six weeks of officer training at Fort Sill, Oklahoma and then six more weeks of advanced officer field artillery training at Fort McCall, North Carolina. By September I had been assigned to the 76th Infantry Division at Camp McCoy, Wisconsin, as the Athletic Director. My job was to help the men have a little fun, learn teamwork and stay in great shape. It was a good short-term assignment, but I wanted something with more meat and more challenge."

When the call came for officers to volunteer for the Airborne – to become a paratrooper – Bill indicated his interest. "I was told I was too big to be a paratrooper, but when I got down to Fort Benning, Georgia, November of '43 they accepted me into class #129. That was a very interesting four weeks," he says with a smile.

"I was with a group of other officers getting instruction on how to pack a 'chute, and the Drill Instructor, a first sergeant, says, 'This is our lucky day. It looks like we're about to see a jump.' He pointed off in the distance to a formation of C-47's headed our way. The drop-zone was just a hundred yards or so from our training area, and we all watched as the men started to jump." He pauses, then continues, "One of the 'chutes didn't open. The lines were tangled, and the paratrooper was plummeting earthward. We watched horrified, as he hit the ground at near free-fall speed. Matter-of-factly, the DI said, 'See what happens when you don't pack your 'chute properly?' He let it sink in for a minute, observing the shocked and pale faces surrounding him. 'Now let's get busy and learn to pack our 'chutes the right way so that doesn't happen to one of you guys!'"

He pauses again and chuckles, "Only later did we learn they'd tossed out a dummy for our benefit. Believe me, it got our attention. We were very attentive and asked a lot of good questions in that class."

By the time Bill graduated from Fort Benning, he had made ten jumps and earned his Parachutist Badge. He was assigned to the 17th Airborne Division Dec. 16, 1943. It had been formed from the 101st Airborne Division at Fort Bragg, NC, mid-April of that year. From the day of its inception it was under the command of Major General William Miley. He is credited with establishing the airborne officer tradition of never asking one of his men to do something he would not do, or would hesitate to do. The 17th's division insignia was a golden eagle talon on a circular black background – "The grasping of golden opportunities out of the darkness by surprise."

Bill says, "We trained hard in the states, and by August of 1944 we moved from Camp Forrest, TN, to Camp Myles Standish at Taunton, MA. We knew it wouldn't be too long before we headed to Europe. And I was having a good time in my new assignment."

He describes how General Miley had made it very clear he would be with his men at or near the center of future battles. "My platoon," said Bill, "would go into action with the rest of the paratroopers, but when the area was secured, it would be my responsibility to protect the area around General Miley's headquarters close to the front lines. I was given the job of hand-selecting my men. I wanted the toughest guys I could find." He laughs, and continues. "All the guys in the 17th were tough. I went to each company commander and asked for his mavericks, and guys that might be a little hard to manage. I wanted to mold my own team."

He continues, "I got what I asked for, including one ex-professional football player. We played a lot of tackle football without pads and helmets to see how tough these guys were. I wound up with a great platoon skilled in offense and defense."

September 17th, 1944 parts of the 17th Airborne Division set sail from New York City aboard the *Queen Mary*. It was the fastest ship afloat and could outrun any enemy vessel. Including crew it could carry almost 16,000 people. Also on board was Winston Churchill, returning from the second Quebec Conference on war strategy. Coincidentally, Ofie Leeper, a friend of Bill's from Leon, Iowa was an officer aboard the ship. "Bill," he joked, "It's your job to protect the Prime Minister."

"I know, Ofie... I know."

They spent the next several months at Camp Chiseldon near Swindon in SW England. That 1944 Thanksgiving the menu included 7 tons of turkey, 703 pounds of dehydrated sweet potato and more than a thousand large cans of pumpkin. A month later Bill and the rest of the 17th would be fighting to stem the German offensive known as The Battle of the Bulge.

The 17th flew to the area near Charleville, France, and further secured the Meuse River allied positions against possible enemy penetration. "It was very cold and very snowy. Some say it was one of the worst winters in memory," says Bill. "Sometimes it was hard to see more than 30-40 feet in front of us." He pauses for emphasis. "We did not look backward. In fact, the 17th never took a backward step... never."

General Miley was true to his word, and as the front moved so did his headquarters – sometimes every few days – from Charleville, France to various towns in the Luxembourg region of Belgium as the German assault was pushed back. Finally, by early February, the division moved back to Chalons-sur-Marne, France for re-organization and rest. It was needed as casualties had been heavy.

On March 24, Lt. Bill Barger and his platoon would participate in the biggest airborne assault in history, Operation Varsity, the Allied push across the Rhine into Germany. The 17th Airborne would team with the 6th British Airborne Division for a daylight assault near the city of Wesel. According to Bill, "The night before the jump there was a large number of clergy to hear confessions and offer solace to those that needed it." The Americans took off from France and the British 6th from England. They joined forces near Brussels.

"My platoon was one of the first to jump. We needed to seize and clear the area for General Miley's command area. Allied bombers and artillery had been hitting the area hard for several days, but there were still plenty of enemy below. As we approached the Rhine, the flak was heavy. But over the drop zone things quieted down.

"As platoon leader I would be the first one out the door. One of my sergeants would be the last, to ensure all made it out okay. It was a low-altitude jump, six or seven hundred feet. On the way down I was worried about my people and hoping I could land so I could come up shooting. The Germans had thought they were being bombed again and had gone to ground. We had about 15 minutes of calm before encountering the enemy. All of my men made it down okay. Actually," he continued, "things went pretty well. We captured 20-30 Germany soldiers the first hour or so.

"We found a suitable house for General Milcy's headquarters a little over a mile from Wesel and secured the area. We were advancing toward Wesel when I was told one of my sergeants had been hit." His voice softens, "He was still alive, but I could see it was hopeless. I held him for a moment, called for a medic and asked where the shot had come from. One of my men pointed to a trench not too far ahead. I left the sergeant with one of my guys and crawled toward and into the trench." Bill described the trench as having cutouts – like cogs in a gear – for a soldier to position himself to face the enemy without impeding those who might want to move up or down the sunken dirt-lined corridor.

"I had left my rifle by my dying comrade and carried only my .45 and about six grenades. In the trench I moved cautiously but quickly towards the enemy, staying below the rim. I think if the German had thrown his rifle down, I would have let him surrender. Instead, he started to swing around pointing the weapon toward me. We were 6-8 feet apart." He pauses again, "My sergeant died, and so did the man who shot him. I lost three of my brave men during the war.

"A few days later, March 26, I was on an advance reconnoiter with four of my men scoping out the area. We were on the high ground, and below us was a German marshaling yard. I sent back for a bazooka and more men and we destroyed a considerable number of buildings, equipment and the enemy."

Bill served in a combat capacity for 16 months. The war in Europe ended May 7, 1945, and he was transferred to the 101st Airborne's undefeated football team. Bill played first-string tackle. The roster included ex-pro and college players from schools like Nebraska, Penn State, USC, UCLA, Ohio State and a host of other formidable football powerhouses. "At one point we challenged West Point and the Naval Academy to a game. We, of course, were in Europe and they were at home. They turned us down. I guess they thought we were kidding," he says with a wink and sly smile.

In December 1945 Bill transferred to the 82nd Airborne Division and returned to the United States as a Unit Commander. His ship for the return leg was also the *Queen Mary*. Jan 12, 1946 he marched with the 82nd Airborne in the huge ticker-tape parade in NYC celebrating the end of the war.

Bill earned three Bronze Stars and one Bronze Arrowhead. He and his unit also earned the Belgian Fourragere during the Battle of the Bulge.

Bill and Susanne, his wife for three decades, have lived in Penn Valley's Lake Wildwood since 1981 and have been very active in the community. They have four children from his first marriage. Bill has served as President of the Interfaith Food Ministry and seems a gentle man. Yet, even at his age one would be foolish to stand opposite him in a three-point football stance. There are things he knows how to do with a forearm that are best left unsaid.

ACKNOWLEDGEMENTS

In my acknowledgements I get to provide one answer to the important question of which came first – the chicken or the egg? That answer might help me arrange subsequent acknowledgements in proper order, or at least have a little fun. It is very clear in Genesis: "...So God created... every winged bird according to its kind." There is nothing about eggs being first. It's the bird.

Therefore, the newspaper came first, thanks to both Genesis and Gutenberg. My initial acknowledgement must be to Mike Dobbins, owner and publisher of *The Wildwood Independent* and the *Penn Valley Courier*. Without his taking a chance on running *PATRIOTS* over a five-year period there would have been no series. Just like attending a sorority dance in my youth I will stay with the one who brought me – my series publisher and dear friend – Michael Dobbins.

While on a media mogul roll I single out Dave Henderson, owner and publisher of Pine Tree Arts of Penn Valley, CA. In addition to publishing he is an accomplished and prolific novelist, non-fiction writer and editor. Without his valuable help and tireless effort, advice and counsel there would be no book – just a drawer or computer file full of old *PATRIOTS* stories. The articles were the eggs... Dave is the winged bird mentioned in Genesis, hatching those written eggs. He, too, has become a dear friend.

Pushing the biblical theme, I fear too far, I thank Marty Martin, a close pal for more than forty-five years. The Sistine Chapel's ceiling boasts the Michelangelo masterpiece painted six-hundred years ago. It shows God extending a hand and finger toward Adam. Marty kept his finger prodding me – reaching out – poking — until I entered the garden of book publishing. I'm glad I did and thank him more than he may ever know.

So, just four short paragraphs, and I have highlighted three wonderful friends. It's a lifetime's worth – a trio of really good eggs.

My spouse Diana deserves special mention. She has helped immensely in bringing the book to fruition and is the apple of my eye. Any thanks are not enough. Note to self: "Must do more to pick up stuff I strew around the house. Must remember cleanliness is next to Godliness."

There are five pillars of their respective communities and professions that must be acknowledged. In alphabetical order they are the men who took their valuable time to provide tributes and endorsements for the book:

Jeff Ackerman, publisher and editor of *The Union* newspaper serving Western Nevada County, CA. *The Union* is one of nearly 30 keenly focused community newspapers in the Swift Communications stable in California, Colorado, Nebraska, Nevada and Oregon. The company is also deeply involved in other 21st century media communications ventures. I respect Jeff very much for what he does for our community as an individual and helping keep strong our area's freedom of the press. It is near impossible to imagine anyone being a better publisher of an important paper, and for that matter, a better and more focused writer.

Jeff served with distinction during the Vietnam War, and has returned in the not too distant past to observe firsthand as that country moves forward in this new millennium.

Jerry Barden, Rotary International Director 1995-97. Of more than 1.2 million Rotarians he was one of only twelve directors in the world. Jerry has been a dear friend for more than 35 years, and his sage advice, sense of humor and wise ways are deeply treasured. His spouse, too, is named Diana and she and my Diana share many of the same outstanding traits.

Jerry and Diana live by the Rotary motto of Service Above Self. Over the years they have visited every continent on behalf of Rotary, including Antarctica. I am very lucky he has taken me on as one of his long-term service projects.

Les Denend, Vice Chairman of the Board, USAA Insurance (Ret. 2010). In addition to Insurance USAA also markets a full range of investment and banking opportunities. It's been an honor to know Les for two decades. He earned a doctorate in economics, public policy and business from Stanford and has had a superb run of dedicated service to industry and our country. He has been an officer, owner or director for a number of companies.

His service to our nation has been exemplary. Les flew 190 combat missions in Vietnam; been a past member of the National Security Council staff; a White House Fellow; Advisor to the Chair of the Joint Chiefs of Staff; Deputy Director of the Cabinet Council of Economic Affairs; Assistant Professor of Economics and Management at the Air Force Academy; Fulbright scholar in economics at the University of Bonn and more.

Richard Landis, CEO and Chairman of the Board, Del Monte Corporation, Ret., and President R.J. Reynolds, Pacific (Pacific Basin and 13 western states), Ret. Dick is profiled in this book for his service to our country as a P-38 and P-51 pilot during WWII and the Battle of the Bulge. While eligible to return home, he was determined to do whatever was necessary as a combat pilot until the war was over. He stayed beyond VE Day. Post conflict he was grounded for a week when he performed a perfect low-level snap roll in his P-51 over Frankfurt's airport.

Dick's strong commitment to doing the right thing, with élan, stood him in good stead then and in his subsequent personal, charitable and business life. Following retirement from the corporate world he assumed, at a cost of one dollar a year to the school, Chancellorship of the prestigious University of La Verne in Southern California. His plan was to stay a year while a going-forward management plan was readied for implementation. It became another mission accomplished.

He and wife Beth live in Penn Valley where they provide support, leadership and sponsorship to key community, education and youth programs across a broad geographic area.

Major General Orlo K. Steele, USMC, Ret. General Steele was keynote speaker for a luncheon Mike Dobbins hosted for the first one-dozen *PATRIOTS* late 2002. General Steele incorporated detailed personal observations about each honoree into his remarks. He had approached his speech preparation job with the same consummate care he took while rising through the ranks from enlisted PFC in 1955 to Major General in 1987.

During his distinguished career he was responsible for commanding Marines around the globe. I first met him in person at his home in Grass Valley, CA. He had just returned with all his climbing gear from doing repairs on the steep roof of his church. Among Marines in our local community he is called the general's general. High praise, I believe, for a man who richly deserves it.

Maj. Gen. Steele also served with distinction during the Vietnam conflict earning the Bronze Star with Combat "V"; Combat Action Ribbon; Vietnam Service Medal with four bronze stars; and more.

Over the years Carol Lynn, Production Manager with *The Wildwood Independent*, has been a treasure. Every photo I ever used for any story – *PATRIOTS* and others – went through Carol. Many were one-of-a-kind provided by my story subjects and were priceless family assets. She treated them as such. Her story and photo layouts showcased every story to perfection, usually on page one.

Former Lake Wildwood resident Bob Carrel would have been on my payroll if I had had one. He provided about a quarter of my leads for *PATRIOTS*. In more than one instance he talked with a reluctant subject in advance to pave the way for the interview. The only quid pro quo I ever provided him was a great news story about his guard dog business – his ten-pound white Miki-Yorkie mix, *Fang* (aka *Cookie*). He and Marilyn relocated their home and business to the Stockton area a few years ago. With cutbacks in law enforcement their business is prospering.

Larry Bailey
Penn Valley, California

THE AUTHOR:

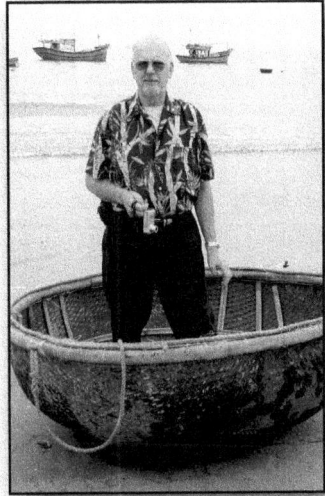

LARRY T. BAILEY spent three decades primarily in the information systems industry. He has a deep background in public relations including executive and political speech writing. He has had responsibility for political contact activities with various levels of government bodies and individuals.

He is skilled at writing for internal and external publications as well as having been a corporate media spokesman, including print, radio and television. He has written award-winning fiction.

The latter years of his career encompassed many of the activities above as well as managing the totality of a hundred million dollar equipment base in a major market area. This included outside and inside sales teams, billing, installation and repair.

Bailey has taught human relations at the university level and English, journalism, creative writing and business classes in high school. He has been active in his communities, having served as a planning and human rights commissioner, fire department elected director and parks and recreation commissioner.

One of his most enjoyable and rewarding activities was interviewing WWII vets in his community. All fought or served in combat zones. Those interviews, over a five-year period, became this book. His activities as an occasional writer for *The Wildwood Independent* have spanned more than a decade, focusing on human and general interest, travel, and the acclaimed *PATRIOTS* series.

Bailey, spouse Diana and two spirited and clever Portuguese Water dogs live in the Sierra Nevada foothills between Lake Tahoe and Sacramento. During the past they spent six weeks of every year out of the country – the more exotic the better.